CYPRUS

Conflict and Negotiation 1960–1980

P. G. Polyviou is Fellow and Tutor of
Lincoln College, Oxford

CYPRUS
Conflict and Negotiation
1960–1980

POLYVIOS G. POLYVIOU

Fellow of Lincoln College
Oxford

DUCKWORTH

TO GEORGE AND THELMA POLYVIOU

First published in 1980 by
Gerald Duckworth & Co. Ltd.
The Old Piano Factory
43 Gloucester Crescent, London NW1

© 1980 by Polyvios G. Polyviou

ISBN 0 7156 1498 3

British Library Cataloguing in Publication Data

Polyviou, Polyvios G
    Cyprus
    1. Cyprus – Politics and government
    I. Title
    956.4'504   DS54.9

    ISBN 0–7156–1498–3

Photoset in Great Britain by
Photobooks (Bristol) Ltd.
28 Midland Road, St. Philips, Bristol
and printed by
Unwin Brothers Limited, Old Woking

Contents

Preface

The problem of Cyprus has evoked different reactions and has been viewed in various ways over the years. Some have regarded it as a nuisance, or as an essentially troublesome thorn in bilateral Graeco-Turkish relations, or as an irksome irritant weakening the NATO alliance and threatening the successful pursuit of western strategic interests in the eastern Mediterranean and the Middle East. For others it is an issue of international dimensions and explosive implications, a crisis owing less to ethnic mistrust and more to the forces of 'neocolonialism' and 'neoimperialist domination', and ultimately a problem relating to the internationally accepted principles of self-determination, freedom from aggression and the right to follow a policy of non-alignment. Consistently with this variety in perception, a bewildering array of designations – such as ethnic conflict, constitutional crisis, political dispute and moral issue – have (all with some justification but none representing the whole truth) been applied. In this book my aim is not the impossible one of offering a complete account or explanation of all the diverse elements that together constitute the problem of Cyprus; my primary tasks, as appears from the title and as I explain further in the Introduction, are the more limited ones of elucidating certain aspects of the political and constitutional conflict and of evaluating the numerous rounds of negotiations held between Greek and Turkish Cypriots for a resolution of their differences.

The book consists of four parts. Chapter 2 examines the independence settlement of 1960, the ensuing strain and breakdown, the proposals put forward by the Greek and Turkish Cypriot sides between 1963 and 1967, and the crisis of November 1967. Chapters 3, 4 and 5 deal with the intercommunal discussions held between the two sides between 1968 and 1974. These talks were first considered in my *Cyprus: In Search of a Constitution* (1976), but my account of them here is more complete. Some of the questions and issues which I explore in these three chapters are: What proposals did the Greek and Turkish Cypriots put forward at the various stages of the intercommunal dialogue? Which were their real views of Cyprus and of the type of political and governmental structure they wished to see emerge from their discussions? What progress was achieved during these years (1968–1974)? Did any definite results emerge? Why did the talks fail to yield agreement? The third part of the book (Chapter 6) describes the Geneva Conference of August 1974, investigating the background against which it took place and assessing responsibility for its collapse. I attended this conference as a member of the Greek Cypriot delegation. This inevitably means that the events of that period are presented through the eyes of a participant; but, as against this, during the plenary sessions of the Conference I kept extensive notes (supplemented at a later stage from the shorthand notes kept by the secretaries of the Greek Cypriot side), which in turn means that for the most part the protagonists are allowed to speak for themselves. In the final section (Chapter 7) I direct my attention to political and constitutional reconstruction. First I put forward detailed views with regard to numerous issues of constitutional structuring and the pattern of the state that Greek and Turkish Cypriots must aim at (and can live with) consistently both with their own interests and with wider considerations relating to the peace and stability of the area. I conclude with a view of the future.

It will become clear that I have had access to many confidential documents and other sources of information. Most of them were made available to me by Mr Gl. Clerides, formerly President of the House of Representatives and Greek Cypriot negotiator. These documents and other materials can be classified as follows:

1. Letters and other communications exchanged between the two negotiators (mainly during 1968–1971).

2. Statements of proposals submitted to each other by the two sides.

3. Lists of points of agreement and disagreement prepared by the two negotiators after the various rounds of talks.

4. Lengthy statements of their positions prepared by the two sides and submitted to each other and the UN mediator.

5. Even more theoretical statements of fundamental constitutional and political attitudes prepared by the two constitutional experts (who assisted the principal negotiators between 1972 and 1974) and submitted to each other and to the UN mediator.

6. Reports by third parties concerning the attitudes and views of western powers towards the negotiations, and other political matters. These reports are included in the files of the intercommunal discussions. Of great assistance also were lengthy papers prepared by the Greek Cypriot representative (Mr Clerides) after the meetings, and various other internal memoranda prepared for the attention of the political leadership.

I have also been fortunate in having had many interesting discussions with officials, both in Cyprus and abroad, regarding the subjects dealt with in this book. Unfortunately, I have not had the chance to hold similar discussions with Turkish officials. It should be noted however that I have seen the relevant Turkish documents (letters, proposals and other communications), and I have made all possible effort to present fairly the views of the two sides, according equal time to the two negotiators and quoting extensively from their exchanges. It should be added that the invariably unpublished documentation on which this study is based is fuller for some parts than others, and on occasion I have had to reconstruct and draw my own conclusions. This is particularly so when I discuss the policies of the Greek military junta and other foreign governments towards the intercommunal discussions.

This book would not have been possible without the private papers of Mr Glafkos Clerides, to whom I am extremely grateful. Miss Katina Kassapi, as usual, transformed my illegible manuscript into a presentable text; and again all kinds of assistance in connection with this book, as with everything else over so long, has come from my parents, George and Thelma Polyviou. It is to them that this book is dedicated, with much affection. But the greatest debt I owe to my wife, Georgia. She not only encouraged the preparation and completion of this book, but also offered invaluable help on matters of both style and substance.

Oxford, September 1979   P.G.P.

1

Introduction

The basic facts about Cyprus[1] – historical, geographic, political and demographic – are well known. The island, strategically located in the eastern Mediterranean, five hundred miles from Greece but only forty from Turkey, has traditionally been inhabited by 80 per cent Greek Cypriots and 18 per cent Turkish Cypriots, the rest consisting of other minorities.

Owing to its privileged geographical position Cyprus, since antiquity, has been coveted by the great powers of the day. As was observed by the German archaeologist Hirschfeld, 'he who would become and remain a great power in the east must hold Cyprus in his hands'. For this reason one conqueror succeeded another. Cyprus was overrun by the Turks in 1571. The present Turks of Cyprus are descendants of those who came and settled in the island during the Ottoman occupation; but, it must be emphasised, the overwhelming majority of the people of Cyprus have always been, and of course still are, Greeks. The last rulers of the island were the British. Cyprus passed to Britain by treaty in 1878, though still continuing to be under the suzerainty of the Turkish Sultans. In 1914, when Turkey entered the First World War against the Allies, Cyprus was annexed by Britain. By the Treaty of Lausanne, signed in 1923, Turkey recognised internationally, without any reservation, that it had no right or claim to Cyprus. Throughout the years of colonialism the Greek Cypriots never wavered in their demand for freedom, self-determination and union with Greece. Finally, in April 1955, after all efforts to achieve these demands by peaceful means had failed, the Greek Cypriots revolted against the British colonial regime, and after a four-year struggle Cyprus was proclaimed an independent state. After three tense years the complex

[1] A full bibliography on Cyprus is provided in Crawshaw, *The Cyprus Revolt* (1978). Particularly interesting are the following: Hill, *A History of Cyprus* (4 vols, 1940—52); Hackett, *A History of the Orthodox Church of Cyprus* (1901); Luke, *Cyprus under the Turks, 1571–1878* (1921); Mayes, *Cyprus and Makarios* (1960); Stephens, *Cyprus: A Place of Arms* (1966); Storrs, *Orientations* (1937); Terlexis, *Diplomacy and Politics on Cyprus* (1971, in Greek); Xydis, *Cyprus: Conflict and Conciliation, 1954–1958* (1967); Xydis, *Cyprus: Reluctant Republic* (1973); Ierodiakonou, *The Cyprus Question* (1971); Crouzet, *Le Conflit de Chypre* (2 vols, 1973); Crawshaw, *The Cyprus Revolt* (1978); Ehrlich, *Cyprus 1958–1964* (1974).

constitutional machinery set up by the independence settlement of 1960 collapsed under the weight of its own unworkability and the continuing mistrust between the two communities. In December 1963 civil strife broke out in the island, Greece and Turkey were inevitably drawn in, Turkey threatening to invade and Greece declaring that in the event of a Turkish attack she would assist the Cyprus government in resisting it, and for the first time the United States and the Soviet Union also became actively involved, the United States attempting to mediate between its two NATO allies and avert a Graeco-Turkish war, while the Soviet Union, fearing the island's incorporation within the western alliance, warned that she could not stand idly by and watch Cyprus being brought within the American sphere of influence. What had been a local ethnic conflict had become a major international crisis.

Equally well known are recent developments.[2] After years of unsuccessful negotiations between Greek and Turkish Cypriots, in July 1974 the junta then ruling Greece staged a coup against the government of President Makarios, and Turkey invaded Cyprus and occupied a substantial part of the republic. Despite the many United Nations resolutions calling upon all parties to withdraw their military forces from the island, to allow the refugees and displaced persons to return to their homes in conditions of safety, and to respect Cyprus' independence and territorial integrity, the Greek Cypriots and the international community have been presented with a series of Turkish faits accomplis. What has now quite generally been agreed to be illegal conquest and occupation of part of an independent and sovereign state has been followed by the expulsion of about 200,000 Greek Cypriots from their homes, the proclamation of a Turkish-Cypriot federated state in the northern part of Cyprus and a large-scale and quite unconcealed Turkish colonisation of the area occupied. According to many statements which either represent or reflect official Turkish thinking, a major effort is being made to increase substantially or even double the Turkish Cypriot population of Cyprus so that the stage will be set for an equalisation of the Greek and Turkish communities and an eventual annexation of the whole island. Small wonder, then, that the Greek Cypriots feel that they are being asked to negotiate under duress and that negotiations between the parties and diplomatic initiatives launched by others have so far failed to yield any progress. But not all parts of the Cyprus tragedy are as well known, and further questions remain totally unanswered: in particular, questions concerning the various constitutional and political proposals put forward by the Greek and Turkish Cypriots after the breakdown of the 1960

[2] See Markides, *The Rise and Fall of the Cyprus Republic* (1977); Polyviou, *Cyprus, The Tragedy and the Challenge* (1975); Polyviou, *Cyprus, In Search of a Constitution* (1976); Stern, *The Wrong Horse: The Politics of Intervention and the Failure of American Diplomacy* (1977).

constitution, the intercommunal negotiations held between 1968 and 1974 which very nearly reached agreement, the Geneva conference which took place after the Turkish invasion of Cyprus and on the collapse of which the Turkish military forces once more began hostile operations, and the complex and involved political developments and machinations, whether Greek, Turkish or foreign, unfolding behind the scenes.

This book aims at a comprehensive constitutional exposition of the Cyprus conflict and at a partial and necessarily tentative political and diplomatic analysis of the surrounding events and developments. A preliminary attempt at conceptual characterisation reveals the size and complexity of the Cyprus problem. What type of crisis is it? How can it best be described?

We can approach it in many ways and at many levels. First it could be regarded as a conflict between two ethnic groups, a majority and a minority. This raises issues that can best be described as constitutional, pertaining to internal or municipal constitutional and political organ-isation, it being well known that 'of all the problems that can confront constitution-makers none can be more difficult than that of finding a formula which will reconcile communities divided into permanent majorities and permanent minorities'.[3] In such situations what system of government should be adopted? If it is not based on simple majority principles, but predicated rather upon the existence of a permanent majority and a permanent minority and the consequent need to protect the minority from the oppression of the majority, what devices should one adopt in order to ensure the necessary security, physical and psychological, without at the same time unnecessarily antagonising the predominant population group to the point that it too becomes alienated from the state and dangerously estranged from the benevolently protected smaller group? But, as is well known, the Cyprus question is much more than a constitutional conflict or a problem in the relations between a majority and a minority. It is also a complicated political issue in Graeco-Turkish relations, centering historically on the fundamental opposition of two incompatible nationalist ideas, enosis and partition, for long professed by the Greek and Turkish Cypriots and actively promoted by Greece and Turkey. Enosis was the demand of the Greek Cypriot community that the island should be united with Greece because, as it was claimed, the Greek Cypriots were ethnically, culturally and spiritually one with the Greek nation; therefore any political arrangements that might be adopted had to reflect this profound identity. The Turkish Cypriots too have long claimed that Cyprus, which was once under Turkish occupation and is so near to

[3] From the Foreword to Polyviou, *Cyprus, In Search of a Constitution*, supra, by Professor H. W. R. Wade.

the Turkish mainland, is in fact geographically an extension of Asia Minor, that they themselves are part of the Turkish nation, and that therefore the island, or at least a part of it, should revert to direct Turkish rule. On the Greek Cypriot side enosis has now certainly been abandoned in favour of a solution of sovereign independence, but the Turkish Cypriot leadership continues to insist that the Turks of Cyprus form an integral part of the Turkish nation; if the island is not to be partitioned, it should therefore be federated between the two communities in a way that ensures Turkish 'rights' and allows the fate of the Turkish Cypriot community to be determined by the Turkish government. Whatever the strength or weakness of these arguments, there can be little doubt that Greece and Turkey, in part because of the inherent emotive appeal and the undeniable political convenience and electoral marketability of the ideas of enosis and partition – but in the case of Turkey, it is thought, mainly because of strategic considerations that have been thought by Turkish strategists to make it vital that Cyprus, or at least its northern coast, should remain under some kind of Turkish political and military superintendence – have long been intimately involved in the affairs of the island. This is particularly so with Turkey, partly because of her closer proximity to the island, partly because of the Turkish Cypriots' small numbers and traditional economic inferiority which make them totally dependent upon mainland support, and partly because of recent developments. For, ever since the island was plunged into catastrophe following the events of 1974, the Greek government, despite continuing economic and military support, has made it clear that the formulation of policy with regard to the Cyprus problem must be the exclusive responsibility of the Cyprus government, while Turkey, as a result of these same events, has in effect annexed the occupied part of the island and is administering its affairs directly. Decisions affecting the Turkish Cypriot community are no longer, if indeed they ever were, in the hands of the Turkish Cypriots themselves. But despite this Greek disengagement from the island the Cyprus problem is still a potent, and at times an explosive, issue of Greek and Turkish internal politics, capable of arousing deep emotions and strong feelings in both countries. Thus, as long as the problem of Cyprus is not satisfactorily settled but the ingredients of ethnic conflict remain, there will be a strong possibility, so disturbing to western policy-makers, of a wider Graeco-Turkish convulsion that would further weaken NATO's already vulnerable and exposed eastern flank.

This brings one to the broader international and strategic aspects of the Cyprus problem. The Cyprus government has often declared itself committed to a genuine policy of neutrality and non-alignment, but it is equally clear that, however insistent Cypriot protestations of neutrality may be, these cannot affect the island's strategically crucial location in the eastern Mediterranean – within sight of the Turkish coast and in close proximity to the Middle East – which unavoidably brings it within the range of American and Soviet strategic and political calculations and thus makes it an object of rivalry and potential conflict to the two superpowers. The main reasons for American involvement in the Cyprus problem are basically two: first, because 'as a result of ethnic ties and a complicated treaty structure',[4] what might otherwise be only a local quarrel could easily trigger a large-scale armed conflict between Greece and Turkey, both of them NATO allies, from which the western alliance would be certain to suffer possibly irremediable dislocation; and secondly because of a feared Soviet intrusion into the eastern Mediterranean as a result, on the one hand, of what American strategists saw as Archbishop Makarios' dangerous flirtations with the Soviet Union and the non-aligned and, on the other, of 'the strength of the legal indigenous Communist party'.[5] In the light of these reasons, American policy has traditionally been based on two principal tenets, one long-term and the other short-term.[6] The short-term aim is to avert a Graeco-Turkish war over Cyprus, both by attempting to contain the conflict between the Greek and Turkish Cypriot communities within the island itself and, if either Greece or Turkey intervenes unilaterally (as happened in 1974 when Turkey invaded), by persuading or putting pressure upon the other not to resort also to military action but rather to negotiate. The long-term objective of American diplomacy is to help bring about a settlement that will finally secure western strategic interests in the area and remove forever the threat of Graeco-Turkish war. Ideally this would consist of an agreed arrangement between Greece and Turkey whereby the island would be divided between them and permanently brought within the NATO alliance. But since any plan to partition the island was certain to founder on the opposition of the Cyprus government and of Archbishop Makarios in particular, American policy-makers have often supported plans, such as federation or systems of communal administration, whereby the semblance of an independent and sovereign state would remain but effective power be held by the Greek and Turkish governments.

The Soviet Union has not been as actively involved in the Cyprus problem as the United States, basically because until recently its aims, both military and political, have been essentially negative, namely to ensure the continued neutrality of Cyprus by preventing either enosis or partition and

[4] George W. Ball, *Address to the Chicago Council on Foreign Relations*, Chicago, Illinois, 18 September 1964 (see Adams and Cottrell, *Cyprus Between East and West* (1968)).
[5] Ibid.
[6] See Van Coufoudakis 'United States foreign policy and the Cyprus question: a case study in Cold War diplomacy', in Couloumbis and Hicks, eds., *US Foreign Policy Toward Greece and Cyprus: The Clash of Principle and Pragmatism* (1975).

to frustrate Anglo-American plans aiming to bring the island within the NATO alliance. At times the objectives of Soviet policy have assumed a more active form, and these then are, first, to sow dissension in the relations between Greece and Turkey, so as to exacerbate further existing divisions and weaknesses within NATO, and, secondly, to penetrate British military installations in Cyprus and gather vital information about western plans for the defence of the eastern Mediterranean, in order ultimately to secure the complete removal of the British bases from the island. Within the constant framework of these basic objectives Soviet strategy has continuously shifted, the Soviet leaders sometimes supporting the Makarios government and independent Cyprus, sometimes switching their attention to Turkey in an attempt to improve relations with Ankara, and on yet other occasions simply issuing angry tirades against so-called imperialist intervention in the affairs of the republic. In any case, despite the occasional manifestation of more active interest in Cyprus in support of collateral policy objectives, Soviet policy has until now been relatively restrained, being confined in general to frustrating American attempts to divide the island between its allies, Greece and Turkey. But with NATO in disarray, with the United States profoundly involved in the Middle East, and with momentous developments unfolding in the Arab world, the possibility that the Soviet Union may decide to pursue a more active policy designed to bring Cyprus within its sphere of influence cannot be discounted.[7] This in turn will increase the strategic significance of the island and add further to the complications of the overall situation.

The problem of Cyprus abounds in difficulties, involvements, paradoxes and contradictions, and no single book can possibly hope to cover and account for all its manifold and baffling complexities, ranging from its broader strategic and political aspects to its domestic, ethnic and constitutional intricacies. Thus it has often been observed that to weave its tortuous strands into a coherent pattern is virtually impossible; and yet so pronounced is the interrelationship of all its elements and so hopelessly tangled are its various strands that no treatment of any single aspect of the Cyprus problem can avoid going into much else besides. The present book is no exception. Still, the topics that form its basic subject-matter are constitutional conflict and constitutional negotiation and diplomacy. Both phrases, it must be emphasized, are used with awareness of their limitations. For not only, as has been seen, is the Cyprus problem much more than a constitutional conflict, and talks and processes directed over the years at its resolution much more than limited constitutional negotiations, but also, like many other constitutional conflicts, sound treatment of the

[7] Kedourie, *The Cyprus Problem and its Solution* (1973) (An International Seminar Report).

Cyprus one, even in its constitutional and legal aspects, depends to a great extent on adequate knowledge of its social context and a full understanding of its political background. Thus other factors and forces have contributed over the years to its present development, and these are still very much in evidence. Domestic politics, ethnic mistrust and suspicion, historical factors, foreign involvement, strategic and economic considerations, international politics, outside interests and much else must surely be included in any overall survey of the Cyprus problem that would aspire to comprehensiveness. Indeed one cannot but wonder whether the problem would be what it is today had all these factors not intruded decisively into the affairs of the island and its people. This is why an effort, however inadequate, will be made to discuss what might be described as political developments and events which either changed the balance of power or had an impact upon the parties' perception of the situation and their overall negotiating strategy. At the same time, whatever the broader international issues and interests on the one hand or what modern sociological jargon refers to as the internal social dynamics of the situation on the other, there can be no denying its political and constitutional dimensions. It is not only that it is basically only 'political' and 'constitutional' disagreements which lend themselves to overt compromise and mediation, without which conflicting interests and passions would run rampant, or even that a viable constitutional and political settlement is also a necessary barrier against direct external intervention, the intrusion of which is normally only made possible by the absence of essential internal stability. The very security of both Greek and Turkish Cypriots depends on a durable political settlement which in turn would make possible the satisfactory functioning of constitutional government. Without this almost nothing else can be achieved. But if the political conflict were resolved and the constitutional problem settled, then it might just be possible both to insulate the ravaged body politic from external erosion and to facilitate orderly government and (ultimately) harmonious social interaction.[8] Without therefore for a moment underestimating the external forces and all-important strategic considerations which must be accorded pride of place in any attempted explanation of Cyprus' misfortunes, there is after all much to be said for a careful study, first, of 'constitutional conflict', defined as the conflict or disagreement between the two communities over important issues of constitutionalism and government, and, secondly, of 'constitutional negotiations and proposals', by which I primarily refer to the attempts over the years on the part of the two Cypriot communities to arrive at an agreed framework of government for the republic.

[8] Ibid. I am indebted to Professor Kedourie's perceptive comments.

Various constitutional phases or periods between 1960 and 1974 can be delineated, and different considerations apply to each.

The first constitutional period extends from the adoption of the 1960 constitution to its functional breakdown in 1963.[9] Until then Cyprus was a colony of Great Britain. It became independent in 1960 after agreement was reached both on independence and the constitutional structure of the island between the United Kingdom, Greece and Turkey without the participation of the people of Cyprus in the talks and discussions that led to the agreement. The resulting constitution was quite generally regarded as unfair to the Greek Cypriot majority, and before long proved seriously defective in operation; but whatever its merits or demerits the 1960 constitution is fundamental for any inquiry into the Cyprus problem, both because all subsequent negotiations until 1974 were essentially efforts directed at its modification or reconstruction, and because this constitution was until recently regarded by the Turkish community as a solemn declaration of its status and rights from which there could be no deviation or departure, at least not without serious concessions. Due to its structural defects, but mainly because of the general state of relationships between the two communities at the time, the 1960 constitution not only failed to bring about the resolution of the constitutional conflict but exacerbated it further. Its artificial and rigid structure could not absorb the intercommunal tension generated by the difficulty of its implementation and operation. Almost all matters tended to become controversial, and the accumulation of unresolved issues resulted in the intensification of existing differences. In November 1963 thirteen proposals to amend the constitution were put forward by Archbishop Makarios, President of the republic, but they were not accepted by the Turkish leadership. The eruption of violence in December 1963 signalled the degeneration of the conflict into crisis and overt confrontation.

The second constitutional period extends from 1963 to 1968.[10] After the outbreak of disorder in 1963 the Turkish Cypriots followed a policy of self-segregation and withdrawal into several 'Turkish' enclaves scattered within the territory of the republic, where they attempted to establish their own governmental and administrative structures. The government of the republic came under the exclusive control of the Greek Cypriots, who proceeded to invoke 'the principle of necessity' in justification of the resulting deviations from the letter of the 1960 constitutional charter. Barriers, both physical and psychological, duly arose. As a result most young Greek and Turkish Cypriots grew up in a situation where there was

[9] See Kyriakides, *Cyprus: Constitutionalism and Crisis Government* (1968); Polyviou, *Cyprus, The Tragedy and the Challenge* (1975).

[10] See Kyriakides, supra. n.9; Ehrlich, supra n. 1; Markides, *The Rise and Fall of the Cyprus Republic* (1977).

almost no ordinary contact between the two communities, and where political estrangement and readiness to engage in conflict, as well as imprisonment within the shackles of narrow political indoctrination, became stronger by the day. Amidst sporadic incidents of intercommunal violence a number of initiatives were launched between 1963 and 1968 for a resolution of the crisis, and widely divergent proposals for constitutional and political reconstruction were put forward by both sides. These positions and proposals will be investigated shortly.

The constitutional conflict entered a new stage in 1968.[11] The two sides, with restoration of 'cooperation' within a common state and political reintegration of the two communities as their main objectives, embarked on the intercommunal negotiations which continued until 1974. These negotiations are the main topic to be considered and analysed in this book, as they were clearly conducted for the purpose of arriving at an agreed internal settlement of the constitutional problem and thus qualify as 'constitutional negotiations' par excellence. It is not claimed of course that these talks, or any others, were, or can be, totally insulated from political pressures and international realities, or that they can profitably be studied in isolation from and without an effort to correlate them to surrounding factors and forces; far from it. But here at last the two Cypriot sides came face to face in order to deal squarely with the major constitutional issue at the time, namely the reconstitution of the 1960 governmental system, and in consequence the intercommunal discussions were almost exclusively concerned with constitutional arguments and proposals regarding internal constitutional reconstruction. These talks finally broke down in July 1974, following the Greek military coup against Archbishop Makarios and the Turkish invasion of Cyprus.

The Turkish invasion on 20 July 1974 dramatically changed the situation. The balance of power shifted decisively in Turkey's favour, and a fundamental reassessment of positions and attitudes became necessary. Turkey, as will be seen, after and as a result of the initial invasion of Cyprus and the first phase of military operations lasting from 20 July to the first week of August, occupied only a comparatively small strip of land in the northern part of the island, but there was little doubt that its army had the capacity to proceed further and occupy, if it so wished, the whole of the island. In those circumstances, and after the Security Council had called upon the parties to enter into negotiations without delay, two Geneva conferences took place for yet another attempt at resolving what was now no longer a local constitutional problem but potentially a major international crisis. Particularly important was the second conference[12] which convened on 9 August 1974 and was attended by the three guarantors of the

[11] Polyviou, *Cyprus, In Search of a Constitution* (1976)
[12] Ibid.

1960 settlement, i.e. Great Britain, Greece and Turkey, and by representatives of the two Cypriot sides; and, among other things, proposals regarding the future constitutional structure of the republic were there put forward. But Turkey had clearly decided to wait or talk no longer, but to solve the Cyprus problem once and for all. Nothing therefore could save the conference, which broke down finally on 14 August when the Turkish army once more started military operations – with three main results: occupation of 40 per cent of Cyprus, 200,000 Greek Cypriot refugees, and a de facto partitioning of the island. Despite its short duration and the fact that in retrospect it was not a bona fide attempt to resolve the political and constitutional problems that had been created but, as will be argued below, nothing short of a cynical exercise in power politics, the Geneva conference was an important turning point in Cypriot history, possibly marking the end of independent Cyprus, and thus constitutes a distinct phase in the evolution of the constitutional conflict. It will be described and assessed in detail later.

The next constitutional phase which is still unfolding could be designated as 'federal reconstruction'.[13] Its essential elements are these. Turkey has effectively partitioned the island. It has established almost complete communal separation through a compulsory population movement and shown complete disregard for UN resolutions calling for the withdrawal of the Turkish forces from Cyprus and the return of the refugees to their homes. Further, the Turkish leadership has declared the northern part of Cyprus a 'federated state', and has announced its readiness to proclaim a completely independent Turkish Cypriot state, or alternatively to annex the occupied part of Cyprus to Turkey. The government of Cyprus, in its turn, has accepted what it had resolutely resisted until then, namely the 'federal principle', but has also declared strong insistence on a return of all displaced persons to their homes in conditions of safety, a constitutional reconstruction of Cyprus that does not amount to disguised partition, and strong guarantees safeguarding the territorial integrity, sovereignty and security of the republic for the future. The intercommunal negotiations, at least in form, have been resuscitated by order of the General Assembly of the United Nations, but they have so far failed to yield any progress on the constitutional issues. Half-hearted international initiatives have also dismally failed.

It will readily be seen that the realities and circumstances within which the Cyprus constitutional conflict has developed and in the context of which the various constitutional negotiations and proposals have taken place or been put forward have undergone very substantial changes. The

13 Ibid.

two related consequences of this are first that no constant statement of the problem is possible and secondly that the constitutional and political issues themselves have materially changed. Thus, to take one example, one of the most important features of the situation until recently was that the two communities were not physically separated from each other. Greek Cypriots and Turkish Cypriots were spread widely over the island, 'not according to any fixed geographical pattern but rather as a result of the usual factors behind the movement and settlement of people over many generations', and as a result there was 'islandwide intermingling of the populations'.[14] Within such intermingling there naturally did exist local concentrations of people where one community or the other sharply predominated, i.e. there were quite a few villages that were either wholly Greek or wholly Turkish but, in their turn, these villages themselves were not usually to be found in clusters, the more general pattern in any given area being a mixture of Greek Cypriot, Turkish Cypriot and mixed villages. There was thus no fixed territorial pattern on the basis of which ethnic federal arrangements could be made, and the most that could be contemplated was recognition of a degree of local government that would not contravene the principles of a unitary state which, the Greek side believed, were the most appropriate way of expressing and articulating the population intermingling and the social and economic cohesion that were an established and prominent feature of Cypriot society. This has now changed. For not only has an almost complete compulsory population movement taken place with the consequent imposition of two distinct geographic and communal zones but also recent proposals put forward by the Greek Cypriot side, both in their acceptance of federal geographical arrangements and in their resignation to the inevitability of a substantial population exchange entailing the creation of cohesive Turkish areas, have irrevocably changed both the parties' and the international community's political perception of the overall situation and their related conception of the constitutional issues at stake, on the one hand, and of the range of available solutions, on the other. At the same time it goes without saying that neither all variations in factual content nor more or less temporary advantages of one party or the other must necessarily be reflected either in a sound political assessment or in a neutral juridical analysis of the constitutional conflict; in general, only fundamental or irreversible developments, particularly when these have already influenced the parties' own demands and positions, need be taken as part of the framework or context within which a solution must be sought. Further, in contrast to important changes in the wake of recent events, other elements have remained more or less constant. Thus, to begin with, Greek Cypriots

[14] *Report of the United Nations Mediator on Cyprus to the Secretary-General*, UN doc. S/6253 (The Plaza Report).

within Cyprus substantially outnumber Turkish Cypriots, which means that no system of government that ignores the interests of Greek Cypriots can be viable. Secondly, Turkey is considerably closer to the island than Greece, which means both that Greece and the Greek Cypriot side cannot in the last resort, whatever their temporary advantage, impose a long-term solution that is not acceptable to Turkey, and that in case of a confrontation the Turkish population of the island can count on immediate support from Turkey mainland, unlike the Greek Cypriots; and thirdly, and as a result of the transformation of what some viewed in the past as a minor ethnic quarrel into what almost all now accept to be a world crisis, only that solution can prove durable which both satisfies local demands and does not threaten wider international political and strategic concerns. This solution is likely to be a sovereign, independent, integral, demilitarised and non-aligned Cyprus, with the most exacting guarantees of human rights for all, protection from all types of discrimination, and the absolute security of all ethnic groups within the republic. But agreement on abstract generalities does not dispose of the need either for the detailed resolution of many difficult problems or for compromise by the various sides on almost all issues. Against this background, discharge of the twin tasks of a neutral and balanced exposition of the constitutional and political conflict on the one hand and of the principled enunciation and development of criteria on the basis of which constitutional proposals can be put forward and evaluated on the other presents great difficulties but must none the less be attempted.

2

Independence, Breakdown, and the Uneasy Years

1. *The 1960 constitution*

The 1960 constitution of the republic of Cyprus has its roots in the Zurich agreement reached between the Greek and Turkish governments on 11 February 1959 which in turn was incorporated in the agreements reached between these governments and that of the UK in London on 19 February of the same year. On that date also the representatives of the Greek and Turkish communities of Cyprus 'accepted' the accords reached, and eventually these agreements were embodied in three treaties and a constitution, normally called the 1960 or Zurich constitution, which were all duly signed at Nicosia on 16 August 1960 and thus became the legal framework of the republic of Cyprus.

Was the Zurich and London settlement an imposed one, or was it freely accepted by the Greek and Turkish Cypriots? On this, traditionally one of the most furiously contested issues of the Cyprus problem, as on so many others, Greek and Turkish Cypriot spokesmen have disagreed. But the following points are not open to dispute.[1] The Zurich accord was a compromise negotiated between the Greek and Turkish governments in the absence of Greek and Turkish Cypriots. Meetings between the Greek and Turkish foreign ministers had begun in early December 1958 at the United Nations and continued at the NATO meeting in Paris in late December 1958. The talks between the Greek and Turkish governments continued throughout January, and in early February 1959 the Greek and Turkish Prime Ministers, Messrs Karamanlis and Menderes, met at Zurich, where they drew up the outlines of a comprehensive settlement of the Cyprus dispute. The agreement was announced in a joint Graeco-Turkish communiqué issued on 11 February. The British government, which had already made it clear that any agreement reached between Greece and Turkey would be acceptable to it provided it could maintain sovereign British bases and a military presence in the island, was immediately informed, and it was only then that Greek and Turkish Cypriot leaders were fully brought into the picture. Archbishop Makarios at a meeting in Athens with the Greek government accepted, with some

[1] See Mackenzie, *Cyprus: The Ideological Crucible* (Conflict Studies) (1972); Stephens, *Cyprus: A Place of Arms* (1966); Crawshaw, *The Cyprus Revolt* (1978).

reluctance, the principles of the Graeco-Turkish agreement, since it was now clear that outright rejection of the plan and continuation of the armed conflict would mean partition, but, as he himself said later, he expected further negotiations to take place at the London conference which had already been called. At this conference at Lancaster House in February 1959 the Archbishop did indeed raise a number of objections and expressed strong misgivings with regard to certain provisions of the Zurich agreement.[2] He accepted the Graeco-Turkish accord *as a basis* for the solution of the Cyprus problem, he stated, but he could not accept without further discussion the details of the Zurich settlement in which he had not participated. But the Greek Prime Minister told him that further negotiation was not possible, that the Greek government had committed itself in the eyes of its allies and could not go back on its word, and that if he did not accept the Zurich settlement as it stood Greece would abandon both him and Cyprus. The Turkish and British Foreign Ministers, Zorlu and Selwyn Lloyd, could not accept any further discussion or negotiation. They demanded in almost brutal terms that the Archbishop should either sign the agreement or reject it, in which event, it was already clear, Great Britain would withdraw from the island and Cyprus would be partitioned. 'You expressed your views and expressed disagreement on certain points', Selwyn Lloyd told Makarios at the last meeting. 'We don't agree with you. You have to take it or leave it'. When Makarios realised that he had been confronted with a fait accompli, he asked for more time to consider the situation, but even this was refused. Lennox-Boyd said that both he and Mr Macmillan were to leave the next day for the Far East and Moscow respectively and that the Archbishop had to give his answer immediately. 'If you want my answer now,' Makarios retorted, 'my answer is 'No'.' The meeting was adjourned and it was agreed that the Greek Cypriot leader should give an answer by 10.30 a.m. the next morning. During the night, as the Archbishop was reflecting on 'the agonizing dilemma'[3] facing him, further pressure was brought to bear upon him by the Greek government, the Greek Prime Minister telling him that if the agreement was not signed the consequences for Cyprus would be unpredictable and possibly disastrous, and that he would be held responsible for any repercussions that followed. Makarios, as he stated later, was sure that if he did not sign, there would be catastrophe for Cyprus. The island, still a colony, would in all probability be divided, and that would have been the end of the matter. 'In the circumstances', he regarded himself as having 'no alternative but to sign'.[4] It does therefore appear that whatever the juridical validity of the

[2] Makarios, 'Proposals to amend the Cyprus constitution', *International Relations (Athens)*, April 1964; see also the account in Stephens, supra n.1, at 165–7.

[3] *Daily Telegraph*, 20 February 1959 (see Crawshaw, supra n.1, at 345).

[4] Makarios, supra n.2.

overall settlement, and irrespective of whether subsequent Greek Cypriot attempts to amend the constitutional arrangements should have been embarked upon given international realities and domestic tension, the Zurich and London agreements were basically negotiated and concluded between Greece and Turkey and not between the Greek and Turkish Cypriots. The Zurich agreement was therefore 'essentially an imposed settlement',[5] imposed by the Greek and Turkish governments, and this fact must be borne in mind in attempted explanations of the constitutional and political breakdown of 1963.[6]

In any case the overall political and constitutional settlement that has its basis in the Zurich and London agreements is set at two levels – the international, which is demarcated by the three treaties, and the internal, which is fixed by the 1960 constitution. The three treaties, the treaty of establishment, the treaty of alliance and the treaty of guarantee, reflected the uneasy compromise negotiated at Zurich and London, and effectively shackled the newly born state. The treaty of establishment, between Cyprus and Great Britain, sets up the republic of Cyprus and provides that its territory 'shall comprise the island of Cyprus . . . with the exception of two areas', which remain 'under the sovereignty of the United Kingdom'. This treaty of course secures British military interests in the area, and in effect provides for the retention of British influence in the Middle East. It could perhaps have been thought that the recognition of British sovereign bases was an additional military guarantee of the integrity of Cyprus and its constitution. If this was indeed one of the objectives of the treaty of establishment, this has obviously not been carried out. The treaty of alliance was concluded between Cyprus, Greece and Turkey. By this the contracting parties undertook to resist any attack or aggression directed against the independence or territorial integrity of Cyprus, and for this purpose it was further provided that a tripartite headquarters should be established and that Greek and Turkish military contingents, consisting of 950 and 650 officers and men respectively, should be stationed on the territory of the republic. Finally, by the treaty of guarantee, the most controversial of all, enosis and partition were excluded, the republic of Cyprus undertook the obligation to maintain its independence and the constitutional order created, and the three guarantor powers, Great Britain, Greece and Turkey, guaranteed the continuation and maintenance of 'the state of affairs established by the basic articles of its constitution', as well as the independence and territorial integrity of Cyprus, and reserved to themselves the right to take steps for the restoration of Cyprus' status in

[5] Mackenzie, supra n.1, at 2.

[6] See Kedourie, *The Cyprus Problem and its Solution* (1973) (An International Seminar Report).

case of any change or disturbance, or in the event of a breach of the provisions of the treaty. The final clause of the treaty of guarantee which was later to be invoked by Turkey in justification of its military intervention provides that in the event of a breach 'Greece, Turkey and the United Kingdom undertake to consult together with respect to the representations or measures necessary to ensure observance of these provisions'. In so far as common or concerted action may not prove possible, 'each of the three guaranteeing powers reserves the right to take action with the sole aim of re-establishing the state of affairs created by the present treaty'.

As far as internal constitutional and governmental arrangements are concerned, these are contained in the 1960 constitution, which was drafted within the rigid and narrow framework of the Zurich and London agreements. There have been a number of extensive commentaries[7] on this constitution and there is almost universal agreement about its incredible complexity, overwhelming (bi)communal character, and sui generis provisions. Its central principles were, first, that the state being set up was a bicommunal one, and secondly that there had to be the most minute and detailed regulation of every issue in the relations between Greek and Turkish Cypriots that could ever become controversial and a possible bone of contention between the two communities. Its very first article provides that the state of Cyprus is an independent and sovereign republic with a presidential regime, the President being Greek and the Vice-President being a Turk elected by the Greek and Turkish communities of Cyprus respectively; and there follow a group of provisions which establish the communal character of the state. Thus, the two communities are first defined, and an equal status is accorded to them with regard to a great number and variety of matters, including the official languages of the republic, the choice of its flag, the right to fly the national flag of Greece or Turkey as the case may be, the celebration of Greek and Turkish national holidays, and many others. Other provisions entrench the recognition of the two communities' separate existence, particularly in the political and cultural areas. Thus, to take but two examples, all elections take place on the basis of separate communal electoral lists and separate voting, and sound and vision broadcasting hours are allocated between the two communities according to a complicated formula. Additionally, the constitution provides for an exclusively communal level of political and social activity. It does so by demarcating special communal competencies and jurisdictions, and by establishing organs and structures which are

[7] Polyviou, *Cyprus, The Tragedy and the Challenge* (1975), 55–108; Polyviou, *Cyprus, In Search of a Constitution* (1976), 13–26; de Smith, *The New Commonwealth and its Constitutions* (1964), 282–96; de Smith, *Constitutional and Administrative Law* (1977), 22–3; Friedrich, *Trends of Federalism in Theory and Practice* (1968), 123–8; Kyriakides, *Cyprus: Constitutionalism and Crisis Government* (1968).

purely communal in representation and function. Thus, provision is made for two communal chambers, each elected separately by its own community and having exclusive legislative competence with regard to religious, educational, cultural and teaching matters, personal status, the composition of courts dealing with civil disputes relating to personal status and to religious matters, and matters 'where the interests and institutions are of purely communal nature'. With regard to all these the two communal chambers are declared to have power to impose direct taxation on the members of their respective communities and are also given competence both to direct policy within their communal laws and to exercise administrative powers in the manner that, and through such persons as, may be provided by a communal law, provided that no law or decision of a communal chamber shall contain anything contrary to the security of the republic or its constitutional order or public safety, or anything which detracts from the fundamental rights and liberties guaranteed by the constitution. As is apparent, the communal chambers, entrusted with jurisdiction over communal matters, are special legislative assemblies, their range of competence being of a personal rather than a territorial kind, or, to put it somewhat differently, the legislative competence of the communal chambers is limited by reference to two general criteria, the subject matter of legislation and the communal status of the persons to whom their enactments are addressed. In this connection one should also note the provision regarding the creation of separate municipalities in the five largest towns of the republic. Whereas in all other matters what is established is a functional separation or differentiation, in the municipal case, and it is the only one, the relevant constitutional provisions are based on a supposed territorial separation of the two communities. Finally, the two communities are accorded rights of special relationship with Greece and Turkey respectively. It is thus provided that the two communities have the right to receive subsidies from the Greek and Turkish governments for institutions and purposes of education, culture, athletics and charity; and where necessary, Greece and Turkey may also provide schoolmasters and clergymen for the functioning of the relevant communal institutions. Education and culture are thus viewed as strictly communal concerns, which in turn means that no state responsibility in this connection is recognised and no effort is made to integrate communal institutions and processes within the scope of state activity. Education in particular is obviously conceived in a very narrow sense, as simply the transmission of communal cultural and religious values from which the state must strictly abstain. What appears only too clearly from the above is that communalism was the basis of the 1960 constitutional arrangements, everything else being pitilessly and shortsightedly sacrificed on its altar.

When one now turns to an examination of the political system and its distribution of governmental powers, the following features are particularly noticeable. To begin with, almost all state organs are designed to ensure the participation of the two communities as such in both their composition and functioning. The basis and extent of this participation vary from organ to organ. Thus, in the area of the executive, there are both a Greek President and a Turkish Vice-President who jointly 'ensure' executive power and who have, for this purpose, a Council of Ministers composed of seven Greek Ministers and three Turkish ministers. These ministers should be designated respectively by the President and the Vice-President, who shall then appoint them by instrument signed by them both, and may be dismissed at will by the relevant appointing authority. It is further provided that the decisions of the Council shall be taken by absolute majority and must, unless the right of veto or return is exercised by the President or the Vice-President, be promulgated immediately by them both. As regards legislative power, it is provided that this shall be exercised by the House of Representatives, consisting of 50 representatives of whom 35 should be Greeks and 15 Turks, 'in all matters except those expressly reserved to the communal chambers'; further, the President of the House is to be a Greek, to be elected by the Greek Cypriot representatives, and the Vice-President must be a Turk, to be elected by the Turkish representatives. In the area of the judiciary, authority is vested in the Supreme Constitutional Court and the High Court. The former is to be composed of three judges, a Greek, a Turkish and a neutral judge, the neutral judge to be the President, and the latter is to consist of two Greek judges, one Turkish judge and a neutral judge, the neutral judge again to be the President and to have two votes.

The public service under the 1960 constitution was to be composed of Greek and Turkish Cypriots according to a ratio of 7 : 3. This same ratio is also prescribed for the security forces of the republic, these being divided into the police and the gendarmerie. In the armed forces the relevant ratio was 6 : 4. In charge of appointments to the public service was to be a public service commission consisting of ten members. In general, its decisions were to be taken by simple majority but this was qualified by other provisions making it necessary that in matters of appointment, promotions and transfers, and in questions of discipline this majority had to include a minimum number of Greek and Turkish votes depending on whether the decision related to a Greek or a Turk. In short, a power of veto was given to a section of the Greek or Turkish members to frustrate majority decisions on the basis of collateral political considerations. In the case of the 'independent officers' of the republic, namely the Attorney-General, the Auditor-General and the Governor of the Issuing Bank, as in the case of the heads of the army, the police and the gendarmerie, the relevant appointment may by and large be made from either community, but each of the above-mentioned officials must have a deputy appointed from the other community. It can thus be seen that communal participation in governmental organs takes a number of forms. In some it is represented by numerical equality, as in the Supreme Constitutional Court; elsewhere it is based on a fixed ratio that, again, varies with the different organs and departments; and in areas such as the executive or some of the other independent offices of the republic two positions are recognised and set up, and the relevant power is shared between them more or less on a basis of equality.

A second characteristic feature of the 1960 constitution is that through a multiplication of checks and balances most of the major affairs of state are effectively subject to the agreement or concurrence of the representatives of the two communities. Thus, in the executive area, both the President and the Vice-President have the right to delay decisions in many matters and to veto them in others, and these powers can be exercised either separately or jointly. In greater detail, either the President or the Vice-President may veto a decision of the Council of Ministers concerning foreign affairs, defence or security, or return any other decision for reconsideration. This executive right of final veto is also extended to any law or decision of the House of Representatives or any part thereof concerning foreign affairs, defence or security. Further, the President and the Vice-President also have the right, either separately or conjointly, to return any law or decision or any part thereof of the House of Representatives to the House for reconsideration. In such a case, the House of Representatives must pronounce on the matter so returned within fifteen days, and if the House persists in its decision the President and the Vice-President shall then promulgate the law or decision as the case may be, unless in the meantime they exercise, separately or conjointly, the right of veto or their right of reference to the Supreme Court so that the question of constitutionality may be adjudicated upon. In addition, a number of decisions or acts within the authority of the President and the Vice-President, such as the choice of flag, the promulgation of legislation and of decisions of the Council of Ministers, the appointment of ministers and of many high public officials, and many others, also require the agreement or joint action of both. Similarly, in the legislative area, three important classes of legislation, namely any attempted modification of the electoral arrangements, the adoption of any law relating to the munici-palities, and the enactment of any law imposing duties or taxes, require 'a separate simple majority of the representatives elected by the Greek and Turkish communities respectively taking part in the vote'; separate two-thirds majorities are required for the amendment of those relatively less important articles of the constitution which are in fact capable of amendment; but a great number of the 1960 constitutional provisions are designated as basic and are declared to be unamendable.

A third obvious and important feature of the Zurich constitution is the fragmentation of what might be thought to be integral functions and their dispersal among a great number of governmental and communal bodies. Thus, to take the most obvious and important example, in the area of the executive there is a bewildering variety of powers allocated to the various executive organs. There are thus (i) separate presidential powers, (ii) separate vice-presidential powers, (iii) powers belonging to the President and the Vice-President jointly, (iv) limited executive powers belonging to the Communal Chambers, (v) executive powers vested in the individual ministers, and (vi) general executive power 'in all other matters' which belongs to and can be exercised by the Council of Ministers. These executive arrangements have no exact parallel elsewhere. The constitution supposedly establishes a 'presidential regime', but this must be viewed rather sceptically. Perhaps it would be more correct to describe it as a vice-presidential one,[8] so inflated are the powers of the Turkish Vice-President and so great the obstructive potential of his prerogatives, the final and unqualified veto given to him in the vital areas delineated above being but the culmination of this unparallelled constitutional generosity. It might perhaps be argued that since it is the Council of Ministers that is entrusted with general and residual executive power, all other fields of executive competence being specifically enumerated, it is this body which in reality is the chief executive organ of the state. But this is at most the facade, not the reality of power. It is not only that the Council's meetings are convened by the President and the Vice-President, or even that the two of them are the ones who 'ensure' executive power. The most significant provision here is the one that allows the termination of ministerial appointments by the President, in the case of Greek Ministers, and by the Vice-President, in the case of the Turks. The inevitable result is that Greek Ministers derive their authority from the Greek President and Turkish ministers from the Turkish Vice-President; this in turn makes impossible the development of genuine collective responsibility. There is a similar fragmentation and dispersal of responsibilities elsewhere. There are thus three legislative bodies, the House of Representatives and the two communal chambers, and the House, in those cases when separate majorities are necessary, is in effect required to divide into two separate communal groups, which naturally means that the number of bodies which exercise or can frustrate legislative authority is correspondingly increased. More remarkably, not only are two superior courts plus a substantial number of subordinate civil and criminal tribunals set up, but also the jurisdiction of the latter is

---

[8] de Smith, *The New Commonwealth and its Constitutions*, supra n.7. at 286.

declared to vary with the communal or ethnic origin of the defendant(s) or litigants. Even the holding of routine inquests is not immune to this illiberal provision. Where the deceased belongs to one community the inquest must be conducted by a coroner from the same community, and in cases where there are more than one deceased belonging to different communities special arrangements for the appointment of a coroner must be made by the High Court.

Finally, as has already been mentioned, many articles of the constitution, included in a special annex, are described as 'basic' and 'cannot, in any way, be amended, whether by way of variation, addition or repeal'. This is the feature of constitutional unamendability, yet another of the extraordinary characteristics of the 1960 arrangements.

There has been almost unanimous agreement that the 1960 constitution was unsound and seriously defective in terms of both political balance and functional capacity. It has thus been described as 'the most rigid, detailed and complicated constitution in the world',[9] and even the UN mediator called it an 'oddity'[10]. This is not the place for an elaborate investigation. Suffice it to say that the 1960 constitution failed to provide a sound framework for the government of the republic, and that it is open to numerous objections, the main ones of which are the following.

To begin with it is strikingly (and what is more important *unnecessarily*) undemocratic and inequitable, and not simply anti-majoritarian, the most pronounced of its many undemocratic and politically controversial features being the absolute veto given to the President and the Vice-President, the legislative separate majorities, and the inflated percentage of the Turkish community's participation in the public service and security forces. It cannot be denied that the 1960 constitution gave excessive powers to the Turkish community, then not more than 18 per cent of the total population, and deposited with their leadership obstructionist potential out of all proportion and indeed totally unrelated to the Turkish Cypriots' admitted need for security. This iniquitous imbalance caused the frustration of the larger ethnic group, the Greek Cypriots, and the accumulated tension and stress could not be absorbed by the constitutional structures and institutions. In no state is it possible in the long run for a smaller ethnic group, particularly if it is as small in comparison to the main group as the Turkish Cypriots vis-à-vis the Greek Cypriots, to enjoy rights and exercise powers which the larger group is unwilling to recognise, and again no larger group, particularly if it is over 80 per cent of the population, will willingly recognise excessive rights to a smaller ethnic group by which moreover it will be seriously limited in the pursuit of its

[9] de Smith, *Constitutional and Administrative Law*, supra n.7, at 22.
[10] *Report of the United Nations Mediator on Cyprus to the Secretary-General*, UN doc. S/6253.

interests. At the same time, despite this unprecedented constitutional generosity, not enough was done to give the Turkish community both the reality and the psychological assurance of security. Ample political power was given to it, it is true, but this could not be exercised directly for its protection. Its use or abuse could bring the state to a standstill, as it actually did, but this did not and could not provide security.

Further, the 1960 constitution is open to serious objections in so far as both its general approach and its particular dispositions with regard to the special problems posed by the existence within one state of two politically opposed ethnic groups of substantially different sizes are concerned. For, if a general theoretical statement of the objectives, orientation and funda-mental premises of the Zurich settlement is attempted, it can more or less accurately be said that the 1960 constitution was intended as the legal and political framework for what was conceived to be in important respects a bicommunal society. This perception can of course be questioned and has indeed often been strongly objected to by the Greek side on the ground that no society composed as to more than its four-fifths of one ethnic group should be designated as bicommunal; but what cannot be doubted is that the 1960 order was supposed to provide, among other things, for the resolution of what was thought to be a dangerous and potentially explosive constitutional and ethnic conflict between the island's two communities, and can therefore legitimately be judged as such. In this respect, it is abundantly clear, the 1960 constitution miserably failed. Its artificial and rigid structure could not cope with the stress of the continuing inter-communal conflict, and its complicated and uncoordinated mechanisms could not absorb increasing tension or resolve outstanding disputes.

The constitutional perspective[11] must be widened. What are the essential constituents of a sound constitutional strategy or policy in cases such as Cyprus? As has been pointed out in the introduction, phrases such as 'constitutional strategy' and 'constitutional policy' must be used with caution and with awareness of their limitations. One should not be deluded into placing too much trust and confidence in the value and efficacy of constitutions as such. However well balanced, they are no panaceas, and no constitution can artificially create social unity and political harmony if in fact the operative currents are flowing too strongly in an opposite direction. Nor, as has been seen, is the Cyprus problem exclusively legal. Its international repercussions and ramifications are there for all to see and are such that even what might be regarded as viable constitutional settlements are not necessarily final political solutions. Yet, on the other hand, the value of sound constitutional arrangements cannot and should not be underestimated; it is a serious mistake to underrate the role and

[11] See de Smith, supra n.7; Polyviou, supra n.7.

psychological importance of legal and institutional forms in social and political behaviour; and it should not be forgotten that the Cyprus conflict, despite its other characteristics, does present important constitutional issues the satisfactory resolution of which is nothing short of crucial. The central one can be formulated as follows: states built upon the political integration of two ethnic groups substantially varying in size often go through phases of acute constitutional conflict even when there are no opposing national policies endangering the independence and integrity of the state. In these the fundamental constitutional problem is related to the pattern that their structure and institutional apparatus should have so that potential conflict situations can be avoided and inevitable intercommunal tension absorbed and legitimated through regular constitutional and political channels. More specifically, a sound constitutional policy with regard to bicommunal societies in general and Cyprus in particular should, at the very least, be directed towards, first the successful institutional-isation of the cooperation of the various ethnic groups in the running of governmental affairs and the sharing of power; secondly, a fair allocation of the structures and functions of the state, and the achievement thereby of a satisfactory power balance between the various ethnic groups excluding both political dominance over and oppression of the smaller group(s) as well as the frustration and alienation of the larger and major group(s); and thirdly the provision of revision procedures and adequate readjustment machinery for the amicable resolution of inevitable disputes and the renegotiation of the political and constitutional arrangements in the event of their proving unworkable or unsatisfactory.

The 1960 arrangements failed on all three scores. To begin with, instead of attempting to institutionalise bicommunal cooperation by workable provisions and living institutions based on the traditions and realities of the island, rigid and unworkable patterns and structures were set up. No incentives for cooperation were provided, and functions and responsi-bilities were not in general coordinated. Government itself was conceived of not as a process based on compromise and mutual accommodation but as a static amalgamation of checks and balances, the underlying theory apparently being that only through neutralization of the power of the larger group would there be security for the smaller one. Further, as demonstrated above, too many governmental bodies and organs were provided, and these made up a heavy and expensive state machinery which was disproportionate to the size and resources of the island, and, in many respects, devoid of functional relevance. These structures moreover were unfairly distributed with the result that a false intercommunal balance of power was established, out of tune both with the real strength of the two communities and with their genuine needs, and this in turn could only be maintained at the original position by obstructionist and obstinate use of power on the part of the minority. So erratically divided was the system of distribution of power and so delicately balanced the various governmental and communal jurisdictions that what was clearly needed was rational machinery for resolving disputes and readjusting positions. Instead, the Zurich constitution provided for unnecessarily involved processes which, in the final analysis, not only could provide no answers to intercommunal problems but themselves had a seriously adverse effect upon the capacity of the state. Nor could fresh political or communal bargains be negotiated by the two sides since, in addition to all else, the 1960 constitutional arrangements were, in all essential respects, meant to be forever binding and non-negotiable. All in all, under the Zurich constitution, because of the absence of correction devices and sound adjudicatory procedures, disagreements could only become unresolved deadlocks; and these breed conflict and confrontation.

It will be seen that it is not necessary to base a damning indictment of the 1960 constitution on simple majoritarian lines, even though that is what the Greek Cypriot side mainly did in the years following independence. For surely it cannot be doubted that in a society where majority and minority are permanent, and where as a result there is a real danger that at least for the time being political decisions will follow automatically from deeply ingrained notions of community and ethnic allegiance instead of representing the electorate's shifting preferences according to the issues placed before it, the principle of majority rule must be substantially modified by the pressing claims of a different set of principles. Some of these are: permanent ethnic, racial or communal minorities must be positively protected; in many cases this positive protection cannot be guaranteed in the context of a regime of pure majoritarian democracy and must therefore not be left to the vagaries of popular rule; and the problems of a permanent minority that is suspicious of the majority must be dealt with by all available means and devices, such as the entrenchment of certain clauses in the constitution, the recognition of adequate local government, the necessity in some cases for reinforced or even concurrent majorities before legislative or constitutional changes can be effected so that legislation considered detrimental by one side or the other can be blocked, the reservation of seats in the legislative and executive organs, in some cases separate electoral rolls, provision for adequate participation in the public service, and others.[12] But if the legitimate claims of the major group are not also respected, if care is not taken to promote (at least some) political interaction between the various communities, if the constitution is generally seen not as a necessary attempt to mediate fairly between conflicting political demands and ethnic aspirations but rather as an

[12] Kedourie, supra n.6.

expedient device for reconciling external interests, and if moreover the eventual political and constitutional compromise does not emanate from the free will of the people most directly affected but has instead been negotiated behind their backs, then it is almost certain that the necessary goodwill for operating complicated constitutional provisions will not be there, with the equally inevitable result that the provisions themselves will ultimately become the breeding ground for deadlock and breakdown. This is precisely what happened with the 1960 constitution.

2. *The constitutional crisis and the 13 proposals*

Both because of Greek Cypriot resentment of the way in which the 1960 accords had been negotiated in their absence, which made them unwilling 'to exert much effort in order to perpetuate an arrangement for which they did not have any great affection',[13] and because of Turkish Cypriot intransigence and mistrust, which made them 'suspicious, unaccommodating, and inclined to adopt a rigid attitude'[14] on those governmental and constitutional problems which soon (and indeed inevitably) arose after the establishment of the republic (as well as because of the inherent complexity and unworkability of many of the constitutional provisions) it was not long before serious disagreements began to appear and divide Greek and Turkish Cypriots. The first issue to cause 'genuine difficulties'[15] was the attempted implementation of the 70 : 30 ratio in the public service. The Greek Cypriots looked upon this provision as causing their community a loss of jobs, and as being clearly discriminatory. In addition, the Greek Cypriot side maintained,[16] the allocation of 30 per cent of the posts in the civil service to the Turkish Cypriots created serious problems for the state. It made it necessary, in considering appointments and promotions, to use criteria other than those universally accepted, such as qualifications, efficiency and the general suitability of candidates, because, obviously, the appointing authority had to take into consideration and indeed give primacy to ethnic and communal factors. It was an inevitable result of the attempted implementation of this provision that the best candidates simply could not be selected. Particular hardship was created in the case of promotions. Public servants who possessed all the required qualifications and experience for promotion to higher grades were overlooked in favour

[13] Ibid, at 4.

[14] Ibid.

[15] Crawshaw, supra n.1, at 365

[16] Makarios, 'Proposals to amend the Cyprus constitution', supra n.2. These proposals appear in summary form in P.I.O., Republic of Cyprus, *Cyprus: The Problem in Perspective* (Nicosia 1968); see also Polyviou, *Cyprus, In Search of a Constitution*, supra n.7, 38–41

of less qualified public servants solely for the purpose of giving effect to an artificially fixed communal ratio of participation. The Turkish Cypriots, in public, disagreed violently.[17] They, as they then said, looked upon the 70 : 30 ratio as essential for the purpose of securing 'for the Turkish community adequate representation in all spheres of governmental activity'. Without this the Greek Cypriots would be enabled to gain complete control of the governmental machine, and this in view of 'past experience' could not be tolerated. Controversy over appointments continued, the Turkish leadership complained that positions in the public service were not being filled on the basis of the constitutionally prescribed ratio, and in retaliation the Turkish members of the House of Representatives refused to vote for the budget, with the result that the republic was left without tax laws, to the serious detriment of the economy.[18]

A somewhat different source of tension was the proposed creation of a Cyprus army. The question was whether this army, whose formation was envisaged in the constitution, was to be formed on a separate or a mixed basis. The Turkish side insisted on separation, namely that soldiers of Greek and Turkish origins could not be quartered together because 'of linguistic and religious differences'. The Council of Ministers however decided that there should be no separation, but that the army should be integrated. This was vetoed by the Turkish Vice-President, with the result that the plan to form a Cyprus army was abandoned.

But the issue which above all others led to the constitutional breakdown of 1963 and proved to be the most volatile of all was the separation of the municipalities. Article 173 of the 1960 constitution provided that separate municipalities were to be created in the five largest towns 'provided that the President and Vice-President of the republic shall within four years of the day of the going into operation of this constitution examine the question whether or not this separation of municipalities shall continue', and Article 177 provided that each municipality should exercise its jurisdiction within a region (of the relevant town) the limits of which should be fixed by agreement between the President and the Vice-President. If one were to examine Article 173 in isolation one would no doubt say that its application should be simple since it clearly declares in imperative language that separate municipalities should be established. Difficulties arose however from the fact that in none of the towns concerned did the population live exclusively in 'ethnic' areas, and indeed in most urban regions Greeks and Turks lived together.[19] The President and the Vice-President appointed committees in each town which met and

---

[17] The Turkish Communal Chamber, *The Turkish Case: 70 : 30 and the Greek Tactics* (1963).
[18] Ehrlich, *Cyprus 1958–1967* (1974), at 43; Crawshaw, supra n.1, at 366.
[19] Clerides, *Outline of the Negotiations Regarding the Question of Municipalities in the Five Towns*, at 1.

tried to reach agreement on defining the areas of the municipal councils, but without success. This remained a highly contentious issue. Therefore the President, in order to resolve the deadlock that had developed, made on 19 March 1962 certain proposals to the Vice-President which were designed both to by-pass the difficulty of defining separate Greek and Turkish regions and to make adequate provision for Turkish Cypriot interests. Archbishop Makarios expressed the view that the geographical separation of the municipalities was difficult to bring about without severe detriment to both communities. He therefore suggested the establishment of a united municipal authority in each town and the proportional representation on it of Greeks and Turks. With a view to safeguarding the rights of Turkish citizens, he also suggested that the staff to be employed by the municipal authorities should be in proportion to the Greek and Turkish populations in each town, that a percentage of the annual budget of each municipality, to be fixed in advance, should be made available for the needs of Turkish citizens in ways to be suggested by the Turkish members of the municipal council, and that in each of the five towns where the mayor was a Greek the deputy mayor should be a Turk, if this was justified by the proportion of the Turkish population. On 20 March 1962 the President of the Turkish communal chamber, Mr Denktash, described President Makarios' statement as 'unrealistic'. During subsequent negoti-ations Mr Clerides, President of the House of Representatives, expressed the view that in his opinion there was a duty on the President and the Vice-President under the constitution to consider whether separate Municipali-ties should exist or not. He advised that it was desirable for the two sides to solve the problem by first carrying on an experiment for a limited period and then by proceeding accordingly. In his view the right approach was to set up mixed councils to administer the municipal affairs of the five towns with proportionate representation on each based on population, enacting at the same time all necessary safeguards to assure the Turkish side that no discrimination whatsoever could be practised against them, and leaving entirely for the Turkish members of each council to decide the manner in which a certain percentage of the estimates, fixed by law, would be disposed of.[20] The whole exercise would be reconsidered after an experimental period. Apparently Mr Denktash expressed the view that this was an interesting compromise, worthy of further consideration. Shortly thereafter a more detailed paper was prepared by Mr Clerides expounding further these proposals which, it can be seen, had a number of advantages. They would have reduced financial expenditure with regard to the burden of maintaining separate municipalities, they would have avoided the thorny problem of geographical division, and they would have

[20] Ibid.

adequately safeguarded the interests of the Turkish community. And, had they been finally accepted and implemented, there would have been an important indication that the two communities were at last prepared to work together in the interests of a more efficient performance of governmental functions. Indeed the Turkish side initially accepted the Clerides suggestions and an announcement was made to the press that 'common ground' had been found paving the way for eventual agreement. Yet, not long afterwards the Turkish side reverted to its old position, demanding geographical separation of the towns. A significant opportunity for a decisive breakthrough in intercommunal relations was lost.

This is not the place to apportion responsibility or establish the specific causes of the many constitutional difficulties. What cannot be denied is that by 1963, partly because of the parties' mutual suspicion, hostility and absence of good will which made them adopt rigid and uncompromising positions and partly because of the complexity of the constitutional arrangements which themselves proved a fertile source of disputes, key governmental operations had come 'to a virtual halt'[21]. On many vital issues, including financial legislation, the composition of the public service, and the separation of the municipalities, Greek and Turkish Cypriots were 'at an impasse'.[22] The state could not function. On 30 November 1963, some three years after the constitution came into force, President Makarios made certain proposals[23] to the Turkish Vice-President, Dr Kutchuk, for the revision of 'at least some of those provisions of the constitution' which impeded the smooth functioning and development of the state. He said in a preamble to his proposals that he believed that the intention of those who drew up the agreements at Zurich and London was to create an independent state, in which the interests of the Turks would be safeguarded, but 'it could not have been their intention that the smooth functioning and development of the country should be prejudiced or thwarted, as has in fact been the case'. He continued by observing that the main consequence of the difficulties created 'by certain constitutional provisions' was 'to prevent the Greeks and Turks of Cyprus from co-operating in a spirit of understanding and friendship, to undermine the relations between them and to cause them to draw further apart instead of closer together, to the detriment of the well-being of the people of Cyprus as a whole'. It was therefore essential to consider remedial modifications to the constitutional structure of the republic.

The Greek Cypriot proposals were that the executive veto and the

---

[21] Ehrlich, supra n.18, at 38–9.

[22] Ibid.

[23] Makarios, 'Proposals to amend the Cyprus constitution', *International Relations (Athens)*, April 1964, 8–25; see also *Cyprus: The Problem in Perspective*, supra n.16, 9–15, and Polyviou, *Cyprus, In Search of a Constitution*, supra n.16, 27–43.

constitutional provisions regarding separate majorities should be abolished; that the administration of justice and the organisation of the municipalities should be unified; that the proportion of Turkish Cypriot participation in the public service and the forces of the republic should be brought down to 20 per cent; that the positions of the Turkish Vice-President and of the Turkish Vice-President of the House of Representatives should be upgraded by providing first that the Vice-President of the republic should deputise for the President in the case of the latter's temporary absence or incapacity to perform his duties and secondly that the Turkish Vice-President of the House should similarly deputise for the Greek President; that the number of the members of the public service commission should be reduced and that all its decisions should be taken by simple majority; that the division of the security forces into police and gendarmerie should be abolished, and that the numerical strength of the security forces should be determined by an ordinary law; and that the Greek communal chamber should be abolished. It was not the intention of his proposals, Archbishop Makarios concluded, to deprive the Turkish Cypriots of either their just rights and interests or of proper safeguards. Their purpose was only to remove certain causes of friction and various obstacles to the smooth operation of the state.

Shortly after the circulation of the proposed amendments the Turkish government announced that they were utterly unacceptable, that they should not even be discussed, and that the 1960 constitution should not be modified in any way, however minor. The Turkish Cypriot side soon followed suit, and Vice-President Kutchuk in a subsequent memorandum[24] accused the Greek Cypriot side first of intentionally not implementing those parts of the constitution which had favoured the Turkish community and then of attempting to overthrow it completely by the submission of 'sweeping amendments'. It was true, he admitted, that the constitution contained many *sui generis* provisions, but this had been necessitated by the peculiar nature of the Cyprus problem, i.e. the existence of two communities, the geographical proximity of Turkey and the intention on the part of Greece to annex the island. 'It was the aim at Zurich that the Cyprus ailment should be cured by the proper administration of a detailed regime,' the Vice-President remarked. 'But the medicine was deliberately withheld'. And now those who had been guilty of this neglect were saying that the constitution was useless and were advocating a more drastic remedy, 'amendment'. But this could never be accepted, as it would involve 'amputation' of Turkish rights. Dr Kutchuk concluded by refusing to hold any discussions with the Greek Cypriot side regarding the proposed constitutional amendments. He saw in them 'a predetermined policy to

[24] Kutchuk, *Cyprus: Reply to President's Memorandum.*

abrogate the agreements which had brought about the republic of Cyprus and to create an independent Greek State in which the Turks would be left at the complete mercy of the Greeks'. His own proposal was that the Greek Cypriots should abandon any thought of amendment, accept the Turkish Cypriots as full 'partners' and resign themselves to the immutability of the 1960 constitution.

Whatever possibility may have existed at the time for rational discussion of the proposed amendments between the two sides disappeared with the outbreak of violent disturbances between Greek and Turkish Cypriots on 21 December 1963.

How should Archbishop Makarios' 13 proposals be assessed politically and legally?

The basic position of the Cyprus government was that the constitution had been imposed on the republic; that the combined operation of the constitution and the treaty of guarantee meant that a situation had been created whereby constitutional and political development had been arrested in its infancy and the republic itself placed in a straitjacket; and that, as regards its internal operation, the 1960 constitution had proved both unworkable and grossly unfair. Clearly, various options presented themselves to the Greek Cypriot leadership and Archbishop Makarios in particular. One solution would be to do nothing and always attempt to solve outstanding problems by compromise and mediation. This, in the eyes of the Greek Cypriot leadership, was undesirable and unsatisfactory, for a number of reasons. It would not cure the underlying causes of friction, would do nothing to bring about essential constitutional reforms, and, through the separatist tactics of the Turkish Cypriot leadership, the two communities would draw further apart, with a real danger of total constitutional deadlock eventually leading to partition. In turn, to allow the constitution to be used or abused for communal purposes, President Makarios believed, would permit further intrusion by Turkey in the affairs of Cyprus.

A second option was to identify the specific issues on which there had been serious disagreement in the attempted implementation of the 1960 constitution and proceed to deal with them either one by one or in a gradual and phased way. On this model, no general plan for constitutional reform would be put forward, but a gradual and lengthy process of amendment would be embarked upon. An essential element of this process would be the taking of measures for assuring the Turkish Cypriots that any constitutional modifications would be reconsidered after a fixed period of time, including a guarantee that there would be a return to the previously existing position if the amendments failed to work satisfactorily. This, too, was not considered acceptable by the Greek Cypriot leadership. Its view was that the whole constitutional framework was fundamentally defective and that no meaningful progress could be achieved unless its basic imbalance was corrected. Wholesale and drastic amendment was therefore necessary.

This brings one to the third possible decision available to, and actually followed by, Archbishop Makarios – the submission of comprehensive proposals for a general overhauling and amendment of the constitution. This had the twin advantages of comprehensiveness and candour. It had the weakness that it made no secret of the ultimate intention of the Greek Cypriot side, namely to secure a more 'progressive', 'democratic' and 'unitary' constitution that would with time lead to internal and external conditions favouring the exercise of the right of self-determination, something that was unacceptable to the Turkish side. But since what was really needed, according to the Greek Cypriot side, was in effect a new constitution, the circulation of full proposals would both give the whole picture and facilitate discussion.

A fourth possibility would have been to proceed to a unilateral abrogation of parts, or even of the whole, of the 1960 constitution. Indeed, this seems to follow logically from the view of the Greek Cypriot side that the 1960 accords had been imposed. The 1960 constitution, it will be recalled, did not allow for any amendment or variation of its basic articles but, had the course of unilateral abrogation been followed, it could have been plausibly maintained, in addition to the argument concerning the imposition of the agreements, that perpetual constitutional restrictions 'agreed to in exchange for the grant of independence'[25] are invalid both on the ground of undue influence and by reason of their inconsistency with the doctrine of sovereignty; and in that case a suitable amending procedure might have been provided either by a referendum or by the calling of a constituent assembly. A final possible decision would have been to abrogate unilaterally all the accords of Zurich and London, namely the 1960 constitution and the associated treaties. Indeed, quite often during the years that followed, Greek Cypriot spokesmen referred to the 1960 accords as 'unequal' and 'inequitable', and, to the extent that they did not allow for any amendment, these, it was contended, could not but be null and void. This last course would have been the most drastic of all. For, even though the previous one, i.e. unilateral abrogation of the 1960 constitution, would also have involved unilateral action and constitutional revision that had not been agreed to by the Turkish side, still, an argument that at least some internal constitutional amendment should be possible whatever the restrictions that the initial constituent power has burdened itself or its

[25] See Ehrlich, supra n.18, at 53; and see Lester, 'Bizerta and the unequal treaty theory', 11 *I.C.L.Q.* 847, 855 (1962).

successors with is substantially more powerful than arguments favouring or supporting unilateral revision of treaties on the ground of inequality or inequity. Further, unforeseeable international complications would certainly attend this last course whereas the Greek Cypriot side could always maintain that internal constitutional revision, even though unilateral, had not encroached upon the external guarantees of Cyprus' independence and nonalignment. But however attractive and consistent arguments of unilateral abrogation might be in theory, Turkey had made it clear that any unilateral action would inevitably be followed by military intervention under the treaty of guarantee. And even though Greek Cypriot spokesmen had always argued that the treaty had given or could give no such right of military action, there was little doubt that in the event of unilateral abrogation or revision the pressures on any Turkish government to launch military operations would be irresistible – and the Greek Cypriot leadership and Archbishop Makarios knew this. In addition, there were other considerations militating in favour of less drastic courses. Thus, Greece wanted to avoid military complications with Turkey, and Great Britain, a party to the 1960 settlement, would not have readily acquiesced in unilateral action or accomplished facts. Finally, arguments alleging that the 1960 accords had been imposed or that they were unjust and inequitable, even though strong, were not conclusive; and to *propose* revision and agreed amendment rather than to proclaim unilateral abrogation was more likely to obtain international sympathy for the Greek Cypriot case. Thus, political and international factors effectively excluded the last two possible solutions and narrowed the range of available options to the first, second and third ones; and since the Greek Cypriot leadership was determined to embark upon some kind of constitutional revision, only the second and third courses offered themselves for serious consideration.

It is thought that choice of the third course on the part of the Greek Cypriot side was a grievous error, and that the second, namely a piecemeal and gradual amendment process, would have been much preferable, both because it was milder and because in the then overcharged atmosphere proposed wholesale revision stood little or no chance of acceptance.[26] The same conclusion can be obtained from a constitutional evaluation of the thirteen proposals. For a start, some of them are undeniably more controversial politically than others, the potentially adverse impact on bicommunalism of specific proposals being taken here as the relevant test of political acceptability. Thus, 'that the administration of justice should be unified' cannot have been regarded by the Turks, whatever their declarations and statements to the contrary, with the same aversion as the proposal that 'separate legislative majorities should be abolished'. The

[26] Polyviou, *Cyprus, The Tragedy and the Challenge*, supra, at 39.

demand for separate majorities was both much more significant politically, in that it was the chief support for the maintenance of the constitutionally enshrined communal balance of power, and moreover, on a different level, convincing practical arguments could be adduced that judicial separation was not only illiberal but also expensive and a positive nuisance. Furthermore, the administration of justice had always been more success-fully insulated than other services from the influence of communal factors, and the traditional cohesion of the legal profession in Cyprus could have allowed greater scope for the operation in this area of practical arguments and considerations of utility. Likewise, using now a different criterion, the proposed reduction in Turkish participation in the public service was, from the Turkish point of view, not as objectionable as efforts to democratise the processes and deliberations of the public service commission. To bring down simply in terms of percentages Turkish Cypriot participation would not have essentially modified the bicommunal character of the state, as seen by the Turks, nor would it have placed substantially greater political powers in Greek Cypriot hands. Indeed, as Turkish Cypriot spokesmen later admitted, a reduction in their public service participation would not have been entirely unwelcome as it would have 'liberated' many young Turks for various forms of private enterprise potentially more important to their prosperity as a community. But abrupt democratisation of essential state processes and their remodelling on majoritarian lines could not but have appeared to the Turkish Cypriots as a dangerous development that might change the internal balance of power and be taken internationally as a sign that the bicommunal nature of the state was giving way to unitary and majority principles.

In view of the above an alternative method of amendment that might have had better possibilities of being considered could have been one that initially only proposed that the Turkish Vice-President should deputise for the Greek President of the republic and that likewise the Turkish Vice-President of the House should deputise for the Greek President. In this way, the representative capacity of these organs, which were always looked upon as primarily communal ones, would have been expanded and their constitutional base broadened. What in other words should have been aimed at, at least as a first step, should have been a conversion of communal instrumentalities into political ones, but without any reduction in their powers or change in the way they would be elected. This would have been a start in the right direction both because of its generous nature and because of its likely integrative effects. Once this was accomplished, further politically neutral changes could have been considered, such as balanced reduction of the Turkish-Cypriot participation in the public service, and only after a considerable improvement of intercommunal relations, partly as a result of the successful operation of the above, should the amendment process have ventured into the sensitive realm of the exercise of political powers, such as the veto, and the crucial area of the security forces. And, wherever possible, proposed removal of what the Greeks viewed as excessive rights from the Turkish Cypriots should have been followed by a proposed increase in effective protection for their community. Instead for instance of proposing a total abolition of the provisions regarding separate majorities, as was done, an effort should have been made to replace them with a stiff requirement of an increased general majority which would also include a specified number of Turkish Cypriot representatives. Wholesale amendment of the 1960 constitution, it is believed, would at some point have been essential, but should only have been attempted at a much later stage, only when existing mutual suspicion had been reduced and the confidence of the Turkish Cypriots secured, and additionally only if iron-clad guarantees had at the same time been given that enosis would not be sought and that the status of independence would not be endangered. For these reasons the decision of the Cyprus government to circulate at that time of serious tension comprehensive proposals for amending the constitution, particularly since firm international support for such drastic changes had not been positively obtained beforehand, was a political miscalculation of the first order. In any case the Turkish Cypriot leadership, at the prompting of the Turkish government, absolutely rejected all proposals for amendment and made it clear that the 1960 constitution, as it stood, was perfectly satisfactory and should not be submitted to any change whatsoever.

The effort of the Greek Cypriot side to do away with the separatist character of the 1960 constitution and democratise it was unceremoniously rejected. The time had not yet come when the two sides would be able to meet in direct negotiation and hold detailed discussions on the constitutional future of Cyprus.

3. *The uneasy years*

A trivial incident seems to have sparked off the outbreak of intercommunal violence.[27] Some Turkish Cypriots were asked to produce their identity cards. They refused. The (Greek-Cypriot) policemen insisted. There was an argument. Shots were fired, it is not clear by whom. There were injuries on both sides. Given the prevailing atmosphere of tension it did not take long for serious fighting to engulf the island. Turkey threatened to invade, and Greece made it clear that she would come to the republic's assistance in

[27] See Foley, *Legacy of Strife: Cyprus from Rebellion to Civil War* (1964); Ehrlich, supra n.18, at 45 et seq; Crawshaw, supra n.1, at 366 et seq.

the event of Turkish aggression. Early in January 1964 most but not all Turkish officials withdrew from their positions, alleging that the government was no longer legitimate, and in a number of areas, mainly in the cities, fortifications and barricades went up. In late January 1964 the United States government suggested to President Makarios that a NATO peacekeeping force, mainly consisting of American and British troops, should be established and sent to the island. The Cyprus government had no hesitation in rejecting this proposal, which was again put forward, this time by Under-Secretary of State George Ball, in February. The American proposal was again rejected, and in March 1964 the Security Council set up a UN force in Cyprus. But Turkey once more threatened to invade and forcibly partition the island. In the summer of 1964 the situation once more became critical. In June the Turkish government of Ismet Inonu was ready to mount an invasion, only to be stopped by President Johnson's forthright intervention, but in August Turkish air force planes bombed Greek Cypriot villages, causing a heavy loss of civilian life. During the next two years sporadic incidents of violence continued, armaments and irregular forces accumulated, and the two sides drifted further apart. By the beginning of 1965 the 1960 constitution, whatever the formal legal position, was effectively dead. It was inevitable that the constitutional views of the two sides would also change.

In January 1964 a conference was called in London, known as the London conference, for the purpose of making another attempt to reach a settlement. By this time the positions of the representatives of the two communities concerning the future structure of the republic had greatly hardened and drawn much further apart. A settlement was therefore impossible and the London conference ended in complete failure amidst extreme tension and increasing hostility.

At this conference positions were advanced and proposals were made on the part of both sides. From the Greek Cypriot side there was now a demand that the state should be allowed to take an independent, unitary, integral form, with all legislative power vested in a parliament elected by universal suffrage on a common electoral roll, with executive power residing in a Council of Ministers responsible to Parliament and with judicial power exercisable by completely unified and independent judicial organs. In this connection, the Greek Cypriot side declared its readiness to consider a number of devices for ensuring Turkish representation in the legislature and the public service; and the Turkish minority would continue to enjoy full autonomy in matters of religion, education and culture. Universally accepted human rights would be maintained as integral parts of the constitution and, in addition, there would be the recognition of a right of appeal to an international tribunal against violations of those rights. As regards the external aspects of the problem, the treaties of alliance and guarantee would be revoked because they were incompatible with the notions of independence and sovereignty.

The Turkish Cypriots, in their turn, now abandoned insistence on the 1960 constitution and reverted to the previously proposed concept of partitioning/federating the island and separating the two communities. Recent events, in their view, had made it clear that the two communities could not live together in peace and that the Greek Cypriot side would attempt to bring about union with Greece. The 1960 constitution was not enough for protecting the Turkish Cypriots and for frustrating schemes for a Greek annexation of the island. Complete communal separation had therefore become necessary. On this view, the two ethnic groups would be concentrated, by compulsory population exchange if necessary, in two cohesive geographical areas, and a completely new political and administrative structure would be created on that basis. The treaties of alliance and guarantee, which, the Turkish side believed, alone ensured the security of the Turkish community by allowing military intervention by Turkey, would continue in force.

The deterioration of the situation was dealt with by the Security Council of the United Nations which, in its resolution of 4 March 1964, recommended that the Secretary-General should designate, in agreement with the government of Cyprus and the governments of Greece, Turkey and the UK, a mediator who should use his best endeavours with the representatives of the communities and the interested four governments in order to promote a peaceful solution and an agreed settlement of the problem. Impending UN mediation, particularly since it was expressly directed towards the finding of a solution, led to a further elaboration of the positions which the two sides had put forward at the London conference.

The Greek Cypriot side

The basic attitudes and arguments of the Greek Cypriot side regarding the political future and constitutional reconstruction of Cyprus, as explained orally to the mediator and other UN authorities and as formally stated on 13 May 1964 by Archbishop Makarios, President of the republic, can be set out as follows:[28]

(i) The Zurich and London agreements, on which the republic of Cyprus was founded, did not emanate from the free will of the people but were imposed on them. In the circumstances prevailing at the time Greek Cypriot 'acceptance' of the accords had been dictated 'by necessity'.

[28] *Certain Aspects of the Political Problem of Cyprus* (13 May 1964).

Further, the resulting constitution had been put into force without being approved by the people.

(ii) The 1960 constitution had put the Turkish minority, substantially, on the same level with regard to the exercise of political power with the Greek majority. This had been done despite its numerical strength, 18 per cent of the total population, its small proportion in land ownership and contribution to public expenditure, and 'contrary to every democratic principle'. This, the Greek Cypriot side alleged, was 'completely wrong'. Nor could the argument that the Turks of Cyprus had to be treated differently from other minorities because they formed either a part of the Turks of the mainland or a distinct ethnic community be accepted. To begin with, the existence of minorities in close proximity with their mother country was not a phenomenon peculiar to Cyprus. One came across similar situations in many other countries in the world. But the extraordinary proposition had never been put forward that such minorities should be given a privileged position with regard to their participation in the exercise of political power or that they should be under the protection of the foreign country from which they derived their ethnic origin. What should be accorded to minorities, including the Turkish Cypriot one, was protection of individual and communal rights and no discrimination in the matter of political participation. In addition, the Greek Cypriot side stated, from the moment that a section of the community was singled out and treated differently from the rest, that section was bound to acquire a 'separateness', something which would pose dangers and cause complications. 'If such section is given different rights from those of the rest of the community, as happened in the case of Cyprus, then artificial, unrealistic and unworkable means have to be devised in order to implement and safeguard such rights. Such a system is essentially unjust, in that citizens are given unequal treatment, and the inevitable consequence is conflict. The majority feels unfairly treated and therefore aggrieved, while the minority is forever suspecting the majority of endeavouring to take its privileges away'. The separate treatment demanded for the Turkish minority under the 1960 constitution, Archbishop Makarios continued, was wrong because it prevented integration and 'the development of unity and of a public conscience', accentuating in this way differences and perpetuating conflict.

(iii) The Greek Cypriot side maintained that, besides its many *sui generis* provisions and negative elements based on the concept of 'political communal segregation', the 1960 constitution suffered from the further fundamental defect that its basic articles could not be amended. This, the Greek Cypriots thought, did not have 'legal value' because, in their view, a present constituent power had no right to restrict the constituent power of the future. 'Furthermore, to preclude amendment of a constitution is to ignore reality and to deny progress'. But it was not only certain elements of the constitution which were defective. The whole concept on which it was based was entirely wrong. For this reason it was necessary to lay completely new foundations.

On the basis of these premises and arguments, concrete principles and proposals for constitutional and political reconstruction were put before the UN mediator on 13 May 1964. Since one of those principles was that the constitution, any constitution, had to be approved by the people of Cyprus, no details were formulated. These general principles, an elaboration of what had been proposed at the London Conference, were the following: Cyprus should become a completely independent, unitary, integral, sovereign state; all state powers should emanate from the people who would be entitled to decide the future of their country on the basis of the internationally accepted principle of self-determination; and no treaties with Greece or Turkey or any other country should form part of the final solution if these would, 'in any way', limit the independence or sovereignty of the state and prevent the people of Cyprus from amending, modifying or altering the constitution or from deciding, in a free and sovereign way, upon their future. Secondly, the constitution should as a general rule be based on the democratic principle that the political majority, at any election, should govern and that the political minority should constitute the opposition. Thirdly, all legislative power should be exercised by a parliament consisting of one elected chamber, executive organs should be answerable to the legislature, and judicial functions should be exercised by an independent and unified judiciary. Finally, the universally accepted human and communal rights should be suitably entrenched in the constitution and, in addition to any municipal remedies, individuals should also be able to obtain appropriate redress by recourse to suitable international bodies.

The Turkish Cypriot side

In their own proposals to the UN mediator on 2 June 1964[29] the Turkish side first outlined what they considered to be the 'root causes' of the Cyprus problem as this had developed in recent years, and then responded to the principal points made by Archbishop Makarios in his own memorandum.

The 'root causes' of the problem and the basic causes of conflict, according to the Turkish Cypriot side, were the following:

[29] *Some Comments by the Vice-President of Cyprus on Archbishop Makarios' Memorandum on 'Certain Aspects of the Political Problem of Cyprus'* (2 June 1964).

(i) The Greek Cypriots appeared to demand full independence for the island but this was only a tactic to deceive world public opinion and the UN; their true aim was to achieve enosis. Therefore, what the Turks were being asked to accept was not 'to become the integral part of a sovereign state, but a small permanent ethnic "minority" in Greece.'

(ii) The Turkish Cypriot side could not accept the assurances of the Greek Cypriots concerning their security and protection. 'In civilised countries where the government comprises civilised people, minorities have nothing to fear and can entrust their rights and interests to the safekeeping of the majority government. We know from long bitter experience, however, that the Greeks of Cyprus are by no means civilised as far as the protection of the lives and of the fundamental rights and interests of the Turks are concerned.'

(iii) Apart from the above two 'root-causes' of the problem, there was a very important factor, 'an immutable factor', which could never be ignored in any attempted settlement of the Cyprus problem. This factor, the Turkish side informed the UN mediator, was 'the proximity of the island to Turkey and its vital strategic importance for the latter country'. This was primarily because 'the western and south-western coastlines of Turkey are surrounded by Greek-held islands many of which are so close to Turkey that they fall within Turkish territorial waters.' In the event of Greece falling into the hands of a government hostile to Turkey, 'the western and south-western approaches of Turkey would be controlled entirely by hostile forces and, therefore, Turkey's southern approaches would be of vital importance for maintaining Turkey's communications with the western world'. It was for this purpose that 'very important ports and naval and air bases' had been established in southern Turkey and 'all these could be threatened by a hostile Cyprus'. Consequently, it was essential for Turkey's own security that this country should possess 'some degree of control over the destiny of the island of Cyprus'. Indeed, the Turkish side announced, one could go even further. 'The fact is that Cyprus has always been part of Turkey, historically, strategically and geopolitically, and this fact, which is a consequence of the geographical position of Cyprus, can never be changed'.

As to the other points raised by Archbishop Makarios, the Turkish side wished to point out the following:

(a) The Greek argument that the independence granted to the island in 1960 was not a 'full one' and that the Zurich and London agreements 'were imposed' had no foundation in truth. The only serious curtailment on the independence of Cyprus was that the republic could not opt for enosis or taksim (partition), and this was not so much a restriction on sovereignty as a safeguard for Turkish rights.

(b) As regards the argument that the agreements were 'imposed', it was true that no referendum was held but, on the other hand, there was very considerable participation in the first elections held under the 1960 constitution, and this was 'a clear indication of the people's approval of the constitution and of the new regime established on the basis of the agreements'. Further, it was totally unacceptable in international relations for any party to an agreement to claim that it had put its signature because there was no other alternative. Most international agreements were signed by the parties to them precisely because there 'was no other alternative', and it would throw the entire system of international relations into turmoil if everyone tried to abrogate international agreements unilaterally on the basis invoked by the Greek Cypriot side. 'What if Turkey, for instance, decided to abrogate the Treaty of Lausanne claiming that she had signed it because there was no other alternative?'

(c) The 1960 constitution was not unworkable as the Greek Cypriot side had claimed. It had been subverted by them. The Turks, the Turkish Cypriot memorandum continued, had only used their safeguards to protect their interests against unconstitutional encroachment by the Greeks.

(d) 'The Turks were too big a community to be treated as a simple minority'. There was a separate Turkish community in Cyprus, and it had to be accorded separate juridical recognition and allowed to exercise its share of political power separately. As to the legal basis of this claim, this was the force of numbers. 'We claim that one fifth of the population of any country has to be treated as a separate entity over and above the individuals who form the community in question'. Indeed, instead of talking of a 'majority' and a 'minority', the Turkish side wished to point out that 'Cyprus is not a country and is not populated by a Cypriot nation'. It should instead be treated as 'an off-shore island of Turkey in which case the Cypriot Greeks themselves become a small minority in the population of Turkey as a whole'.

The point of departure for the formulation of the Turkish proposals was that the 1960 constitution had not provided adequate protection for the Turkish Cypriot community and had not satisfied the wider strategic and other considerations mentioned above. What it was now necessary to establish was 'a geographical basis for the state of affairs created by the Zurich and London agreements'. These agreements, the Turkish side believed, had recognised the independence and autonomy of the Turkish Cypriot community, and the time had now come when such independence and autonomy had to be given a geographical foundation. They therefore called for the physical separation of the two communities within secure geographical boundaries, the creation of a federation within which would exist the Greek Cypriot and Turkish Cypriot states, and the continuation and strengthening of the guarantees and restrictions on sovereignty included in the treaties. The federation proposed by the Turkish side was a very loose one, with regional administration covering most of the subjects that are normally allocated in federations to the central government. Further, each of the two areas, on the Turkish proposals, would be able to have cultural and other relations directly with Greece and Turkey as the case might be, and each would be allowed to enter into international agreements with Greece or Turkey for the purpose of regulating 'relations of neighbourhood', including the provision of a 'special pass system' between that area and the respective 'mother' country.

The Greek Cypriot side, in a further memorandum it submitted to the UN mediator, declared itself as absolutely opposed to any federal solution to the Cyprus problem.[30] The main objections to federal proposals, the Greek Cypriot side stated, were, first, that their implementation would require an inhumane compulsory population movement, secondly, that the particular federal scheme proposed by Turkey had no purpose other than to promote the virtual partitioning of the island, with eventual annexation by Turkey of the Turkish region, and thirdly, that the Turkish federal proposals, instead of promoting the well being of the people of Cyprus as a whole, were sure to create an unhappy people, kept divided by enmity and hatred and permanently apart, the communities looking upon each other across their artificial borders as antagonists instead of working together for their common interests.

In September – October 1964, when a new round of intensive consultations on the part of the UN mediator with all interested parties took place, and for a substantial time thereafter, the initial positions of the parties, as outlined above, maintained their original substantive rigidity. The two sides, however, now seemed willing to make some concessions and adjustments with regard to the manner of the implementation of their demands in order to facilitate a solution.

The Greek Cypriot side, throughout the years 1963–7, continued to insist on the negotiation of a solution of true independence, in the sense that the republic should be liberated from the limitations imposed in 1960, on the completely unitary character of the state and on the right of self determination which indeed would be an inevitable corollary of unfettered independence. But in order to facilitate a settlement the Greek

[30] The various objections to a federal system of government are marshalled in Tornaritis, *Constitutional and Legal Problems in the Republic of Cyprus* (Nicosia, 1972), 19–24; Tornaritis, *Cyprus and Federalism* (Nicosia, 1974); Polyviou, *Cyprus, The Tragedy and the Challenge*, op. cit, 108–19. See Palley (1975) *MLR* 485–88.

Cypriot side expressed its willingness to the UN mediator to make a number of concessions. Thus, agreement was expressed with the proposition that Cyprus, so long as it remained independent, should be demilitarised and non-aligned. Also, additional guarantees for the protection of individual human and communal rights would be enacted, and these would include an invitation to the United Nations to appoint a commissioner who, assisted by a staff of advisers, would observe on the spot the authorities' compliance with the relevant constitutional provisions. Finally, Archbishop Makarios assured the UN mediator, ways and means should be discovered for ensuring, for a transitional period at least, representation of the Turkish Cypriots in governmental institutions. This could be done for instance by the reservation of seats in the House of Representatives or by a system of proportional representation, and also by the appointment of a Turkish Cypriot Minister who would be responsible for the affairs of his community – all these of course would be without prejudice to other Turkish Cypriots being elected or appointed on merit. Also, 'sympathetic understanding' was shown towards a UN suggestion that in addition to the above 'some satisfactory measure of local government' should be recognised so that in areas where one community or the other predominated it would feel that it was playing an effective and equitable part in the management of local affairs.

There was no change in the Turkish Cypriot stand. The Turkish Cypriot side throughout the years 1963–7 held firmly to its position that the Cyprus problem could only be solved through the establishment of a biregional federation based on the geographical separation of the two communities. In a memorandum submitted to the UN mediator on 22 February 1965 Vice-President Kutchuk reiterated his views on the matter.[31] The Greek Cypriot side had not abandoned enosis, he claimed, nor was it likely that it would ever do so; and the security of the Turkish community could not be safeguarded in the context of a unitary state, whatever the legal and constitutional guarantees. Constitutional safeguards were bound to be quite ineffective unless they were expressed in terms of geography. The time had come for.a final settlement based on a rigid federal system with communal separation. The necessary population exchange, Dr Kutchuk now suggested, could be a 'voluntary' one or a phased one, i.e. one to be carried out over a period of five to ten years; and as the UN mediator reports, at one point, there seemed to be an admission on the part of the Turkish government that the extent of the area that had been claimed (over 36 per cent) had been fixed at an unrealistically high level for bargaining purposes, and that the Turkish government would be prepared

---

[31] I have not been able to obtain this memorandum, but Dr Kutchuk's arguments are summarised by the then UN mediator, Dr Plaza, in his *Report*, supra n.10.

to agree to a reduction of this to about 750 square miles or about 20 per cent of the total area of the republic. But nothing further was heard in this direction; and as has been already mentioned, all 'federal' solutions had been completely ruled out by the Greek Cypriot side, whatever the extent of the area claimed.

An important landmark in the Cyprus problem was the report of the UN mediator[32] which was submitted to the UN Secretary-General on 26 March 1965. In his report the then mediator, Dr Plaza, first described the 1960 constitution as a 'constitutional oddity' and could not help wondering whether 'the physical division of the minority from the majority', which was sought by the Turkish side, was not 'a desperate step in the wrong direction'. He was moreover reluctant to believe, as the Turkish Cypriot leadership claimed, in the 'impossibility' of Greek Cypriots and Turkish Cypriots learning to live together in peace. For this reason he could not accept the federal schemes proposed by Turkey or any other federal solutions since all these would involve 'a compulsory movement of the people concerned contrary to all the enlightened principles of the present time,' would be open to serious security objections, and would bring about 'a state of affairs that would constitute a lasting, if not permanent, cause of discontent and unrest'. Dr Plaza was of the clear view that the only viable solution was an independent and unitary Cyprus, with effective protection of individual and minority rights, and expressed his satisfaction with the various assurances which Archbishop Makarios had given. As to the external aspects of the problem, the UN mediator concluded that both enosis and partition had to be excluded. But would not exclusion of enosis, desired after all by the majority of Cypriots, encroach upon that other fundamental UN principle, the principle of self-determination? Dr Plaza thought that just as the enjoyment by the citizen of his fundamental rights is not an absolute matter but is governed by considerations for the legitimate interests of others, so also the exercise by the state of its right of self-determination should not be absolute but should be governed by its obligations as a state, including those pertaining to the well-being of all its citizens and the cause of international peace. In the light of such considerations he thought that it would be both an act of enlightened statesmanship as well as a sovereign act of self-determination in its highest sense if the government of Cyprus were in the superior interests of the security of the state and the peace of the region to undertake to maintain the independence of the republic by, among other things, renouncing enosis. Finally, Dr Plaza recommended, establishment of guaranteed independence should be followed by demilitarisation of the island. Both

[32] *Report of the United Nations Mediator on Cyprus to the Secretary-General*, UN doc. S/6253.

the governments of Cyprus and Greece thought that the mediator's find-
ings constituted a constructive approach to the problem and, in conformity
with the wishes of the UN, wished his mediation to continue. But this
proved impossible. The Turkish government and the Turkish Cypriot
leadership asserted that the report went beyond the mediator's terms of
reference and stated that they considered Dr Plaza's functions as mediator
to have come to an end. The Secretary-General rejected Turkey's assertion
regarding Dr Plaza's alleged excess of his mandate and in a letter to him
which was circulated as a Security Council document U Thant referred to
the report as 'a most important contribution to the search for a just and
lasting solution to the Cyprus problem'. Further, expressing regret for the
fact that Turkey and the Turkish Cypriots had reacted negatively to the
report, the Secretary-General repeated his belief that efforts for a solution
should continue 'as recommended by the mediator and in the light of his
analysis', and stated that at his request 'the mediator would remain
available to the parties for the continuation of the mediation effort'.[33] This
offer too was rejected by Turkey.[34] The mediation effort of Dr Plaza was
thus brought to a premature end.[35]

Meanwhile bilateral Graeco-Turkish talks, without the participation of
the republic, took place in a number of contexts. Already in Geneva in the
summer of 1964 an unsuccessful attempt had been made under the aegis of
the then UN mediator, Mr Tuomioja, with the presence of the former
American Secretary of State Mr Acheson,[36] to find a solution based,
effectively, on double enosis (or partition). Further Graeco-Turkish talks
covering the whole range of relations between the two countries were
initiated in late 1965. The Government of Cyprus reluctantly 'agreed' to
these talks taking place and announced that, to the extent that they could
reduce tension in the area and contribute to the creation of a more peaceful
atmosphere, they were indeed welcome. But it was strongly felt that
better procedures for seeking a satisfactory solution to the Cyprus problem
should be sought, and Archbishop Makarios left no doubt that his

[33] A/60001/Add.1 (20 September 1965). Other related documents appear in *Cyprus: The Problem in Perspective*, supra n.16.

[34] Despite this, Archbishop Makarios, following the suggestion of Dr Plaza, made a declaration of intent concerning the measures that he was ready to adopt regarding the protection of minorities: see *Letter by President Makarios to U Thant* (4 October 1965).

[35] In late 1965 the government of the republic placed the question of Cyprus on the agenda of the 19th Session of the General Assembly. The resulting resolution, taking cognizance of the fact that the republic was entitled to the enjoyment of full sovereignty and independence and calling upon all states to refrain from any intervention directed against it, was very favourable to the position of the Cyprus government. The events surrounding the Recourse to the General Assembly are recounted in *Cyprus: The Problem in Perspective*, supra n.16, at 25–6.

[36] Adams and Cottrell, *Cyprus Between East and West* (1968), 65–6.

government would not be bound, as a non participant in the talks, by any solution agreed upon which was inconsistent with the wishes of the people of the island. Finally the Graeco-Turkish dialogue which had intermittently continued since May 1966 culminated in a meeting held in Thrace in September 1967 between the Prime Ministers of Greece and Turkey. It there emerged that the gap existing between the basic positions of the two countries, Greece still making efforts to achieve enosis and the Turkish government steadfastly adhering to partition or at least geographical federation, was unbridgeable. The Graeco-Turkish talks therefore came to an end. In the meantime, as a result of a coup on 21 April 1967, a military junta took power in Greece. From the start its undisputed leader was the former head of military intelligence, Colonel Papadopoulos. It was announced that Greek policy towards Cyprus would not change, but, as will appear shortly, this was not borne out by subsequent events.

The collapse of the Graeco-Turkish dialogue strengthened the hand of those who were insisting that the Cyprus problem could only be solved by reference to UN procedures and in the context of efforts to be primarily undertaken by the two Cypriot sides themselves. Dr Plaza himself had called for informal meetings between representatives of the two principal parties, namely the Greek Cypriots and the Turkish Cypriots, and indications had been given as early as 1964 that the two Cypriot sides did not, on principle, reject direct meetings and consultations. But in the past there had been serious procedural and other difficulties regarding both the jurisdiction and the precise objective of direct negotiations between the two communities, the Greek Cypriots insisting that the only matter to be discussed would be the question of 'minority rights' within a completely unfettered and unitary state, whereas the Turkish Cypriots demanded, among other things, that no talks could take place unless there was an immediate restoration of the 1960 constitution and an 'equalisation' of the positions of the two sides. But it was now felt, particularly among UN authorities, that there was urgent need for some new procedure for a peaceful settlement of the problem that would fill the vacuum which had been created by the failure of Graeco-Turkish bilateral talks and the frustration of Dr Plaza's mediation. The UN Secretary-General duly began consultations with the interested parties to see whether some kind of dialogue could be initiated.

4. *The crisis of November 1967*

Efforts in this direction however were overtaken by the outbreak of serious incidents of intercommunal violence in the Kophinou – Ayios Theodhoros area and the resulting imminent full-scale military confrontation between Greece and Turkey.[37] For once there is much evidence about what happened even though again ultimate apportionment of responsibility is not easy. Turkish Cypriot 'fighters' objected to the resumption of patrolling by the Cyprus police in the area of the mixed village of Ayios Theodhoros situated near the main road between Nicosia and the coastal town of Limassol. Patrols there had been conducted regularly since the events of 1963–4, but after a number of incidents in July 1967 the Cyprus police decided on its own initiative not to continue patrolling until calm was restored. In the meantime evidence began accumulating that during July and August Turkish-Cypriot irregular forces were preparing to organize yet another enclave in the area near Kophinou and Ayios Theodhoros. The Cyprus government approached UNFICYP, the UN force, complained about the paramilitary activities and asked that steps should be taken so that ordinary police patrolling should be allowed to resume. The leadership of UNFICYP shared the anxieties of the Cyprus government since it was now becoming clear that the local Turkish 'security forces' in refusing to allow police patrols through the mixed villages of the area had the support of the Turkish Cypriot leadership and of Turkey who wanted through the establishment of new fortifications to establish control over the vital Nicosia-Limassol highway. UNFICYP officers told the Turks that the request of the police authorities that they should resume patrolling was quite innocent, that the police patrol near Kophinou and Ayios Theodhoros was neither new nor sinister as 'it had been running quite happily each week for the past two and a half years' and had only been suspended temporarily, and that 'their denial of freedom of movement was unjustified and unwarranted'.[38] But the Turks would not be convinced, their main argument being that similar restrictions were being placed on Turkish Cypriots elsewhere and that in any case resumption of police patrolling should be made dependent on the withdrawal of the National Guard from positions the latter had occupied in Larnaca during that same summer. After consultations with all interested parties and after UNFICYP made numerous representations to the Turkish Cypriot leadership and the Turkish government, the UN representatives in Cyprus took the view that 'the status quo ante 30 July 1967 should be restored and that the Cyprus police should be in a position to patrol to Ayios Theodhoros via the main access road, as it had done in the past, approximately twice a week'.[39] The Ayios Theodhoros and the Larnaca situations which had been linked by the Turks were regarded by

[37] See particularly Harbottle, *The Impartial Solider* (1970), 145–67; Ehrlich, *Cyprus 1958–1967* (1974), 90–116. I have also derived much useful information from *The Times* and *The Economist* of this period.

[38] Harbottle, supra n.37, at 149; see also UN doc. S/8248, 16 November 1967.

[39] S/8248, 16 November 1967, para. 4.

the United Nations as completely distinct, UNFICYP taking the view that in the case of Ayios Theodhoros and Kophinou the main problem was the restoration of the freedom of movement of the Cyprus police whereas in Larnaca it was not a question of freedom of movement, which had never been hindered, but of a new confrontation area which had arisen lately and which would require separate negotiations. When it became apparent not only that no progress was being made in restoring freedom of movement in the area but also that a new Turkish-Cypriot military enclave was being organised in Kophinou and Ayios Theodhoros the Cyprus government became impatient and made urgent representations to the Secretary-General of the United Nations, asking that police patrolling should be resumed at an early date under UN supervision and protection. After further consultations UNFICYP, on 18 October, proposed to the Cyprus Government and the Turkish side a time-table for the gradual resumption of Cyprus police patrols as from 2 November. The Cyprus government immediately accepted the proposed time-table, but the Turkish side expressed reservations, only agreeing to review the matter again. By this time, mid-October 1967, the UN Secretary-General was himself becoming increasingly impatient with the procrastination of the Turkish side, and finally on 27 October he addressed an urgent personal appeal to the Turkish government requesting its cooperation with the UN authorities in Cyprus and their efforts to restore freedom of movement in the Kophinou area. The reply of the Turkish government on 3 November was that Turkey would be prepared to accept the proposed time-table only if the Larnaca situation was resolved simultaneously.

On 13 November, at a meeting between on the one hand Archbishop Makarios, General Grivas, then Commander of the National Guard, and Polykarpos Georkadjis, then Minister of the Interior, and on the other Mr Ozorio Tafall, the UN special representative, and General Martola, commander of the UN force in Cyprus, the Cyprus government expressed deep concern at the delay in the resumption of Cyprus police patrolling to Ayios Theodhoros and indicated that 'it might not be in a position to wait any longer'.[40] The UN special representative requested that the resumption of patrolling should be postponed, making the point that after the release on 12 November by the Cyprus government of the Turkish Cypriot leader, Mr Rauf Denktash, who had attempted to come into the island secretly on 31 October and had been apprehended, the Turkish government might be prepared to reconsider their until then negative attitude on the question of Cyprus police patrolling to Ayios Theodhoros. The Cyprus government however decided to wait no longer and on 14 November sent two police patrols to the village. At this point a crucial mis-

[40] Harbottle, supra, at 150; S/8248, para. 7.

understanding arose. It appears that the Cyprus authorities believed that the patrols would be protected by UNFICYP since 'it had been made known to the Cyprus Government that UNFICYP would be prepared, if necessary, to take appropriate measures to restore the status quo ante in Ayios Theodhoros and enable the Cyprus police to resume patrolling, and in particular it had been made clear that UNFICYP was ready to escort the patrol again as it had done on 16 September'.[41] But UNFICYP itself, despite its policy (which it had communicated to the Cyprus government) that it was prepared to offer military protection to ordinary police patrols, seems to have taken the view that it was only to offer such assistance if there was an official request for its participation. Since there had been no official request it was not going to offer the required assistance. In any case at about noon of 14 November the UN commander at Kophinou was informed by way of the commander of the local National Guard troops that during that same afternoon the police patrols would move into Ayios Theodhoros and was asked to provide UN protection. Otherwise the National Guard would escort the patrols. The UNFICYP local commander, observing National Guard military movements in the area, refused to provide the requested protection. On that day, 14 November, police patrolling proceeded without incident, but on the following day, 15 November, the police patrol was fired upon by the Turkish Cypriot 'fighters', the National Guard immediately opened fire, and during the hours that followed the fighting became intense as General Grivas ordered his troops to launch an attack on the Turkish Cypriot fortifications above Kophinou. There is evidence that the retaliatory attacks of the National Guard had been planned by General Grivas before the police patrols were sent in, even though he himself blamed UNFICYP for not having prevented what had happened. What had happened, according to the General, was that 'the Turkish Cypriots had fired on the National Guard and all (that) the latter was doing was to defend itself'.[42] Impartial eyewitnesses have suggested that two events were primarily responsible for the crisis and the full-scale military confrontation that threatened to ensue, first, 'the stubborn opposition of the Turks to the early resumption of the patrols',[43] as well as their unprovoked attack on the police, and, secondly, the 'excessiveness of the National Guard attack'[44] once the Turks had fired the fatal shots. The stubborn resistance of the Turkish Cypriots to the resumption of police patrolling is not difficult to explain. The Turkish Cypriot leadership had obviously decided first that its position was becoming increasingly weak as a result of the introduction of a

[41] S/8248, para. 8.
[42] S/8248, para. 22.
[43] Harbottle, supra, at 160.
[44] Ibid.

number of normalisation measures brought in by President Makarios in the preceding months and the consequent partial restoration of freedom of movement in various parts of the island and secondly that this would best be strengthened if another Turkish Cypriot enclave was organised near the important road linking Nicosia and Limassol. The excessive retaliation of the National Guard is more difficult to analyse. A number of possible explanations offer themselves. One is that General Grivas was acting in collusion with Archbishop Makarios, but this is most unlikely, Makarios' government having nothing to gain from a new outbreak of inter-communal violence that would jeopardise its earlier efforts to reduce tension in the island and initiate some kind of intercommunal dialogue. Another possibility is that the General was acting in agreement and after consultations with the Greek junta or at least some of its more extremist members. This too is unlikely. General Grivas was not known to enjoy good relations with the Greek military regime, he apparently never consulted them on military matters, and, equally important, he doubted the strength of their commitment to the idea of enosis. It therefore appears that the General, in ordering extensive military attacks upon the Turkish positions in Kophinou and Ayios Theodhoros, was acting very much on his own. Equally intriguing is an inquiry into the General's precise objective. Some have suggested that Grivas had been offended by Makarios' release of Mr Denktash in October 1967 and had therefore decided to stage a punitive raid on Turkish Cypriot villages.[45] Another possibility is that Grivas, far from acting impulsively and in a fit of anger, was aiming at nothing short of provoking a full-scale war between Greece and Turkey that might pave the way for enosis. It is thought that a far more likely explanation given his temperament, his well-known hostility to Makarios and the situation in the island during the summer of 1967 was that Grivas became alarmed by what he regarded as a 'drift' towards independence and by the Archbishop's consolidation of his position as undisputed head of an independent Cyprus, most of the people of which appeared by now to regard with equanimity, if not with outright relief, the indefinite postponement of enosis and its virtual consignment to the unfulfilled 'dreams' (or nightmares) of history. It may therefore be that General Grivas, a life-long champion of enosis and an implacable opponent of any solution other than that, planned (and was only too happy when the opportunity was given for) the National Guard's excessive retaliation in response to admitted Turkish Cypriot provocation, in order both to thwart Archbishop Makarios personally and to torpedo the latter's policy of independence.

Whatever the correct explanation, serious hostilities broke out between

---

[45] *The Times* (London), 29 November 1967; see also Ehrlich, supra n.37, at 97.

the National Guard and the well-armed Turkish Cypriot 'security forces'.
A ceasefire was quickly negotiated, but in the meantime the Turkish
government sent military aircraft flying low over Cyprus, mobilised the
Turkish invasion force stationed on a more or less permanent basis at
Mersin only forty miles away from northern Cyprus, and warned the UN
Secretary-General that the events of the Ayios Theodhoros area had
introduced 'an element of complication such as ha(d) not been seen since
1964' and made 'a crisis which will go beyond the borders of the island'
almost unavoidable.[46] Full-scale war between Greece and Turkey was
imminent. Some of the Turkish military obviously felt that this was the
time to settle the Cyprus problem once and for all and that with a weak and
internationally isolated Greek regime an invasion of Cyprus should be
launched immediately. Prime Minister Demirel decided not to do so right
away but rather to make stiff demands of the Greek government regarding
the withdrawal of Greek troops from the island and the dissolution of the
Cyprus National Guard, and only to authorise an invasion if the Greek
regime, as seems confidently to have been expected, did not capitulate.
Accordingly, in a note to the Greek junta, the Turkish government
demanded that General Grivas should be recalled back to Greece and not
allowed back to Cyprus, that all Greek soldiers present in the island
otherwise than in accordance with the treaty of alliance should be
withdrawn, that the Cyprus National Guard should be disbanded, that
Turkish Cypriots should be allowed to set up their own governmental and
administrative structures in their enclaves, that Turkish Cypriots who had
suffered in the Kophinou and Ayios Theodhoros incidents should be
compensated, and that the UN peacekeeping force should be enlarged.[47]
The Greek government swiftly recalled General Grivas but did not at first
seem willing to sanction an ignominious withdrawal of its armed forces
from Cyprus. Indeed there were serious doubts among western diplomats
whether Greece could give in to some of Ankara's demands, particularly
under constant Turkish threats of war. On 20 and 21 November there were
unconfirmed reports of partial Greek mobilisation and troop movements,
and some of the members of the junta appear to have taken the view that
the price Turkey was asking was too great and that it was better to go to
war. The turning point may well have been the appointment of Mr
Panayotis Pipinelis as Foreign Minister on 20 November. Mr Pipinelis was
known to be on excellent terms with the Turkish government and a firm
supporter of the NATO alliance and western interests. He immediately
initiated consultations with the Turkish and American governments and
seems to have persuaded Colonel Papadopoulos, the principal figure in the

[46] This can be found in S/8248, para. 15.
[47] See Adams and Cottrell, *Cyprus Between East and West* (1968), at 71, and Ehrlich, supra
n.37, at 105.

military regime, that war with Turkey over Cyprus would be inconclusive at best and most probably disastrous, that a Graeco-Turkish military conflagration in the area would weaken NATO and destroy any chance of support that the American government might be inclined to extend to the junta in the future, and that it was therefore vital to swallow national pride and at all costs come to an accommodation with Turkey, however humiliating this might be.

Simultaneously with these early contacts between the Greek and Turkish governments a number of urgent mediation efforts were being made to bring about an agreement between Greece and Turkey. On 21 November discussions took place in London between the United States, Britain and Canada, Canada finding itself in the position of a mediator because of the presence of Canadian troops in Cyprus as part of the UN contingent and the respect felt by both Greece and Turkey for the Canadian Prime Minister, Mr Lester Pearson, and as a result of these talks a plan consisting of five propositions was put to the governments in Athens and Ankara. These were that Turkey should reaffirm her respect for the territorial integrity and sovereignty of Cyprus and should dismantle her invasion force; that Greek and Turkish troop levels in Cyprus should be reduced to the levels specified by the treaty of alliance; that the UN force in the island should be expanded and strengthened; that those Turkish Cypriots who had suffered losses during the recent fighting should be compensated; and that the future security of the Turkish Cypriot community should be assured. Mr Pearson suggested these points as a basis for further discussions between the Greek and Turkish governments, but even though, as will be seen, the eventual outcome was not significantly different to the Canadian formula, such was the volatility of the situation that it was clearly not possible to arrange meetings between Greek and Turkish representatives, Turkey demanding that discussions with the Greek government could only be held after the withdrawal of the Greek troops from the island while Greek officials rejected the Turkish position, insisting that there could be no military withdrawal without prior discussions. 'In these circumstances, third-party mediation efforts were essential',[48] and these were provided by the United Nations, U Thant appointing as his special representative his Under-Secretary for Special Political Affairs, Jose Rolz-Bennett, the United States, President Johnson sending to the island Mr Cyrus Vance, and NATO, whose Secretary-General, Mr Manlio Brosio, undertook to mediate between Greece and Turkey, both of course members of the alliance. On 22 November, as a military confrontation loomed nearer and nearer, the UN Secretary-General addressed his first urgent appeal[49] to the President of Cyprus and

[48] Ehrlich, supra, at 111.
[49] S/8248/Add. 3, 22 November 1967.

the Prime Ministers of Greece and Turkey asking them to act in full compliance with the charter of the UN which called upon all states to settle their disputes only by peaceful means and to refrain from the threat or use of force. The three governments, the Secretary-General continued, had a special responsibility to check what seemed to be, more and more, a rapid deterioration of relations which was clearly leading towards an outbreak of hostilities. In the interests of peace it was his earnest hope that all interested governments would avoid any provocative action and exercise 'the utmost restraint in the present explosive circumstances', and it was in view of the prevailing danger and his natural desire to do everything possible to avert war that he was taking the exceptional step of sending quickly to the three capitals his personal high level representative to convey directly to the three governments his grave concern and his urgent appeal for moderation. For the next two days exhaustive discussions took place between the envoys, particularly Cyrus Vance, and the governments of Greece, Turkey and Cyprus, with Turkey continuing her military preparations for an invasion. Indeed at one point it seemed as if this could no longer be averted. On 23 November President Sunay of Turkey sent messages to the leaders of the great powers and the Moslem states announcing that his country had decided 'to solve the Cyprus problem once and for all'. Upon this British and American citizens were evacuated from the island. The situation was so ominous that on 24 November U Thant thought it necessary to address a new appeal[50] to the President of Cyprus and the Prime Ministers of Greece and Turkey in which he again asked them, 'in the strongest possible terms', 'to exercise utmost restraint', 'to avoid all acts of force or the threats of recourse to force', and 'to be temperate in their public utterances relating to the Cyprus problem and to relations among them'. Otherwise war would be unavoidable. The problems of Cyprus, U Thant went on, were numerous and complicated and demanded urgent solution if peace was to be preserved. One of the most critical, if not the most critical, at that time was the presence of non-Cypriot armed forces, other than the UN force which was a peace force, on the island, and there was little doubt that such forces exceeded the previously agreed allowable numbers. As a result the Secretary-General was of the view that the prevailing tension could be eased and the imminent threat of war removed by 'a reasoned and earnest effort by the three parties directly concerned to agree upon and arrange for a substantial reduction of the non-Cypriot armed forces now in hostile confrontation on the troubled island of Cyprus'. Practically, such reductions had to be in stages, but it was nonetheless important that they should envisage the ultimate withdrawal from the island of *all* non-Cypriot

[50] S/8248/Add.5, 24 November 1967.

armed forces other than those of the United Nations, something which in its turn would make possible 'the positive demilitarisation of Cyprus'. U Thant therefore appealed 'most urgently' to all three governments to agree to the military evacuation he was suggesting and 'to undertake to work out a programme' for the phased reduction of Greek and Turkish military forces, offering his assistance towards this end 'to the fullest extent'. In a final (and obvious) reference to the ongoing war preparations by the Turkish government, the UN Secretary-General called upon all parties to act in accordance with their obligations under the charter, to 'desist from the use of force or the threat of the use of force,' to 'respect the sovereignty, independence and territorial integrity of the republic of Cyprus', and to 'refrain from any military intervention in the affairs of that republic'.

At about the same time Cyrus Vance, shuttling between Athens, Ankara and Nicosia, seems to have proposed to the Greek and Turkish governments a plan very similar in its basic thrust to the suggestion contained in the second appeal of U Thant. Under the American formula, which may have been supported by the threat of sanctions and the withholding of military aid against both Greece and Turkey, in response to a new appeal by the United Nations Greece would agree to withdraw her troops from Cyprus, and in response to the same appeal Turkey would also agree to call off her plans for an invasion of the island. This formula, intended to satisfy Turkish substantive demands without heaping unnecessary public humiliation upon Greece, was first put by Mr Vance to the Turkish side who apparently showed interest. The American envoy, who by now was acting in concert with U Thant even though the two of them had apparently acted independently during the early exchanges, then flew to Athens and persuaded Mr Pipinelis, the Greek Foreign Secretary, that acceptance of the proposed plan was the only way in which war could be averted. The Greek regime at first agreed that in response to a fresh appeal from the Secretary-General it would make a substantial but phased withdrawal of her troops, provided that at the same time Turkey would also dismantle her own war preparations and agree to negotiations on all further outstanding points. Mr Vance flew back to Ankara where the Turkish side declared itself dissatisfied with the Greek suggestion that the 'illegal' troops should be withdrawn from the island in a phased way. What was necessary, the Turkish government insisted, was that Greece should agree to withdraw, and actually withdraw, her troops from Cyprus 'within the shortest possible time' and before any direct negotiations between the Greek and Turkish governments. Furthermore, the Greek Cypriot National Guard should also be disbanded, but some Turkish forces would have to remain in the island and protect the Turkish Cypriot community. These Turkish counterproposals were transmitted, through Cyrus Vance and Manlio Brosio, to the Greek military regime which on 28 November, at a crucial two-hour meeting of the inner cabinet, decided to spare no effort to avoid war with Turkey and therefore to accept the new Turkish demands, provided that its withdrawal of the troops would be made to appear as having been decided in response to a United Nations appeal. On 29 November the Greek government notified the Turkish side that it had accepted in principle its demands and that it was now prepared, as soon as the UN Secretary-General issued his final appeal embodying what was agreed between them, to proceed with the swift evacuation of the 'illegal' Greek troops from the island provided that Turkey would also do so and stop her preparations for an invasion. The Greek regime was apparently also willing to use its 'authority' to dismantle the Cypriot National Guard even though the latter was under the control of the Cyprus government. President Makarios was informed of this on 28 and 29 November and immediately expressed serious reservations about disbanding the National Guard and proceeding to unilateral disarmament unless all Turkish troops left the island and the United Nations gave firm guarantees about Cyprus' future security. Despite the Archbishop's reservations Greece and Turkey reached a final agreement on 30 November 1967 the basic elements of which were the following: Greek and Turkish troops in excess of the allowable limits under the treaty of alliance would be withdrawn from Cyprus within a very short time; Turkey would not mount an invasion; the Greek Cypriot National Guard would be disbanded and all its weapons would be surrendered to the UN peace force which would assume fuller responsibility for law and order in Cyprus; and the independence and integrity of the republic of Cyprus would be reaffirmed. But Archbishop Makarios refused to agree to the Cyprus National Guard being disbanded unless there were new and more extensive guarantees concerning the island's territorial integrity and sovereignty, preferably in the context of a comprehensive UN arrangement. The preferable solution in his view would be the complete demilitarisation of the island through the withdrawal of all the Greek and Turkish troops, including the authorised contingents under the 1960 settlement; failing that he would not willingly sanction the dissolution of the National Guard, particularly since Ankara had indicatd on 1 December that it would not make any fresh pledge regarding the need to respect the independence, sovereignty and territorial integrity of Cyprus (the Turkish side viewing any new guarantee to this end as a tacit renunciation of its rights under the 1960 treaties of alliance and guarantee). Intense pressure was then put on Makarios. Mr Cyrus Vance had a number of additional meetings with him, and at some point Greece and Turkey threatened to proceed without him. Eventually the Cypriot government indicated its willingness to accept those sections of the Graeco-Turkish agreement providing for the withdrawal of the 'illegal' Greek and Turkish military forces but, in the absence of satisfactory guarantees concerning Cyprus' independence and security and since some Greek and Turkish troops would remain in the island, refused to go along with the 'understanding' that the National Guard should be disbanded.

The crisis was effectively over with the acceptance on the part of all three countries, Cyprus, Greece and Turkey, of the third appeal[51] of the Secretary-General of the United Nations of 3 December 1967 in which U Thant, consistently with what had been agreed upon, asked the parties, and particularly Greece and Turkey, to take 'prompt and positive actions for the preservation of peace', 'to take immediate measures to end any threat to the security of either one by the other as well as of the republic of Cyprus', and 'as a first step' to carry out an 'expeditious withdrawal' of those of their forces that were in excess of their respective legally allowable contingents. Both Greece[52] and Turkey[53] immediately accepted the prearranged contents of the Secretary-General's appeal. The Cyprus government, in its reply[54] of 4 December, told the Secretary-General that it also accepted his appeal concerning 'the withdrawal from Cyprus of the forces of Greece and Turkey in excess of their respective contingents', but this development, welcome though it was, could only be regarded as a first step towards 'the ultimate and complete withdrawal from the republic of Cyprus of all non-Cypriot armed forces other than those of the United Nations'. It was only by such 'complete demilitarisation' that the cause of peace in Cyprus would be served. Further, the Cyprus government welcomed the UN appeal for prompt and positive action for the preservation of peace, and particularly the reference to the need for immediate measures to put an end to the threat to the security of Cyprus. It was this threat that was the main danger to international peace in the area, the Cypriot reply continued, and in this respect the Cyprus government was convinced that the establishment of effective guarantees against any military intervention in the affairs of Cyprus was a demanding necessity, to be effected and ensured through the Security Council. The Greek troops were withdrawn from the island in early December.

A number of important facts and lessons emerged from the events of November–December 1967. To begin with, it was once more demonstrated with dramatic clarity how easily trouble could flare up in the island and how swiftly it could escalate into a major international crisis. Two ways suggested themselves for pacifying the immediate situation and for

[51] S/8248/Add.6, 3 December 1967.
[52] S/8248/Add.7, 3 December 1967.
[53] S/8248/Add.7, 3 December 1967.
[54] S/8248/Add.8, 4 December 1967.

averting similar catastrophes in the future, either a comprehensive political settlement which was clearly impossible at the time or at least the adoption of measures of demilitarisation and pacification that would both reduce possibilities for intercommunal violence and ease the prevailing tension by restoring freedom of movement, by encouraging more frequent exchanges and greater all-round interaction between Greek and Turkish Cypriots, and most important of all by inducing the Turks to come out of virtual isolation in their enclaves and villages, abandoning in the process the siege mentality that went with it. In the present crisis since the threat of war was imminent and the speedy negotiation of an overall settlement not feasible the withdrawal of the various hostile troops on the island presented itself as virtually the only way out. The three connected questions of course were, first how much demilitarisation would (and could) be agreed upon, in other words would all security forces be withdrawn from the island and disbanded or only Greek and Turkish forces in excess of their allowable numbers under the 1960 arrangement, secondly on what basis would demilitarisation proceed, in other words would foreign troops simply be withdrawn because their presence endangered the peace and sovereignty of an independent state, as Archbishop Makarios wished, or would they be withdrawn on the basis of the 1960 accords, as the Turkish side demanded, and thirdly how would the eventual agreement that in effect represented an almost total capitulation by the Greek side be presented without triggering off unpredictable domestic upheavals – as the assumption of interrelated commitments (in this case to withdraw troops) on the part of Greece and Turkey or as the supposedly independent statesmanlike responses of the parties to an appeal to be made by the United Nations Secretary-General? All these issues have been discussed above. Suffice it to say that the outcome of the November crisis represented a comprehensive Turkish victory both in terms of the type of demilitarisation that was brought about (since it was primarily Greek troops that were withdrawn) and in terms of the legal basis on which the military evacuation proceeded, namely not in the context of the security of an independent state but in purported affirmation of the 1960 accords which the government of Makarios regarded as impermissible fetters on sovereignty. As a concession to President Makarios and Cyprus' sovereign status the National Guard was not disbanded, and ironically it was this same National Guard which seven years later would turn against the Archbishop and his government and bring about the Turkish invasion so narrowly averted in November 1967. As to the Greek side, two things made possible its capitulation without endangering its domestic position, first the masterly diplomacy of Cyrus Vance and the United Nations envoy whose collective efforts provided the military regime with a ladder it could climb down, and secondly the fact that the Greek military dictatorship, unlike the then Turkish government, did not have to worry about an irate press and an inflamed public opinion.

What was the resulting balance of power both in the island and in the region after the withdrawal of the Greek troops? In one sense the Cyprus government was weakened enormously by the departure of 'friendly' military forces that could at least be trusted to provide substantial assistance in repelling a Turkish invasion. President Makarios would now have to negotiate with the Turkish Cypriot community whether he liked it or not and would no longer be able to rely on the deterrent effect of a sizeable Greek military presence that formed a sort of local counterweight to the threatening proximity of Turkey and the ease with which Turkish military superiority could be deployed against the republic. But in another sense President Makarios was actually strengthened by the departure of the Greek troops. When these troops first came to the island their primary function was to protect the Greek Cypriots from the threat of a Turkish invasion but gradually, with Makarios pursuing an aggressive non-aligned policy abroad and a conciliatory pro-independence line at home, they came to view their main function as that of a watchdog on the activities of a 'recalcitrant' Cypriot government which, it was feared in Athens and by NATO, was flirting dangerously with the non-aligned and even some members of the eastern bloc. Their departure, it was therefore widely believed, might make it possible for the Cyprus government to move unhindered towards a compromise constitutional settlement with the Turkish community without fearing either the probability of political subversion directed from Athens or that the island might suddenly find itself within NATO's orbit. Three other things that emerged from the November crisis were, first that the relationship between Athens and Nicosia had changed completely and had indeed become distinctly cool, with Archbishop Makarios assuming now primary if not yet sole stewardship of efforts directed at a settlement of the Cyprus problem; secondly, that the Turkish Cypriots, even though heavily outnumbered in the island itself, could always count on support from Turkey mainland; and thirdly that in case of any future crisis the American government, already heavily committed to a highly unpopular military adventure in Vietnam, might not be willing to become actively engaged in preventing a Turkish invasion, or, alternatively, that next time Turkey would not be put off, particularly with the well equipped Greek troops no longer in the island.

Despite the fact that it would obviously have been unrealistic to expect that a complete solution to the Cyprus problem would have been negotiated in the wake of the November crisis it is thought that a number of opportunities were missed to improve the situation in ways that, with the benefit of hindsight, would almost certainly have proved beneficial, not to say salutary. It is thus a pity that it was not found possible to proceed to a complete demilitarisation of the island (including the National Guard as well as Turkish Cypriot paramilitary forces), subject of course to a substantial enlargement of UNFICYP and its mandate. Similarly, it may have been rational at the time if the way was paved for direct discussions regarding the political future of the island between the Cyprus government and Turkey. At the time sentiment in Nicosia in favour of enosis was at a low ebb, the Greek government had apparently decided that it wished for the time being to disengage itself from the affairs of the island, and it was only too clear that the Turkish Cypriot community was totally dependent on Turkey for both military support and political direction. Indeed hints were apparently dropped by Cypriot ministers immediately after the November crisis that President Makarios was ready to talk directly with the Turkish government, but there was no response at all from Ankara. What must surely be regretted most is that there was at this crucial stage no concerted effort by those with power and leverage, mainly the American government and the NATO Alliance, to help remove the Greek junta and have it replaced by a more acceptable regime. The time for such an initiative was ripe and western interests themselves demanded it. What is more important, there were many indications that this could have been achieved with relative ease. The junta had just suffered a stunning setback, most of its conservative support at home had quickly evaporated after its capitulation in Cyprus, and there were widespread rumours of a power struggle among senior army officers. What was more, in early December there was a scathing attack upon the junta from Mr Karamanlis, the conservative leader then in exile in Paris. His denunciation of the junta as insincere, incompetent, demagogic and dangerous stripped the Greek regime of the last remnants of respectability and tolerance, and had a profound effect on international opinion. But the American government and other western powers on whom the Greek military depended once more failed to act decisively, and an opportunity to rid Greece of the junta that was before long to destroy Cyprus was lost.

5. *The aftermath of the crisis*

As a result of the November crisis and the withdrawal from the island of the Greek and Turkish troops, a major impetus was given to further efforts for resolving through negotiation outstanding differences, including political and constitutional ones. Thus, during January and February 1968, the Greek and Turkish Cypriot sides held a number of meetings with the Secretary-General and other UN authorities and once more put forward their views on the various points at issue in an effort to see whether it would be possible to stage some kind of direct political dialogue. Clearly such views could not remain unchanged. Once more Archbishop Makarios took the initiative. On 12 January 1968 he issued a statement[55] to the people of Cyprus and in this he stated the following: The Cyprus problem had entered a critical stage. The two main factors which had contributed to this development were the failure of the direct Graeco-Turkish dialogue and the withdrawal from Cyprus of military forces, these forces being mainly Greek. These two factors had created circumstances and conditions 'dictating a realistic reappraisal of the handling of the Cyprus problem'. A solution had to be sought 'within the limits of what was feasible' which did not always coincide with the limits of what was desirable. The feasible was sovereign independence. As to the constitutional position and prospects, his Beatitude wished to reiterate that Greek Cypriots desired to live in harmony with the Turks of Cyprus. 'We do not wish to deprive them of their rights as equal citizens, far less do we aim at their extermination.' On the contrary, he was prepared to extend to them additional privileges. He also wished to emphasise that the constitution of Cyprus as of any other independent and unitary state should be governed by democratic principles, be approved by the people and be subject to amendment by democratic machinery, in accordance with the will of the people as a whole. That part, however, which would constitute the 'Charter of rights of the Turkish community' would be entrenched. In the very near future, his Beatitude concluded, a document would be drawn up on the above lines and he hoped that this would form the basis for further discussions within the framework of the good offices of the Secretary-General.

Following presidential elections which were held on 25 February and which resulted in a renewal of his mandate by a 96.4 per cent majority, Archbishop Makarios reaffirmed before the House of Representatives his willingness to discuss with the Turkish Cypriots ways of ensuring their legitimate rights and certain additional privileges, provided that these were kept within the limits of a unitary, democratic and independent state. Further on 7 March Makarios lifted all restrictions on the Turkish community and announced a great number of other normalization measures.[56] This was praised by U Thant, but the Turkish side still refused to open up their enclaves. Finally, on 12 March 1968, new proposals were submitted to the Secretary-General on the part of the Greek Cypriot side. In an accompanying letter, Archbishop Makarios repeated his full support for the efforts being made by the Secretary-General in the exercise of his good offices for finding a peaceful and just solution to the Cyprus problem and summarised the new Greek-Cypriot positions. The underlying concept was that Cyprus should be a unitary state, fundamental rights and

[55] This can be found in *Cyprus: The Problem in Perspective*, supra n.16, at 62–3.
[56] Harbottle, supra n.37, at 166.

freedoms were to be guaranteed to all citizens, and, in addition, the Turkish Cypriots were to enjoy full communal autonomy and certain other rights to an extent and degree not incompatible with unitary administration.

The Greek Cypriot proposals of 12 March 1968 dealt only with the constitutional aspects of the problem and their main features were the following: The state of Cyprus should be a unitary democratic republic; the structure of the state and the form of its governmental institutions would be subjects for consideration and discussion, and any proposed constitution should be approved by the people either directly or indirectly through any recognised democratic machinery; the members of the Turkish community, in addition to all fundamental rights and freedoms, would enjoy complete autonomy and freedom in matters relating to their religion, education, culture and personal status and in similar matters where the interests and institutions were of a nature exclusively connected with the Turkish community; the Turkish Cypriot community would also be proportionately represented in the House of Representatives (but elections would be on a common electoral roll, thus ensuring that the persons seeking election would aim at gaining the support of the people as a whole, irrespective of race or creed), there was to be a Ministry for Turkish Cypriot Affairs headed by a Turkish Cypriot Minister, (in addition to the right enjoyed by any citizen of the republic of equal access to the public service of the republic and the police on the basis of qualifications, merit, competence and ability) special provision would be made for the fair representation of the Turkish Cypriots, and, similarly, their fair representation on the judicial organs would also be recognised; further there was also to be recognised a wide field of local administration for carrying out the usual local government services; and finally the republic, through its appropriate organs, would be bound to secure the enjoyment of the rights and freedoms guaranteed to the Turkish community, and in particular, in addition to the remedies available under the European Convention for the Protection of Human Rights, to which the republic was a party, the republic had already accepted as a further safeguard of the rights of the Turkish Cypriots that a UN Commissioner, with an adequate staff of observers and advisers, should be stationed in Cyprus for as long as reasonably necessary, for the purpose of observing, on such terms as the Secretary-General of the United Nations might direct, faithful adherence to all such rights.

Various important concessions were thus made by the Greek Cypriot side on its previously taken positions. Thus, it was expressly declared that Cyprus was to be an independent republic i.e. that enosis, unfettered independence, self-determination or other such solutions would no longer be sought; it was announced that 'the structure' of the state and the form of its governmental institutions would be subjects for discussion, whereas previously the declared Greek Cypriot stand was that only minority rights could be discussed; and throughout the proposals the term 'community' was used. This of course was a major advance or concession in as much as until then the fundamental theme of the Greek Cypriot side was that the Turks of Cyprus were only a 'minority' and nothing more. But now both the designation of 'community' is applied to the Turkish Cypriots and furthermore rights are declared for them which go beyond those normally accorded to minorities. In this context the right of proportional participation now conceded to the Turkish Cypriot side was of particular significance in that it would be taken as representing and would in fact itself constitute a strong bicommunal element that went well beyond all previous Greek Cypriot proposals.

At about this time the Turkish Cypriots themselves seemed willing to abandon their insistence on a geographical federation. They also seemed aware of the fact that, as had been openly acknowledged by the UN mediator in his report, there could be no return to the 1960 constitution. It had been universally accepted that the Turkish community had obtained from the Zurich and London agreements a series of rights far superior to what could realistically be contemplated for it in the future, and the Turkish community itself seemed to realise that excessive rights might actually be counterproductive in that they could provoke rather than efficaciously protect. From their point of view what was essential was that any new settlement should (a) still be a bicommunal one and (b) contain more effective safeguards for their protection. Further, on the issue of procedure, both sides now indicated that they would not be unwilling to take part in local talks provided this did not jeopardise their 'rights'.

The political climate thus became distinctly more favourable. In particular, Greek and Turkish troops were withdrawn from Cyprus and an imminent Graeco-Turkish military confrontation had been averted; it became obvious that no settlement could be a viable one unless it was reached after direct negotiations between the parties principally concerned, i.e. the Greek and Turkish Cypriots; and the Greek and Turkish Cypriot sides now made in the context of consultations with the UN authorities reciprocal concessions, abandoning their initial positions of a completely unitary and independent state that would be free to exercise in an unrestricted manner its right of self-determination, on the one hand, and a federal system with communal separation, on the other. The two sides were in fact moving gradually towards the wide range of alternatives included within the vague formula of a unitary and integral state with some bicommunal participation. It remained to be seen whether direct negotiations after five years of separation and tension could come up with a settlement.

3

The Intercommunal Discussions 1968 – 1971

1. *Early exchanges*

After the crisis of November – December 1967 the Security Council, in its effort to find a peaceful solution to the Cyprus problem, adopted by its resolution of 22 December 1967 the procedure 'of the good offices of the Secretary-General of the United Nations' on the basis of appeals that had been made by the Secretary-General himself. The Secretary-General, having made various soundings, put forward at the beginning of 1968 a suggestion for the commencement of local talks in Cyprus under the aegis of his special representative. An exploratory first meeting of the representatives of the Greek and Turkish communities, Messrs Clerides and Denktash, took place in Beirut on 11 June 1968, and here the way was paved for the opening of substantive negotiations in Cyprus between the two sides, the first meeting in Nicosia taking place on 24 June 1968. From the very beginning, consistently with the consensus reached as a result of the Secretary-General's consultations, it was agreed that the aim of the local talks would be the exploration of various possibilities for the solution of the constitutional problem on the basis of an independent, integral and sovereign state. Once the internal constitutional problem was settled, Cyprus' international position and more particularly the question of the treaties of alliance and guarantee would be the subjects of discussion by the interested governments.

The first phase of talks

At the preliminary meeting in Beirut, Mr Denktash recognised that the Zurich settlement contained unjust provisions both for the Greek Cypriots and for the Turkish Cypriots; as examples of the latter he gave the maintenance of separate municipalities which would, in the long run, mean a heavy financial burden which the Turkish community would not be able to bear and the provision for 7:3 participation in the public service which, if it ever came to be fully applied, would deprive the Turkish community of its young, able and educated members who would otherwise be

All quotations in this chapter come from the documents of the intercommunal files (see Preface).

extremely useful for its development and the improvement of its living standards. The Turkish side, Mr Denktash assured Mr Clerides, was fully aware of the defects of the Zurich and London agreements. But it had not been prepared to accept modifications in 1963 because it strongly believed then (and still believed at the time of the negotiations) that the real purpose of the Greek Cypriot side in 1963 had not been the genuine improvement of the 1960 constitution but the abrogation of essential constitutional safeguards and the bringing about of enosis. In addition, the Zurich and London agreements did not extend sufficient and effective protection to the Turkish Cypriots, Mr Denktash observed. The veto rights of the Vice-President and the provision concerning separate legislative majorities were not capable of safeguarding in an adequate manner the rights of the Turkish Cypriots. A way could always be found to evade them and, moreover, resort to these obstructive prerogatives was 'bad publicity' as it gave the impression internationally that the Turks were intransigent. It was therefore vital that any new set up should include provisions capable of assuring the Turkish Cypriots of effective protection.

As regards Greek Cypriot grievances and demands, the Greek Cypriot side had already, on numerous occasions, voiced its dissatisfaction with many of the provisions of the 1960 constitution, and had given (particularly in the 13 proposals of Archbishop Makarios) clear indication of the kinds of reform it would insist upon. Almost all the points Mr Clerides appears to have raised at this preliminary meeting were points on which the Greek Cypriots had called for amendment in 1963. The Zurich and London agreements and the 1960 constitution, Mr Clerides pointed out, were replete with separatist and objectionable elements, which not only obstructed the operation of the state, but also harmed (on the admission of the Turkish Cypriot side itself) the interests of the Turkish community. Why, then, had the Turkish side never consented until then to a limited modification of the constitution? The impression of the Greek Cypriot side was that the Turkish Cypriot leadership insisted on the rigid implementation of the 'unworkable' elements of the 1960 constitution and on the extension of the communal separation represented by them in order to create further divisive situations and set in motion partitionist schemes. What the Greek Cypriot side wanted was simply to remove what it considered to be 'the anomalies of the constitution' and to improve the administrative machinery of the state; and the Greek Cypriot representative expressed the hope that the Turkish Cypriot side would cast aside its prejudices and evaluate any proposals for constitutional change that might be made on their merits.

At the end of the first meeting in Nicosia the Turkish Cypriot representative, in a clear indication of his side's real worries, brought up his community's serious economic difficulties. He observed that the economic gap between the two communities was widening. The Greek side, despite what he called the 'internal revolution', had achieved remarkable economic success. As a result, its living standards had risen out of all recognition. In contrast to this prosperity, the Turkish side continued to be financially and economically underdeveloped. There therefore had to be substantial economic assistance to the Turkish community. Indeed, Mr Denktash himself observed, it would be in the interests of the Greek Cypriot side to assist financially the Turkish Cypriots, for only in this way would their economic and political reliance on Turkey be reduced. Mr Clerides readily agreed with this. He assured Mr Denktash that his government was all in favour of Turkish economic development. But this and the narrowing of the gap between Greek and Turkish living standards could only be effected in the framework of a unitary state and in the context of unified economic policies. The Zurich and London agreements with their divisive elements and communal narrowmindedness had not been up to the task.

At this early stage the Turkish side seemed amenable to considerable constitutional amendment of the Zurich structure and indeed seemed resigned to the inevitability of many of the reforms that the Greek side had in mind. Mr Denktash made it clear that his side could agree to 'a great number of (constitutional amendments) provided that the intercommunal balance set out under the 1960 agreements was not upset'. He emphasised that the Turkish 'communal political status entrenched in the 1960 constitution' could not be abandoned and indicated that a compromise solution would become possible if certain 'concessions on (Turkish) entrenched rights at government level' were exchanged for a degree of local autonomy. He therefore asked, in one of the very early meetings, whether the Greek side was prepared to examine the subject of local government. Mr Clerides replied in the affirmative, pointing out that 'the institution of local government was a characteristic of all advanced systems of administration, and that it has certain practical advantages in that it decentralises authority and gives more say in matters of administration to the inhabitants of the areas concerned'. He also pointed out that local government, 'as it exists in other countries', was not normally based on ethnic, religious or racial criteria, but on the principles of topography and on the similarity of administrative, economic and social problems.

The first phase of the talks was mainly concerned with a rather untidy preliminary exchange of views and an exploration of the attitudes of the two communities. The general attitude of the Greek Cypriot side was well known, its main objective being to obtain a substantial amendment of the 1960 constitution along the lines of the 13 proposals while at the same time extending adequate protection to the Turkish Cypriots. During this first period, it also transpired from the discussions that the attitude of the Turkish Cypriot side with regard to various issues was the following:

(1) The Turkish side had agreed to a reduction of the percentage of its participation in the civil service, the police and the legislature to that of its population ratio.

(2) It was also accepted that the election of the President and the Vice-President of the House of Representatives would be made by all the members of the House. Where the President was a Greek the Vice-President would be a Turk and vice-versa. But the retention of separate electoral rolls for elections to the House would be insisted upon.

(3) The Turkish side did not object to the unification of the courts on condition, first, that the percentage of the participation of Turkish Cypriots in the judiciary would be on the basis of population and, secondly, that in serious criminal or civil cases the accused or the litigant would have the right to apply to the Supreme Court for the appointment of a judge speaking his language to sit as a co-judge, in which case the Supreme Court would have the discretionary power to accept or reject such an application.

(4) On the subject of the executive, the Turkish side asked for Turkish participation in accordance with its population ratio and insisted on the retention of the office of the Vice-President, this office to belong to the Turkish community. On this last point, in the course of one of the meetings during the first phase, Mr Denktash intimated that if the Greek Cypriot side were to accept the office of a Turkish Cypriot Vice-President, the Turkish Cypriot side would concede that the Turkish Cypriot Vice-President would not be a member of the Council of Ministers, that the President of the state would appoint all ministers, that the right of veto of the Vice-President would be given up, that the President alone would sign laws and the decisions of the Council of Ministers, and that the President alone would appoint high-ranking officials.

(5) On the subject of local administration, Mr Denktash stated in one of the early meetings that the Turkish side did not demand the setting up of areas for local administration on racial grounds provided that there would be agreement as to the areas in which the Turks would be in the majority and that these would not be subject to modification by ordinary legislation. Some kind of qualified majority should be necessary for this purpose, so that a number of Turkish Cypriot votes would be required before any alteration of local authority boundaries could be effected. On the subject of powers and functions for local authorities, Mr Denktash accepted that these would be exercised in accordance with laws enacted by the House of Representatives and mentioned nothing about police or judicial responsibility for local organs. At this stage the Turkish Cypriot negotiator had

made it clear that he wished to dissolve Greek Cypriot fears concerning alleged Turkish plans for the creation of a cantonal system. But at another meeting a few weeks later Mr Denktash said that his side wanted after all the creation of courts in areas of local administration which would try violations of the rules and regulations issued by the local government authorities. Further, his side wanted the setting up of local government police to investigate alleged infringements of these rules. Later on, reverting to the question of the structuring of local government, Mr Denktash introduced the idea of 'groups of villages'. This envisaged not so much the demarcation of areas as the grouping together of a number of villages so that they would form units of local administration. The formation of groups of villages was to be based on ethnic or communal criteria. But at the same meeting as the one in which he introduced the idea of groups of villages Mr Denktash accepted in principle a unified police. The necessary supervision for the observance of local regulations and other similar quasi-police functions, the Turkish Cypriot negotiator suggested, could be entrusted to civilian inspectors, employees of the local authorities.

The Greek Cypriot side, even though in full agreement that complete protection and security should be extended to the Turkish Cypriots and their community, could not agree with Turkish proposals on the suggested structuring and powers of local administration and had strong reservations about the retention of the office of the Vice-President. The view was expressed by Mr Clerides that the demands of Mr Denktash regarding the formation of communal groups of villages, apart from the fact that they conflicted 'with the principles of a unitary state and the accepted forms of local administration', were objectionable on the following points: They were 'entirely unworkable and highly impracticable because of the distribution of the population', the Turkish Cypriots being scattered all over the island; they failed to safeguard the economic viability of the areas and their effective administration, since 'their formation would not be based on the local, administrative, economic and social problems of the inhabitants of the area as a whole, but only of one national group'; the setting up of such groups of villages on racial criteria would constitute 'a constant source of friction and conflicts of jurisdiction' and would result in an unjustified and costly duplication of work; and serious obstacles would be caused to the need for effective planning for the development of the island as a whole.

On the completion of the first phase of the talks a joint statement was issued by the two sides through their representatives. They were able to say that there had been identity of view on a number of points, and that on other issues it would not be very difficult to establish common ground; but there remained certain problems, the importance of which could not be minimised, which would require patient negotiation. Only in this way would the existing gap be narrowed.

At this stage the attitude of both Greece and Turkey towards the intercommunal discussions was very positive. The talks clearly enjoyed the full support of the Greek Government. Mr Pipinelis, the Greek Foreign Secretary, was the architect of Greek policy in this regard. His views (and the basic premises of Greek policy at the time), as communicated to the Cyprus government on the completion of the first round of the talks, were the following:

(a) Enosis was not possible as recent political and military developments had unfolded. It might possibly be considered in the future if international realities allowed. Anyway, it was most unlikely that enosis would ever become possible without the agreement of Turkey or without important reciprocal Greek concessions (whether in Cyprus or elsewhere). Therefore enosis for the foreseeable future had to be shelved and all efforts devoted to a strengthening of the unitary character of the republic. The slogan of enosis itself, Mr Pipinelis believed, had to be abandoned, as high-sounding statements and declarations did nothing but harm.

(b) Military confrontation between Greece and Turkey would result in irreparable harm to Greece and Cyprus. Indeed, it was he himself, Mr Pipinelis informed the Cyprus government, who had averted a Graeco-Turkish war after the Kofinou incidents by persuading the Greek military regime that it was most improbable that enosis would be the result of such a war. Only by complete military annihilation of Turkey and the consequent imposition of peace terms could it be achieved, and this of course was impossible. Even in the case of a Greek victory, it would not follow. Indeed, in this unlikely event, the Greek armed forces would find themselves over-extended and with inadequate supply lines, and further complications might well be caused by the vulnerability of the northern Greek frontiers. Additionally, military confrontation was bound to set in motion an expensive arms race that would disrupt the fragile Greek economy. And, most important of all, the Greek Foreign Secretary warned, whatever the pious rhetoric to the contrary, Cyprus could not be assisted effectively in the event of a Turkish invasion. Greece was too far away to extend a protective air cover and the island would consequently find itself at the mercy of the Turkish Air Force. Great destruction would be caused. Mr Pipinelis was therefore profoundly convinced, both as a result of these factors and in consequence of his broader understanding of Greek interests, that the basis of Greek foreign policy had to be friendship with Turkey. This was the policy of former Greek statesmen such as Ch.

Trikoupis and El. Venizelos, and it was he who would continue their work. If the Cyprus problem could be solved satisfactorily, Cyprus might, even at that late stage, become a bridge of further Graeco-Turkish co-operation.

(c) On the subject of the international implications of the situation, the United States had indicated to the Greek government in no uncertain terms, both before and during the Kofinou events, that a war between Greece and Turkey should never take place. Any such war would be destructive to the stability of the eastern flank of NATO and could well provide the pretext for an irreversible Soviet intrusion in the area. Further, as had become only too clear during the 1967 crisis, America would do nothing either in the event of a Graeco-Turkish war or in case Turkey invaded Cyprus. Genuine accommodation with Turkey, so the Pipinelis doctrine went, was therefore essential.

(d) The Greek government believed that the intercommunal discussions were the most appropriate procedure for arriving at a mutually satisfactory internal constitutional settlement. The question of the treaties and of external guarantees would then be discussed at another level between all interested parties. Meanwhile, everything possible should be done to expedite the progress of the talks. The Greek and Greek Cypriot sides could not possibly afford to miss another opportunity for a final resolution of the Cyprus problem. This, Mr Pipinelis characteristically stated, had already become 'the problem of lost opportunities'; further delay could mean disaster, particularly as there might be unfavourable political developments in Turkey and possibly internal complications within Greece and Cyprus that would impede progress towards a final settlement.

(e) Complete agreement was expressed at this stage with the positions of the Greek Cypriot side on the issue of local autonomy. Local government areas delineated on geographical and not on communal criteria should be insisted upon, Mr Pipinelis informed Mr Clerides. Communal areas, if possible, should be avoided and special care should be taken in the differentiation between state and local affairs. Also, adequate central controls on the exercise of local functions should exist.

As regards Turkey's attitude towards the talks, the positions of Mr Chaglayangil, the Turkish Foreign Secretary, as these were formulated during this time and communicated both to the Greek government and to the UN Secretary-General, can be summarised as follows:

(1) The intercommunal talks should be encouraged.
(2) Both enosis and partition should be excluded. The independence of Cyprus should be maintained and positively ensured. The Turkish Parliament and Turkish public opinion had to be convinced that acceptance of the premise of 'the maintenance of the independence of Cyprus' on

the part of the Cyprus and Greek Governments was genuine. There were still some doubts on this score.

(3) The difficulty of the problem should not be underestimated. The intercommunal discussions were bound to be long and arduous. At the same time, they might be the last chance. The Turkish community should be afforded complete security; and all necessary arrangements in this direction would be strenuously insisted upon.

All in all, the 'reserved optimism' entertained by both sides after the completion of the first round of talks was justified – despite the disagreement that had surfaced with regard to local government – not only by the common ground discovered or achieved on a number of topics but also by the relatively favourable political climate that had developed in the wake of the 1967 crisis and in consequence of the 'moderation' of the Greek and Turkish Foreign Secretaries.

The second phase

After the completion of the first phase both Mr Clerides and Mr Denktash held consultations with the Cyprus and Turkish governments respectively, Mr Denktash flying to Ankara for this purpose. The Greek Cypriot side has since maintained that the hardening of the attitude of the Turkish Cypriot side during the later phases of the talks and its change of view on a number of matters came about after and as a result of Mr Denktash's talks with the Turkish government.

During the second phase the two negotiators exchanged concrete proposals on the executive, the police, the legislature, the administration of justice and local government. On the executive the Greek Cypriot proposals emphasised the presidential character of the regime to be set up, provided for Turkish Cypriot participation on the Council of Ministers in proportion to their population, but omitted all reference to a Turkish Vice-President. The President of the republic, according to the Greek Cypriot side, was to be the head of state and all executive power was to be exercised by him through the Council of Ministers; but he was to have no right to any veto, as opposed to a power to return laws for reconsideration.

On the legislature Mr Clerides' proposals provided for: a House of Representatives consisting of 60 members, of whom 48 would be Greek Cypriots and 12 Turkish Cypriots; common electoral rolls; three officers, a President and two Vice-Presidents, one of the latter to be necessarily a Turkish Cypriot but all to be chosen from among the representatives by majority vote; and all legislative decisions to be taken by majority vote, except in cases where the interests of the Turkish Cypriots were particularly involved. More specifically, in the cases of the electoral arrangements of the republic and of the amendment of constitutional provisions, a two-thirds majority was to be required, and in the case of the amendment of constitutional provisions expressly conferring specific rights on the Turkish Cypriots this majority was to include a specified number of votes from among the Turkish members of the House. Furthermore, as regards education, the House of Representatives was to provide in the budget, in respect of each financial year, a sum for the financing of Turkish education. This sum was to bear the same proportion to the sum to be appropriated for Greek education as the proportion which the number of pupils receiving instruction in Turkish-Cypriot schools bore to the number of pupils receiving instruction in Greek schools.

On the judiciary Mr Clerides proposed the establishment of a system of courts at the apex of which would be a Supreme Court consisting of not more than seven judges, one of whom would be the President, offered representation on judicial organs to the Turkish Cypriots in proportion to their population, and strongly emphasised that justice should be administered on juridical and not ethnic criteria, even though the Supreme Court would have power, either on its own motion or on the application of any party to civil or criminal proceedings, to give such directions as to the composition of any trial court as justice might require. The President and other judges of the Supreme Court were to be appointed by the President of the republic out of a panel prepared by the Supreme Council of Judicature, and this last body, which would be entrusted with the appointment of members of inferior courts, their promotions, transfers, termination of appointments and all disciplinary matters, was to consist of the Attorney-General, the President and judges of the Supreme Court and the Chairman of the Bar Council holding office at the time. Finally, in order to assure Turkish Cypriots of complete judicial impartiality, the Greek Cypriot side proposed the establishment of special appeal procedures from the Supreme Court; in particular, the individual recourse to the European Commission of Human Rights under Article 25 of the European Convention was to be recognised, and for a period of three years from the time when an overall agreement was reached there was to be an appeal from a non-unanimous decision of the Supreme Court to the Judicial Committee of the Privy Council.

As to the police, a unitary force was suggested in which the Turkish Cypriots would be represented in proportion to their population. In this connection arrangements were also promised whereby the police force stationed in parts of the territory of the Republic inhabited by mixed populations would consist of Greeks and Turks, proportionately, as far as practicable, to the population of the relevant part, and whereby the police force stationed in areas inhabited by Greeks or Turks, as the case might be, in a proportion approaching 100 per cent would consist 'in the substantial majority' of Greek or Turkish members of the force respectively.

The detailed proposals of Mr Denktash on these issues diverged considerably from those of the Greek side. On the legislature the Turkish side accepted that its participation should be brought down to 20 per cent of the total number of representatives but insisted that the number of Turks should be not less than 15 'in order to enable Turkish participation at all committees and at any other business of the House'. Further, the House was not to be allowed to legislate on 'any matter specifically reserved in the constitution', local autonomy being such a matter. On this last issue the 1960 'separate majority vote' requirement could only be abandoned, the Turkish side declared, if watertight provisions were worked into the constitution safeguarding to the satisfaction of the Turkish side any agreed electoral system, the existing Turkish municipalities by their incorporation in local authority systems, and other matters of special significance to the Turkish community. As for the system of elections, the Greek proposal concerning common electoral rolls could not be accepted. The Turkish side, Mr Denktash said, could not discover a procedure for general elections capable of satisfying Greek Cypriot wishes for unification while at the same time preventing Greek voters from imposing on the Turks Turkish candidates who might be completely unacceptable to them.

On the executive, according to the Turkish proposals, there had to be a Turkish Vice-President, but the Turkish Cypriot side would not commit itself at this stage on the question of his powers and responsibilities; and in the area of the administration of justice, Turkish and Greek Cypriots had 'to have the constitutional right to have their case tried by a judge of their own language'. This was an important modification of view by the Turkish side which during earlier exchanges had agreed to the primacy of jurisdictional as opposed to ethnic criteria. Further, on the subject of the Supreme Court, Mr Denktash's proposals demanded that the proportion of its Greek and Turkish members should not be below 3 and 2 respectively, unless agreement was reached on the establishment of local administration courts.

But already the emphasis for the Turkish side had shifted to local government. On this Mr Denktash, at the beginning of the second phase, considerably modified his side's position. He demanded that villages should be taken by name and grouped together, that grouping should be effected on communal criteria, that each group of villages so constituted should be a local authority area and that each local authority area should elect a representative or representatives who would sit at a central government authority entrusted with the coordination and exercise of local governmental functions. There would thus be two central authorities, the Turkish local authority council and the Greek local authority council, any coordination between the Turkish local authorities and the central government to be carried on by a Turkish Affairs Ministry, if created, or by the Turkish Vice-President. Thus, Mr Denktash introduced for the first time the idea of a central organ of local administration or, to be more exact, of two such central organs, one for Greek local authorities and another for the Turkish ones; and, as an afterthought, the Turkish side suggested uniting communal chamber functions to the regional set up so as to avoid multiplicity of assemblies. In this way there would be two central bodies, one Greek and the other Turkish, invested with both communal and local governmental powers and responsibilities. With regard to matters falling within the jurisdiction of the local authorities, the Turkish side now asked that the House of Representatives should only promulgate laws concerning general state policy in the barest outline and that the local authorities themselves should be empowered to issue any necessary regulations. Further, in its detailed written proposals on the police and the judiciary, the Turkish side also modified its previous positions. On the police Mr Denktash now asked that 'internal security, i.e. police, should be considered separately at two levels, the governmental level and the local administration level', and specifically demanded the creation of two separate police forces under the control of local authorities. And with regard to the administration of justice, 'communal local courts in local administration areas to try all litigation between the members of their respective communities' were now proposed.

The Turkish side's strong insistence on the question of local government prompted a reassessment by the Greek Cypriot side of its previously expressed views on the subject, and on 24 April 1969 Mr Clerides put forward new comprehensive proposals in an effort to reduce the differences between the two sides. In an explanatory note accompanying the new proposals, the Greek Cypriot negotiator explained that 'the proposed form of local administration, while based on the concept of retaining each village as the basic unit of local administration, also accepts the principle that a number of villages, in geographical proximity to each other, can be grouped together for the purpose of forming a cohesive area of local administration'. Further, the envisaged scheme of local administration, though not based on racial criteria, 'but on the grouping of villages on the principle of geographical proximity, similarity of administrative, economic and social problems and on the consideration that the area unit of local administration to be created must be economically viable', also allowed, 'as far as practicable, the grouping together of Turkish villages, which lie in geographical proximity to each other, into one cohesive area'. This area or administrative region was to constitute the second tier of local government and the third or final tier was to be the district. Considerable powers of supervision over local authorities and units were to be vested in the district officer, the representative of the state, and it was stressed by Mr Clerides that, in so far as powers and functions were concerned, 'local government shall be restricted to administrative and not political local government'. In his letter of 24 April 1969 Mr Clerides asked Mr Denktash to bear in mind when considering his proposals on local administration that, in addition to the above, the government of Cyprus had also proposed that:

(a) complete autonomy should be given to the Turkish Cypriots on matters of education, culture, religion and personal status (and had accepted financial responsibility for Turkish education);

(b) representation in the executive, the legislature, the judiciary, the civil service and the police should be accorded to the Turkish Cypriots in proportion to their population; and

(c) the police force in Turkish villages and areas predominantly Turkish would consist 'in its substantial majority of Turkish police officers belonging to a unified police force'.

Upon receipt of Mr Clerides' April 1969 letter and its enclosures, Mr Denktash decided to seek clarification on the Greek Cypriot proposals before drafting counter-proposals. He therefore, on 20 May 1969, sent a questionnaire to the Greek Cypriot side, expressing the hope that 'clarification of the points raised will somehow smooth the way of negotiations on this subject'. The main inquiries concerned the concept of grouping of villages, Mr Clerides' distinction between 'administrative local government' and 'political local government', and the district officer's powers. On this last point Mr Denktash observed that the 'district officer's powers, as envisaged by the Greek side, put local government authorities in the position – at its highest – of "improvements boards" under the colonial rule', and expressed the general view that separation of functions between first, second and third tiers, as outlined by the Greek Cypriot side, was 'unrealistic'. Mr Clerides' answers to the questionnaire submitted by Mr Denktash signalled the end of the second phase of negotiations. The Greek Cypriot negotiator stated once more the basic Greek Cypriot position on local government. 'The distinction between political government and local government or local administration has been drawn advisedly in the proposals in order to make it clear to the Turkish side that the government is not prepared to accept under the guise of local government or administration either a federal or a canton system'. As to the characteristics of a federal or a canton system which had to be avoided, these were formulated as follows by the Greek Cypriot negotiator:

'(a) A geographical area in which each state of the federation or the canton authority exercises its jurisdiction.

(b) Each state of the federation or canton authority has its own government consisting of all three functions of government, i.e. executive, legislative, and judicial.

(c) Each state of the federation or canton has its own police force and is responsible for policing its area'.

It was also to be noticed, the Greek Cypriot representative proceeded, that normally local government or a local administration authority derived its powers by delegation from the laws enacted by Parliament, could only issue subsidiary legislation in the form of regulations, bye-laws, etc., and was subject to a certain degree of supervision by central authority. These generally recognised principles could not be ignored in the structuring of Cypriot local government. Most important of all, what had to be borne in mind, and was in effect the main organising principle of the Greek Cypriot proposals, was that local government was not a communal arrangement. 'The (Greek Cypriot) proposals do not aim at giving local government to Turkish villages only, but at granting local government to all villages'.

The third phase

The third phase of the talks began on Monday 11 August 1969. At the meeting of the negotiators of this date (their nineteenth meeting until then), Mr Denktash gave Mr Clerides two documents containing the Turkish views, i.e. a letter (dated 24 June) discussing the Greek proposals of 24 April 1969 and Mr Clerides' clarification of them, and a complete set of new Turkish 'Counter proposals on autonomous local government authorities'.

There was still serious disagreement 'on the cardinal principles involved', Mr Denktash stated at the very outset of his letter. The Greek side's offer was, in effect, 'a re-arrangement of the village administration system by the government', and gave 'no basic rights or autonomy to the communities to administer their own local affairs'. The Turkish approach was quite different. 'We are seeking ways and means of accommodating your demand that certain of our 1960 constitutional rights should be amended by rearranging these rights in such a way that (1) the unity of the state is maintained while (2) the political status of the Turkish community is not reduced to that of a minority in a Greek-ruled island'. That is why the Greek proposals did not go far enough. 'The rights which we had indicated willingness to forego if satisfactory arrangements could be made on local autonomy rights are far too important for us to exchange for the local autonomy rights which you have envisaged'. In particular, the

Turkish side could not accept the principle of mixed grouping. Once this principle was accepted 'more than 90 per cent of the Turkish villages would be absorbed into the Greek majority areas by way of a political improvisation and for no good or valid reason at all'. The Turkish community's 'proved and unproved doubts and suspicions' as to what might happen once they lost their identity in a Greek majority area did not permit Turkish Cypriot concessions on this point. But the principle of communal grouping did not mean that the Turkish side was 'trying to pass off to the (Greek) side a "federal" or "cantonal" system under the guise of local administration'. It was with this in mind 'and knowing (the Greek) side's reaction to any idea of setting up geographical boundaries' that the Turkish side, the Turkish Cypriot negotiator explained, 'had offered "grouping" by naming the villages grouped together without bringing them into a geographical boundary'. Each village, according to his own proposals, would have its administrative boundaries and as a result the area of jurisdiction of any local authority in respect of a group of villages would be the totality of the relevant village areas. Mixed grouping should be left to the villagers themselves by way of a referendum, but Greek and Turkish villages should not be grouped together unless two-thirds of the inhabitants of each of the villages involved agreed to be so grouped; and, furthermore, such villages should, by the same means, be given the right to opt out of any 'mixed' group. Having emphasised that in his proposals for local autonomy there was 'no suggestion of having a geographical area', Mr Denktash went on to insist on the local authorities which he envisaged having original legislative capacity in some matters and on any rights and authorisation for the enactment of such legislation arising initially from powers to be embodied in the constitution in detail. Moreover, the local authorities to be created had to have their own police forces, and any 'suggestion that the local authorities should be under the district officer with the powers (the Greek side) envisaged' was simply not acceptable.

It was with all the above in mind that the Turkish counterproposals had been prepared. The main ones were:

(a) Local authorities were to be provided for in the constitution and would not be left to the will of the lawmakers.

(b) The 'currently existing' Turkish municipalities were to be retained.

(c) 'For facilitating the smooth and economic running of the local governments and with a view to making them into viable units able to carry on their constitutional functions and responsibilities villages may be grouped together'. Grouping was to be effected on communal criteria.

(d) There were to be 'two appropriate authorities in Cyprus, one for the Turkish villages and one for the Greek villages or their respective groups'. These authorities were of course the central organs of local administration which Mr Denktash had introduced earlier. These central authorities were to perform agreed functions to be incorporated in the constitution, and provision was to be made for joint meetings of the Greek and Turkish authorities at the highest level for discussing common problems.

(e) Coordination between government and local authorities was to be provided for through a board 'directly connected to the President and Vice-President'.

The detailed Turkish proposals given to the Greek Cypriot side on 11 August 1969 were discussed by the two negotiators at their meeting of 18 August 1969, and in a series of important letters exchanged between them on 1 and 18 September 1969. Disagreement could by now be seen to have focused most clearly on the philosophy and functions of local administration, the structuring of local government authorities, and the supervision or control of the local authorities by central governmental organs.

Mr Clerides made the following observations with regard to these three areas of acute disagreement. The Turkish counter-proposals continued to be based on principles which were unacceptable to the Greek side since they continued 'to aim at the creation in Cyprus of a complicated and unworkable system of government based on the concept of having a separate government for the Turks, a separate government for the Greeks and a central government consisting of Greeks and Turks'. In fact, the Turkish proposals went far beyond what might be termed local government and amounted to the creation of separate governments independent of each other with legislative, executive, fiscal, police and even judicial jurisdiction. The Turkish proposals, in other words, if implemented, would not bring about 'a unitary state'. Yet, it had been made clear to Mr Denktash all along that the Greek Cypriot side was not prepared to accept either a federal or a canton system. What the main characteristics of this were had already been set out, and it seemed to him that the Turkish counterproposals fell foul of them. 'It is clear from your proposals', he told Mr Denktash, 'that a central Turkish local government authority and a corresponding central Greek authority would be created, not for the purpose of decentralising authority from the government to the areas of local administration, but for the purpose of centralising it in the hands of the communities'. It had also been made clear by the Turkish side that these two central authorities were to derive their powers and functions directly from the constitution and would not be subject to any degree of supervision by the government; furthermore, the House of Representatives would have no competence to enact legislation with regard to matters of local government, and it had been candidly acknowledged in the Turkish proposals that the central authorities were intended to have legislative, executive, and possibly judicial powers as well. Given these elements, Mr Clerides had no doubt that the system proposed did not preserve the unity of the state, but created governments independent of each other on the basis of communal or racial criteria. This was 'contrary to the principles of a unitary state and accepted forms of local government'. Further, in addition to being contrary to the principles of a unitary state, establishment of local government areas on a communal basis presented many negative points: It would not ensure the economic viability of the areas or their effective administration; the creation of such areas on communal criteria would be a constant source of friction and conflicts over jurisdiction, and would cause unnecessary and wasteful duplication of services; and establishment of ethnic local authorities would in all probability result in hampering free movement and settlement in any part of the island. Finally, the Turkish counterproposals did not 'provide for any form of control either by the executive or by the legislature through legislation on matters of local government'; and even where some connection with the executive was suggested, 'this (was) merely for purposes of coordination and nothing more'. As a result, the Turkish counterproposals did not offer 'a basis for reaching an agreement on the issue of local government'.

Mr Denktash could not agree with Mr Clerides' evaluation of his letter and counterproposals of 11 August 1969. He termed it as 'too pessimistic'. It was not true, he asserted, that the Turkish Cypriots aimed at the creation of a state within a state. He reminded Mr Clerides that the lists of 'local' functions which had been exchanged between them some time before were not very dissimilar to each other, and that all matters not falling within the sphere of jurisdiction of the local authorities would devolve on the government. Also, 'a machinery of coordination between Greek and Turkish central authorities and vis-à-vis the government' had been suggested. How then could Mr Clerides' argument about the creation of three governments be supported? Nor could Mr Denktash share Mr Clerides' anxiety about the economic viability of the areas to be created. 'I fail to see how the grouping of Turkish and Greek villages separately will hinder their economic viability. The idea behind grouping was to enhance such viability'. Furthermore, mixed boards or councils could be set up for dispensing common services, and other appropriate measures could be taken to allay Greek fears concerning administrative friction or conflicts over jurisdiction or free movement being hampered. But Mr Denktash did not believe that such 'practical factors' were the real reason for Mr Clerides' refusal to accept his proposals. He felt that the Greek side's reasons for objecting to his proposals for local autonomy were 'political' and not based on 'practical considerations'. Had these reasons been merely practical, it would have been quite easy for solutions to be found. But this had not been done because the Greek Cypriot side was still 'unable to treat

the Turkish Community on its existing communal political status' and was
'looking for ways and means of pushing the community into the position of
a minority in the island'. This, for Mr Denktash, continued to be 'the crux
of the matter'. The result of these exchanges was that the gap between the
two sides on the question of local government continued to widen.

2. *Greek Cypriot proposals*

At this point the two interlocutors reexamined all the questions that had
been discussed. This reexamination was long overdue, for so engaged had
the negotiators become with the question of local government that the
other issues, i.e. the executive, the judiciary, the legislature, and the
police, had been for some time now almost completely ignored by them.
Was there perhaps a possibility that if the parties took a fresh look at the
matters that had previously been discussed, some of the differences that
had appeared in the past could now be resolved? When the earlier sets of
proposals regarding the central government had been exchanged, the
parties were, in effect, only engaged in statements of their initial positions
and in an exploration of each other's views; and, at that early time, local
government was only a vague idea which since then, despite the great
divergence of view that had emerged, had assumed more concrete form
both by a differentiation of what had been identified as its main constituent
elements and by essential clarification of many important points. Indeed,
the emphasis had so visibly shifted towards local government that one may
have thought that since, after all, there could be no possibility of partial
implementation of what might be agreed upon, the pressure might have
eased sufficiently for agreement to be reached on many points regarding
the organisation of central government. But this was not so. Positions were
becoming entrenched, attitudes were hardening. What the detailed and
comprehensive study of points of agreement and disagreement that the two
sides embarked upon indicated was that while on certain points of detail
and formulation there was some progress, on many important issues, as
well as on the crucial question of local government, the views of the two
sides continued to remain far apart. Continuation of the talks was in doubt.
Then, on 30 November 1970, the Greek Cypriot side, 'in its desire to avoid
an impasse in the talks and because of its belief that these talks constituted
the most appropriate procedure for the settlement of the Cyprus problem,
exerted a last effort to approach the Turkish points of view'. What Mr
Clerides was offering Mr Denktash was a 'package deal' by which the
Greek Cypriot side substantially modified its position on many issues and
made important concessions:

(a) It accepted the composition of the House of Representatives which had been proposed by the Turkish side, i.e. 60 Greek and 15 Turkish members.

(b) It accepted the Turkish proposal of having a Turkish Vice-President of the House.

(c) It accepted the Turkish proposal of having the Greek and Turkish members of the legislature elected on separate electoral rolls.

(d) It accepted, to some extent, the Turkish position regarding the jurisdiction of the courts by conceding that the Supreme Court could appoint a judge whose mother tongue was that of the litigants in cases where both parties had the same mother tongue.

(e) It accepted the principle of communal grouping, i.e. that Turkish villages could be grouped together to form areas of Turkish local government, contrary to its original position that areas of local government could be designed and demarcated only on administrative, economic and other such criteria, and not on ethnic or communal ones.

As a result there no longer remained any differences on the question of the legislature, and Turkish positions on a number of other topics were accepted. But, in exchange, it was asked that the Turkish side should abandon its proposal of separate central local government authorities for Greeks and Turks, and accept first that the House of Representatives would legislate on matters of local government delegating power to local government authorities to make regulations, and secondly that district officers appointed by the government would have the right to refuse to sign any regulation or decision of the local government authorities, which in their opinion would be outside the powers and functions of the local organs or contrary to the laws of the House, subject to a right of appeal to the Supreme Court by the local government authority concerned.

Before replying to Mr Clerides' proposals of 30 November 1970 Mr Denktash flew to Ankara for consultations with the Turkish government and it was apparently during his stay in Turkey that the Turkish response to the Greek Cypriot proposals was decided. Then, on 27 April 1971, Mr Denktash put forward in the form of a long letter to Mr Clerides not so much answers to or comments upon the Greek Cypriot proposals as independent Turkish Cypriot counterproposals. And before setting out his detailed proposals, Mr Denktash, 'in view of recent public statements by (the Greek) side on the ultimate Greek Cypriot policy on Cyprus' and because he had 'some doubts about the use of continuing the talks', thought it was vital to clarify some important points. First, it appeared to him essential to reaffirm the terms of reference for the intercommunal talks. It was his understanding that what would be sought in their context was 'a permanent solution based on independence', not 'an independence which one side or the other could utilise for furthering "national aims and aspirations",' and he did not think that the Greek Cypriot side had done enough in the direction of assuring the Turkish Cypriots that it too was genuine in its search for an independence settlement. He also wanted to make another point: 'I should like to point out that in trying to settle our problem on the basis of a package deal I have always taken it for granted that the remaining parts of our constitution will stand in (their) present form, subject to such minor adjustments necessitated in the light of agreement on the package deal'. Therefore, for instance, he could not agree to Mr Clerides' general treatment of the Turkish Cypriot Vice-President. He had indeed indicated readiness to forego the Vice-President's veto rights in foreign affairs, defence and internal security, but he could not agree to the Vice-President being 'merely a figurehead'. He was not in any position to write off the existing duties and powers of the Vice-President, since he felt, 'very strongly', that in 'our form of society' peace, understanding and mutual trust could only be cultivated by 'the two Supreme Heads of the executive working in full harmony for the good of Cyprus'. The Greek Cypriot side's basic conception of Cyprus was wrong, Mr Denktash appeared to be telling Mr Clerides, and a new set of proposals was therefore required.

The main points of the Turkish Cypriot counterproposals of 27 April 1971 were the following:

(a) Retention by the Vice-President of his duties and powers as prescribed by the London and Zurich agreements, with the exception of the veto;

(b) the reestablishment of two communal chambers, in other words separate legislative assemblies in charge of communal matters, as under the 1960 constitution, and creation of separate sound and vision broadcasting services;

(c) the setting up of local police forces organised along ethnic lines; and

(d) acceptance by the Greek Cypriot side of the Turkish proposal that trials and other judicial business should be conducted on the basis of communal criteria.

In addition Mr Denktash now demanded the setting up of new communal local courts to deal purely with 'local' or 'communal' matters. Furthermore, and whatever the progress to be achieved on issues in the area of central government, there could be no deviation from previous Turkish positions on local government. In particular, the Turkish side now proposed that:

(a) The powers, duties, and jurisdiction of the local authorities should be embedded in great detail in the constitution. The Greek Cypriot offer that this should be done through legislation to be passed by the House was not acceptable to the Turkish Cypriot side 'in view of the past record of the House which had stalled on the passing of the necessary legislation for the municipalities and had thus created a political impasse on a purely municipal issue'.

(b) There should be central authorities or coordinating bodies for local government and these central authorities should be either the Greek and Turkish communal chambers, or, alternatively, the President and a committee appointed by him from among the elected Greek members for the Greek local authorities, and the Vice-President and a committee appointed by him from among the elected Turkish members for the Turkish local authorities.

(c) Finally, 'the autonomous local bodies should (not) be under the District Officer for any purpose', subordination to central government not being 'compatible with their autonomy', but in alleged cases of ultra vires the courts would have the right to look into any complaint lodged by any person or authority in the republic.

It is clear that the Greek Cypriot side and Mr Clerides in particular were very disappointed with the Turkish response to the Greek Cypriot proposals of 30 November 1970. The Turkish side, Mr Clerides complained, 'for reasons best known to it', had chosen, some time after his package-deal proposals, 'to widen the gap by reopening issues agreed upon and by raising new ones'. Under the circumstances, the Greek Cypriot side 'had either to terminate the talks or to exert one last effort for seeking a settlement of the constitutional problem'. Mr Clerides chose the second course. On 26 June 1971 new proposals were put forward and the Greek Cypriot side expressed the hope 'that the Turkish side would respond positively and that an agreement would be reached'. And, at last, by its new proposals and further concessions, the Greek Cypriot side succeeded in finding common ground on the legislature and in substantially reducing the differences on the police and the judiciary.

The main points of the new proposals of the Greek Cypriot side of 26 June 1971 were the following:

Police

Mr Clerides first pointed out that on this issue the two sides were in agreement on the following points:

(1) Turkish Cypriot participation in the police force should be fixed at 20 per cent.

(2) The police and the gendarmerie should be amalgamated.

(3) Enlistments and promotions should be made on merit by a police commission, due regard being had to the implementation of the 20 per cent proportion of the Turkish Cypriot participation.

(4) Police forces stationed in parts of the territory of the republic inhabited by mixed populations of Greeks and Turks should consist of Greek and Turkish members of the force proportionately, as far as practicable, to the percentages of the population of the relevant area.

He was now prepared to make the following concessions: Further to his previous proposal, he was now ready to accept that where the majority of the Turkish Cypriots in an area approached 100 per cent the police force stationed in that area would consist exclusively of Turkish Cypriots. In addition, provided that Mr Denktash agreed that the numerical strength of the police would be regulated by law and that both the head and the deputy head of the police would be appointed by the President of the republic, he was ready to accept the Turkish suggestion that they should not both be from the same community. Finally, in a major concession, he declared himself prepared to accede to local government authorities having 'civilian inspectors with jurisdiction solely to enforce the bye-laws, regulations and orders made by the local government authorities on matters falling within their competence'.

The judiciary

With regard to the judiciary, Mr Clerides was prepared to accept:

(a) That the composition of the Supreme Court should consist of six Greek Cypriot judges and three Turkish Cypriot judges, as suggested by Mr Denktash;

(b) that the judges of the Supreme Court should be appointed by the President of the republic and that the President should appoint as Turkish judges of the Supreme Court those candidates for whom the Vice-President had expressed preference; and

(c) that Article 159 of the constitution should be optional, in the sense that the judge who had jurisdiction should try the case, irrespective of the community to which the litigant or litigants belonged, unless the litigant or one of the litigants involved invoked its provisions. Further, the Greek Cypriot side was prepared to accede to another of the Turkish Cypriot demands, i.e. to have honorary justices to try cases arising from regulations, bye-laws and orders of the local authorities, provided that their appointment would be made by the Supreme Council of Judicature.

The legislature

There was no longer any disagreement on the legislature, Mr Clerides declared. As a result of the two preceding sets of proposals and many intervening discussions the two sides had reached agreement on all important points relating to the composition and powers of the House of Representatives, and this could be set out as follows: The House of Representatives was to consist of 75 members, 60 Greeks and 15 Turks, to be elected on separate electoral rolls; the House as a whole was to elect its President and two Vice-Presidents, one of them to be Turkish; and decisions of the House were to be taken by majority vote except for the cases of the electoral law and amendments of constitutional clauses where a two-thirds majority would be required, this majority to include in the case of constitutional clauses expressly conferring specific rights on the Turkish Cypriots at least one third of the votes of the Turkish members of the House.

The executive

Mr Clerides summarised what points had already been agreed upon between the two communities:

(a) Turkish participation in the executive was to be fixed at 20 per cent.

(b) There was to be a Turkish Vice-President elected by the Turks.

(c) The veto rights on foreign policy, defence and internal security were to be abolished.

But it was the President alone, Mr Clerides emphasised, who should promulgate the laws and decisions of the Council of Ministers and the House of Representatives, sign the instruments of appointment of ministers, high court judges and independent officers of the republic, and exercise the right of return of laws and decisions of the House for reconsideration. But this, Mr Clerides insisted, did not set up a Vice-President who was a mere figurehead, as had been alleged by Mr Denktash. Indeed, he had proposed that the Vice-President was to recommend to the President, who was to act on such recommendation, Turkish Cypriots to be appointed as ministers, Supreme Court judges and independent officers of the republic, and that he was, additionally, to have the right and duty to challenge before the Supreme Court any law or decision of the House on the ground that it discriminated against the Turkish community. Further, the Vice-President was to promulgate all laws and decisions of the Turkish communal chamber and have the additional right to return them, prior to promulgation, to the Chamber for reconsideration. Surely, Mr Clerides remarked, such functions were 'of substance and not decorative'.

Local government

With regard to local government, Mr Denktash had proposed that the powers, duties and jurisdiction of the local authorities should be embedded in great detail in the constitution. 'If this were to be done, the Constitution of the Republic of Cyprus would have achieved at least one record, that of being the longest and most unwieldy constitutional document in the entire world'. Mr Clerides, in a new effort at compromise, agreed that 'the basic provisions regarding local government should be embedded in the constitution', but, following Mr Denktash's suggestion with regard to the electoral law, expressed the opinion that 'a local government law should be drafted and agreed upon prior to the signing of the general agreement and that for the purposes of its amendment it should require a two-thirds majority of the members of the House', which was also to include one-third of the votes of the Turkish members. Mr Clerides then summarised his final proposals on local government. These were, first, that the House of Representatives would legislate on matters of local government delegating power to local government authorities to make regulations, rules and bye-laws; secondly, that the local government authorities, in addition to the power to make rules, regulations, bye-laws, would have administrative functions on matters falling within their jurisdiction; thirdly, that each Turkish village should form a unit of local government; and fourthly that a number of Turkish villages could be grouped together to form several areas of local government each of which would be under a local government council. But the Greek Cypriot side could not agree that 'there should be a central local government authority either for the Greeks or for the Turks' and therefore could not accept the alternative Turkish proposals on this issue. On this point, Mr Clerides told Mr Denktash, the Greek Cypriot side was adamant, both because the Turkish proposal regarding the creation of communally based central authorities for local government was likely 'to put into slow motion the development of the country' and because it was incompatible with the generally accepted philosophy behind systems of local government, which was to decentralise authority by giving it to the areas concerned and not to take powers and functions from central governmental organs and give them on a centralised system to the communities.

It was clear, Mr Clerides said at the end of his letter of 26 June 1971, that the two sides had succeeded in substantially narrowing their differences. 'On the issue of the legislature there are no longer any differences. On the issues of the judiciary and the police it should be possible to reach an early agreement'. Was agreement on the remaining unsolved issues also possible?

It was not. In a long letter of his to Mr Clerides on 9 August 1971, Mr Denktash, instead of dealing with the points and specific proposals of the Greek Cypriot side, declared himself dissatisfied with the course and progress of the negotiations until then. To begin with, it was not true that the Greek-Cypriot side had been conciliatory; the reverse was the truth, he told Mr Clerides, and even though in a sense the Greek Cypriot side was correct in suggesting that on the difficult issues of the police, the judiciary, the legislature and the executive the two sides had come within sight of a complete settlement, this near-compromise had only been made possible because 'all along the Turkish side had agreed to make important concessions on its existing rights' in exchange for the recognition and establishment of a system of local autonomy. This was vital because it was only by the setting up of a genuine system of local (communal) autonomy deriving directly from the constitution and not subject to central control that the state ultimately to be agreed upon would be 'a Cypriot republic of intercommunal partnership', as insisted by the Turkish side, and not what the Greek Cypriots appeared to want, namely a Greek Cypriot republic. In addition, the Greek Cypriot side seemed 'to have tackled the offers and counter-offers made by either side as if these constituted the sole points of conflict between the two communities' whereas the main cause of conflict continued to be 'in the philosophy of approach to the problem'. The Turkish Cypriots, Mr Denktash emphasised, could not afford to negotiate a settlement in any way or form which did not effectively bar the way to enosis. Furthermore, internally, there had to be some kind of partnership or functional federation. Against this constant background of Turkish Cypriot philosophy and objectives Mr Denktash in his communication of 9 August 1971 could not accept any of the compromise suggestions of Mr Clerides. In particular, in the area of the executive, the Turkish side could not accept the proposed elimination of the 1960 rights of the Vice-President, apart from the veto, and, even more significantly, the existence of the principle of executive 'joint responsibility', which, according to the Turkish side, reflected the bicommunalism of the state and the partnership of the two communities, could never be abandoned. But the most important difference between the two sides related to central authorities for local government. There could be no compromise on this issue, Mr Denktash emphasised. He thought he knew what was the reason for the apparent impasse on this point, he told Mr Clerides. 'You have treated the idea of local autonomy all along as equivalent to limited local government under complete governmental supervision, whereas I have treated it as an added autonomous function to the functions of the communal chambers'. Financial considerations and anxieties about multiplicity of services were unduly exaggerated but in any case 'considerations of self-protection' were paramount. Both central organs for local government and recognition of genuine autonomy, which for Mr Denktash meant the absence of any central controls on the discharge of regional functions, were fundamental and hence non-negotiable.

The anticipated breakdown of the talks was confirmed by an exchange of letters in which the Turkish Cypriot negotiator put forward many new demands, among them that there should be an open and categorical denunciation of enosis before the negotiations could proceed further, that it was not enough for the Greek Cypriot side simply to say that it was aiming at 'an independent state', that the word 'unitary' was meaningless and of no value and that it should therefore be abandoned, that the new system of government had to be a 'partnership' system or a functional federative system, that local authorities should have their own communal police forces and further that local courts should be set up and placed under the control of the central authorities for local administration, that the numerical strength and organisation of the police force should be decided jointly by the President and the Vice-President, that in general executive power should be exercised jointly since the Cyprus state was 'owned' by the two communities, and that there should be an immediate assurance by the Greek Cypriot side that in any case the Treaty of Guarantee would stand.

As can be seen, in consequence of the three Turkish communications of 27 April, 9 August and 20 September 1971, disagreement between the two sides widened further and difficulties multiplied. Thus, completely new demands were put forward, old issues were subtly reopened, and at the same time these disagreements were cleverly linked together and elaborated on the part of the Turkish negotiator so that differences between the two sides appeared not as divergences of view with regard to specific and manageable issues of constitutional structuring, but as the fundamental contrast between two opposing philosophies towards the Cyprus problem. Further, in the last two letters of Mr Denktash, of 9 August and 20 September, the external aspects of the problem were also brought into the picture, and clear declarations of intent on the part of the Greek Cypriot side were imperatively demanded as a precondition to further negotiation. In parallel with these new demands and formulations the Turkish side's approach to the theoretical question of 'the type of state' that should emerge from the discussions diverged further and further from 'the unitary state' formula of the Greek Cypriots. The constitution, according to Mr Denktash, should set up or recognise two autonomous communal administrations, which would, in effect, exercise all powers at the regional level and be linked up at the top by 'a joint proportionate representation'. Whereas the Greek Cypriot side still aimed at the setting up of a unitary constitutional structure within which the two sides would assign recognisably communal powers to the communities and establish an equitable degree of local government that would necessarily be based partly on communal criteria, Mr Denktash and the Turkish side, by the time of their 1971 communications, saw the problem not as one of governmental unification and of the regional devolution of authority but as one regarding the strictly limited governmental reintegration of two politically autonomous communities within a functionally federated state.

After these last exchanges there was clearly no hope or prospect of an agreement. The talks duly broke down. But it could already be seen that, without underestimating the various specific points of acute disagreement in the area of central government as well as in many others, the setting up of local government had firmly emerged as by far the most crucial issue of the discussions; and within the area of local government three questions, first of whether there would be central authorities for local administration, secondly of the type of power that would be exercised by the local organs, and thirdly of what central controls if any would exist over the discharge of regional functions, proved particularly intractable. It was widely believed that accord on local government would effectively solve the internal (constitutional) aspects of the Cyprus problem. But before we turn to the second round of talks (1971–4), we must consider the attitudes, principles and philosophy of the two sides as these were expressed and developed during the period of the intercommunal discussions, particularly in the exchanges between the two negotiators during 1970–2.

3. Philosophy, principles, attitudes

Even when agreement seemed near one gets the distinct impression that a great gulf of irreconcilable objectives and opposing philosophies divided the parties. This becomes clear when one studies the parties' positions on a variety of important points, as these appeared in the documents, memoranda and proposals exchanged between the two negotiators. Some questions which were surely crucial in the attempt to reconstruct the constitution of Cyprus and about which there was for the most part fundamental disagreement were the following: What kind of state was set up by the 1960 constitution? What type of state should the parties aim at? What should the approach to the Cyprus problem be? What was the parties' conception both of Cyprus and of themselves? It is worth considering these questions and the parties' distinct views on them under two headings:

(1) What kind of State was set up by the 1960 constitution? What were the implications of this on the negotiations and the attempt of the two sides to set up new constitutional structures?

The Turkish position was that, basically, the Zurich and London agreements had confirmed the bicommunal character of the Republic of Cyprus. 'The Republic of Cyprus was created by the will of both communities and the Turkish community is a partner community in the state of Cyprus and in everything that this involves'. Moreover, the Turkish community's status of partnership was 'not an improvisation by the makers of the Zurich agreement, but was a reconfirmation of the existing status and relationship of the two communities over the centuries'. Indeed, what had been set up by the 1960 agreements was 'a political, financial and social equilibrium', and no amendment of the constitutional arrangements could be contemplated if as a result the established equilibrium were disturbed. The Turkish side, Mr Denktash often stated, was not interested in describing 'the objective sought' so long as the fundamental 'intercommunal balance' and the basic principles upon which the independence of Cyprus was established and which had been enshrined in the 1960 Agreements were not upset. The Zurich agreement, Mr Denktash maintained, was a 'compromise solution', a kind of pact between the interested parties. What had happened was that 'the political struggle over the Cyprus question' had revealed that there were many difficulties, 'objective political difficulties, internal political difficulties, and psychological and emotional difficulties', and these had necessitated a compromise solution. The principles of this solution, the most important part of which was the recognition which it accorded to the Turkish community, could not be given up, nor would the Turkish Cypriots ever allow them to be modified. Indeed, what had been entrenched in the 1960 constitution was nothing less than the 'communal political status' of the Turkish Cypriots. If this were given up, the Turkish Cypriots would first become 'a minority in a Greek-ruled island' and eventually 'the winds of enosis would sweep away the independence of Cyprus'. Two communities existed in Cyprus, the Turkish side never stopped repeating, and the 1960 system of government reflected precisely this cardinal fact. Equally, any other system imported in place of the 1960 constitution had to conform to the same principles. 'This system emanates from the fact, which cannot be denied, that the independence of Cyprus was won by the two communities and it prevents one of the communities from usurping the rights of the other by destroying the independence in favour of a political settlement acceptable to it, but not acceptable to the other side'. Therefore, political power had to belong to both communities and manifestly be seen to be shared between them, as was the case with the Zurich agreement.

Two things emerge from the above. First, the Turkish side, throughout the intercommunal discussions, believed in the fundamentality and continued essential validity of the 1960 constitution. This constitution, the Turkish side believed, had entrenched, first, the bicommunal nature of the Republic of Cyprus and, secondly, the co-founder partnership status of both communities, and had thus, by implication, given them 'inalienable and indisputable rights in the independence, sovereignty, territorial integrity and security of Cyprus'. These rights were accompanied by 'the duty of protection of (such) independence', and consequently any attempt to reduce the status of the Turkish Cypriots to that of a minority went counter to the spirit, character and 'fundamental structure' of the 1960 agreements and should therefore be resisted. Secondly, according to the Turkish Cypriot side, there was a very close connection between on the one hand the treaties of alliance and guarantee 'which provided for the permanence of the Cypriot Republic' and which had prohibited enosis and partition, and on the other the internal constitutional arrangements. The ousting of enosis was 'the foundation on which bicommunal independence was established in 1960', and no settlement was conceivable which did not, both through the continuation of the same external guarantees and through the internal dichotomy of functions and their distribution to the communities, similarly exclude union of Cyprus with Greece. Rights and guarantees, both internal and external, reinforced each other and could not be given up without great danger to the bicommunalism of the state and the continued independence of Cyprus; some of these 'special protective rights', however, could be recast and reformulated, or more properly exchanged for 'rights' in the area of local autonomy. In line with what has been set out as the basic Turkish Cypriot view of the 1960 arrangements, it was his firm understanding, Mr Denktash pointed out on 27 April 1971, that the 1960 constitution would continue to stand subject to such minor adjustments as would become necessary in the light of any agreement that the two negotiators eventually reached on the central issues. It followed that only those 'rights' should be considered to be abandoned as the Turkish side had indicated express readiness to give up; in all other respects the 1960 constitutional structure should continue in existence and unaltered. This, the Turkish Cypriot negotiator pointed out on 9 August 1971, was 'very important'. No subject could be discussed 'in the abstract'. What was being discussed was 'amendments', the intercommunal negotiations themselves becoming necessary because the Greek Cypriot side had both in 1963 and 1968 asked for specific constitutional amendments. It might be the case, Mr Denktash admitted in his letter of 20 September 1971, that the '13-point plan of Archbishop Makarios' had never been discussed as such in the intercommunal talks. All the points however which Mr Clerides had raised with him in 1968 and since had been those on which the Greek Cypriot side had called for amendment as early as 1963. There was no reason why this should not be borne in mind, and whatever the exact legal position, 'negotiations started not because the Turkish side wanted amendments, but because the Greek Cypriot side claimed that the constitution needed amendment'.

The Greek Cypriot side's views on both the 1960 constitution and the terms of reference of the intercommunal discussions differed substantially from the Turkish Cypriot ones. Mr Clerides' views on these two subjects can be summarised as follows: The negotiations were not being conducted either on the basis of the 1960 constitution or on the basis of the Makarios proposals. Nor was it true that negotiations had begun because amendments to the 1960 constitution had been asked for by the Greek Cypriot side. That constitution had functionally broken down in 1963, and Greeks and Turks had lived apart for the intervening years; it had now been decided to break the impasse and restructure the constitutional arrangements of the republic. This was then the task facing the negotiators. What was to be sought was a satisfactory solution to the problem of Cyprus, and to do this one had to approach the situation free from the prejudices of the past. True, the two parties had not formulated agreed terms of reference, but both understood from the beginning that their common task was to search for a solution to the constitutional aspects of the Cyprus problem in the context of an independent and unitary state. A consensus to that effect had been established as early as 1968, the Greek Cypriot representative maintained, and this could not be altered by late objections on the part of the Turkish side to the use of the term 'unitary'. Indeed, the UN Secretary-General had often said in his reports that the reactivated intercommunal talks were 'the best instrument for achieving a satisfactory, lasting and agreed solution based on the concept of an independent, sovereign and unitary state with adequate participation of the two communities', and this 'clear and unambiguous statement' could not be erased by allegations that the parties had really given different interpretations to the concept of a unitary state. So, the terms of reference of the intercommunal discussions, if any, were to be found in the reports of the Secretary-General, particularly as the talks were being held under his auspices. And the way the talks had in fact been conducted, Mr Clerides stated on 24 August 1971, confirmed that neither the 1960 constitution nor the 13 proposals formed their basis. Thus, during the first phase general exploratory talks had been held and then, after the relevant identification of issues and delimitation of areas of agreement and disagreement, written proposals relating to the various constitutional issues, i.e. the executive, the legislature, the judiciary, the public service, the police and local government, had been exchanged. It was these written proposals which had formed the basis of subsequent discussions, Mr Clerides said, and it was therefore quite wrong to assert that either the 1960 constitution or the 1963 Makarios proposals constituted the framework for the constitutional negotiations. Consistently with this the Greek Cypriot negotiator believed that a new constitution would have to be drawn up once the parties reached agreement on the issues that still divided them. This was inevitable in view both of the changed circumstances of Cyprus, including the admitted breakdown (whatever the cause) of the 1960 constitution, and of the fundamental changes that were bound to be brought about in the event of an agreement in the governmental structure and administration of Cyprus, such as the elimination of many of the earlier separatist features, the introduction of a degree of communal local autonomy, etc. The maximum Mr Clerides was prepared to concede on this issue was that 'though the provisions of the 1960 constitution were not the basis of (the) talks', nevertheless, if agreement were to be reached, the two sides could then set up a joint committee of experts 'to examine, in the light of the agreement reached, what articles of the 1960 constitution could be adopted without amendment, what articles could be adopted subject to amendment, what articles would require complete reformulation and what new articles would be required'. The 1960 constitution itself was the result of 'abnormal political developments', the Greek Cypriot side believed, and should not as a result provide the foundation for what the two negotiators were engaged upon, which was an attempt to set up viable governmental and political structures for Cyprus. 'Any solution that proceeded from Zurich would necessarily reflect the anomalous situation that was enshrined in that settlement and perpetuate constitutional anomaly and intercommunal suspicion'. A fresh start was therefore needed. Was the Zurich set up however that of a unitary state or not? This question was put to Mr Clerides by Mr Denktash in an effort to show that even if a solution to the Cyprus problem had to be sought within the framework of a unitary state, this formula was wide enough to allow a strong bicommunal element both in the allocation of governmental functions and in the structuring of the system of regional administration. Mr Clerides' answer was that 'the Zurich agreement contained many divisive elements' to which the Greek Cypriot side had taken exception as early as 1962. But it was not true that 'the 1960 constitution provided for a federal system of government or for a functional federative system', as had been alleged by the Turkish Cypriot negotiator. Consequently, whatever the basis of the negotiations, there could be 'no obligation for the Greek Cypriot side to negotiate on the basis of a federative solution', as Mr Denktash had demanded. Nor had the Zurich constitution established a full partnership between the two

communities. Mr Clerides agreed of course that the Zurich settlement had
extended distinct communal recognition to the Turkish Cypriots, but this
did not mean that there now had to be territorial arrangements that would
be both economically disadvantageous and politically disastrous. The
correct position was that any solution had to conform to the principles of a
unitary state. The Greek Cypriot side 'would not accept a federal, a
cantonal system or any system that would create a state within a state'; this
was the only guiding principle and any arrangements regarding more
specific issues had to be judged by reference to this general criterion.

(2) What type of state, in the view of each of the parties, should be
created by a negotiated settlement, and what basic approach and principles
should be adopted for this purpose?

It has already been mentioned that the two sides modified their views on
this subject as the negotiations proceeded. It is possible however to
perceive and set forth their basic views as to, first, the kind of state that
should emerge from their negotiations, and, secondly, the type of
constitution that should thereafter be introduced.

The Turkish side's views will be investigated first. What must be
noticed is that in the early documents and correspondence no attempt was
made to set out the nature of the state that was sought. Specific positions
were taken with regard to particular issues, but no comprehensive
formulation as to the type of state that the Turkish side was aiming at was
attempted. Naturally, a general philosophy of approach can be deduced
from the specific positions adopted, but it was only during the later stages
of the intercommunal dialogue that the Turkish side explicitly set out the
specifications to which the reconstructed Cypriot state had to conform.
Thus, in his proposals on regional autonomy communicated to the Greek
Cypriot side in late 1973, Mr Denktash said that it had always been his
understanding that the state should continue to be bicommunal; that the
Turks and Greeks of Cyprus should continue to enjoy the status of
cofounders of the independence of Cyprus; that the permanence of that
independence should continue to be guaranteed as before; and that a
solution should be sought within the concept and framework of the 1960 set
up, i.e. the separation of functions between the government and the
communities. The most important consideration for the Turkish side in
negotiating on a new constitution was what it called 'the political status of
the Turkish community'. Every effort had to be made so that the status
of the Turkish community would not be reduced to that of 'a minority
in a Greek-ruled island'. The main fear was that the Turkish community
might lose its communal and political identity. If that happened, enosis
would become inevitable. There therefore had to be both (a) recognition

that the Turkish community was a partner community in the state of Cyprus (which, in its turn, meant that most problems should not be solved on a numerical basis), and (b) establishment of institutions and structures that would reflect the basic bi-communalism of Cyprus and in their turn help maintain it. As to the first principle, Mr Denktash stated that the partnership between the two communities on which he was insisting did not mean that their numerical strength was of no consequence. 'Partnership' denoted the inherent right of the Turkish community to share the independence of Cyprus with the Greek community on a basis of equality and the consequential constitutional and moral right of the Turks to uphold this independence under all circumstances', and was not to be mixed with the Turkish community's 'proportionate enjoyment of the benefits of the republic and its proportionate contribution to its government'. What, then, was the basis of this 'communal partnership' since, as was fully admitted, the two communities were so unequal in number and in financial contribution to the budget of the republic? The answer to this question related to the way the independence of Cyprus had been acquired, Mr Denktash explained. The independence of Cyprus had not been won either by the Greek Cypriots alone or by the people of Cyprus as a whole. 'Our independence has been won by the two communities and it has been achieved as a result of the conflicting policies followed by them, Greek Cypriots wanting union with Greece and Turkish Cypriots opposing it'. Whether therefore the two communities had desired an 'independence' settlement or not, independence had come about because of the policies and political behaviour of the communities. There was no Cypriot nation which had won this independence and in consequence the Greek Cypriot argument that '(the) democratic rule of one man one vote should settle every issue' was unacceptable to the Turkish Cypriot side. There was, in truth, a compact between the two communities as to the principles on which independence would be shared and power exercised, Mr Denktash claimed, and this could not be abrogated or unilaterally changed by the Greek Cypriot side even though some agreed modifications or revisions not affecting the basic foundations of the settlement could be brought about. 'Partnership' therefore meant that the Turkish community had an equal say in 'the future status of the independence' of Cyprus and entailed the right to demand that this 'could not be settled by mathematical calculations', and did not imply that the Turks wanted an 'equal say in all matters' of government and administration.

As regards the second principle, the establishment and maintenance of social and political equilibrium between the two communities, what was of cardinal significance for the Turkish side was that the strict separation of functions between state and communities should continue and indeed be reinforced (by the addition to traditional communal concerns of regional autonomy). Communal matters had to be left to the communities and there should be no confusion between them and governmental matters. Furthermore, it was not enough to have autonomy in communal matters; 'parity' between the two communities was equally if not more important. Two communal legislative establishments (one Greek and the other Turkish) were in this way absolutely necessary. If there was only a Turkish communal authority or chamber in charge of Turkish communal affairs and similar Greek matters were transferred to the government, 'obvious confusion and injustice' would arise, the state would lose its bicommunal character, 'the partnership image' of the republic would be destroyed and a Greek Cypriot republic would inevitably result. For this reason the Turkish side regarded it as absolutely impermissible that there should be a post of Minister of Education for Cyprus 'in view of the fact that education is a communal matter and not a governmental matter'. Further, it was this necessary separation of functions between affairs of state and communal matters (including now regional self-government) that the Turkish side mainly had in mind when the term functional federation was used, the Turkish negotiator explained. No 'revolutionary change' was sought by this term, but merely a 'continuation' of the basic system of the 1960 constitution 'where communal affairs are in the sole control of the communities who have a proportionate say at governmental level'. What mattered above all else (and much more than the cost of maintaining separate institutions and the possible resulting divisiveness) was the safeguarding of 'communal equality at all levels'.

The basic Turkish approach to the reconstruction of the constitutional system has already been set out. Local autonomy rights were sought in exchange for 'concessions' in the area of central government. The Turkish side, at least in the later stages, does not appear to have seen the issue of local government or local autonomy as one of decentralisation or devolution of central power but rather as a 'rearrangement' of communal 'rights' and 'prerogatives' which had been given to the Turkish community in 1960 and which, in their 1960 constitutional form, the Turkish side was now prepared to give up. 'The philosophy of approach should be to remove what (the Greek) side considers to be "excessive rights" from the sphere of central government and leave these to the Turkish community to arrange at local level'. What the two sides should try to do, Mr Denktash stated in one of his early letters, was to realign or recast the existing communal rights of the Turkish side under the 1960 constitution by distinguishing between central governmental functions on the one hand, and local powers or autonomy on the other. It was a mistake to assert, Mr Denktash stated, that the Turkish side was trying to pass off to the Greek Cypriot side a 'federal' or a 'cantonal' system under the guise of local administration. But, at the same time, genuine and not merely limited autonomy was sought, or, as it was also put, the Turkish demand was for true local or regional autonomy whereas the Greek side was only willing to give 'limited local govern-ment', something that was not acceptable. This genuine regional autonomy meant and necessitated both central bodies with 'independent powers, duties and jurisdiction', and a virtual absence of state control. For if the past had taught anything, Mr Denktash asserted, it was that in areas where the communities were 'their own masters', there had been 'no intercom-munal friction (but) free and voluntary co-operation between the communal organs'. Consequently, this dichotomy of power should 'be encouraged within reasonable limits as a means for inducing voluntary cooperation between the two communities'. Under this 'new system' the recognition and establishment of regional autonomy would, by separating to an important extent the exercise of political power on a communal basis, reduce the areas of daily friction and make the two communities less dependent upon each other. In the ultimate analysis, there had to be communal separation or segregation.

As regards the frequently voiced objections of the Greek Cypriot side that the proposals of the Turkish negotiator both on local government and other issues might make the constitution functionally 'unworkable', Mr Denktash was not perturbed. It is true, he admitted, that his proposals might make the constitution very long and perhaps unwieldy, but this was 'necessary'. In the past, he complained, the 1960 constitution was not sufficiently detailed, and this was one of the reasons it had collapsed. The Turkish community could not 'afford to run the same risk again'. It was not enough that only 'the basic provisions regarding the autonomous local authorities should be embedded in the constitution and the rest left to ordinary legislation'. What guarantee was there that the predominantly Greek legislature would not once more fail in its duty? This time there was to be no doubt, and nothing was to be left to chance. It was therefore essential that the powers, duties and functions of the local authorities, together with all related matters, should be inserted in the constitution in great detail. The basic Turkish position was that Cyprus presented peculiar problems and that the constitution had to be specially modelled so as to accord with the 'realities' of the island. If the negotiators did not see 'the peculiarities of Cyprus and the reasons (organic, psychological, political and factual) which have made the Cyprus problem what it is', it would not prove possible to find a reasonable solution. Indeed, such was the mistrust and the suspicion on the part of the Turkish Cypriots, Mr Denktash often repeated, that what was essential was that the constitution of Cyprus should not have to rely on the goodwill of those who would operate it. This in turn could only be ensured if generous opportunities for separate development, social, communal and political, were provided for and forever placed beyond the reach of both the state and the Greek Cypriots.

The views of the Greek Cypriot side on these matters, i.e. what the future Cyprus republic should be like, what the approach of the parties should be, and how the constitution should be drafted, were concisely summarised by Mr Clerides on 11 June 1974. 'The position of my side is that the solution of the Cyprus problem must be based on the concept of an independent, sovereign and unitary state with adequate participation of the two communities, with complete autonomy on matters provided for by the 1960 constitution (religion, education, culture, personal status etc.) and with a degree of local government compatible with the concept of a unitary state'. Unity and security were the key concepts for Mr Clerides and the Greek Cypriot side. Unity had to be taken both in the sense of a basically unified administrative and governmental machine, and in the sense of avoiding arrangements that would force the communities to draw further apart. Cyprus was both economically and socially a cohesive entity, and this pattern should not be broken up by divisive and illiberal dispositions. Security too, both for Cyprus and the two ethnic groups, would suffer if this unity was artificially and needlessly compromised. Genuine security and long-term protection could only be ensured by rational policies based on the fair participation of both communities in the affairs of state, and on true concern for 'individual' human rights.

The most important element in the Greek Cypriot positions, proposals and formulations was the need to maintain the unity and integrity of the state. What enosis was for the Turkish Cypriots, partition was for the Greek Cypriots. Partition would spell the end of independent Cyprus and therefore no constitutional or political arrangements that facilitated or made inevitable its advent could be considered. There was no need, the Greek Cypriot representative agreed, to give technical names to the 'creations' of the negotiators or to the various constitutional arrangements that were being discussed. But what was of vital significance was whether what the Turkish negotiator had proposed respected the principles of a unitary state, or whether the Turkish positions, in clear defiance of these principles, would inevitably lead to the creation of a Turkish Cypriot state; and, Mr Clerides had no doubt, the system that Mr Denktash had put forward (based as it was on the existence of two effectively independent central communal authorities invested with political, executive, legislative and police powers, and on communal groupings of villages and areas of administration) would not preserve unitary state authority but would lead to the creation of 'cohesive geographical areas of local government on the basis of communal criteria', a development that was neither warranted by the realities of Cyprus nor justified by the experience of other countries. The Turkish negotiator, in an attempt to justify separate geographical areas for Greek Cypriots and Turkish Cypriots, had referred to 'the Turkish community's proved and unproved doubts and suspicions as to what will happen once they (i.e. the Turks) lost their identity in a Greek majority area'. This was not the correct approach, Mr Clerides said. He stated his own starting point to the problem of constitutional reconstruction as follows: 'In my view, if we are to try and find a solution of the Cyprus problem based on the suspicions and mistrust of the two sides, whether actual, imaginary, founded or unfounded, we would devise a system of political and administrative segregation based on racial criteria, which would reflect and perpetuate the anomalies of the times, would result in an unworkable system of government, and inevitably create conflict'. A fresh start was called for, and not yet another false beginning that reflected the animosities of the past. It was true that Mr Denktash had suggested that, in some cases, decisions as to grouping, i.e. as to whether it was to be communal or mixed, could be left to the villagers themselves by way of referendum, but these statements could not satisfy the Greek Cypriots that the intentions of the Turkish side were not separatist and potentially partitionist; for since the Turkish leadership did not accept the principle of mixed areas, their view would naturally be communicated to the various Turkish villages which would, in due course, exercise their 'right' to create areas and groups consisting solely of Turkish villages. And even though Mr Denktash had intimated that in years to come, 'when good government, fair play and justice' brought the two communities together and mutual fears and suspicions proved unjustified, the local authority system might be looked at again, the Greek Cypriot side, Mr Clerides said, could not really take such 'promises' seriously. 'If we followed your suggestions', he told his Turkish counterpart, 'we would be led to the establishment of separate Greek and Turkish areas which would unavoidably become a permanent fixture, despite the fact that they would be impractical and uneconomic. "Personal vested interests" would be claimed in support of the preservation of the set up, and any attempt to alter existing areas would be likely to lead to a new era of tension after a settlement has been found.'

Another related theme figuring prominently in Greek Cypriot arguments concerned the functional capacity of the state. It has already been mentioned that Mr Clerides considered the problem as one of setting up a new system of government for Cyprus more or less unburdened with the sorry legacy of the past, and was unwilling to regard either the 1960 constitution or the 13 points of Archbishop Makarios as the framework or terms of reference of the intercommunal discussions. The system to be imported had to be workable and capable both of speedy implementation and of effective and satisfactory operation. For since both sides were in agreement that Cyprus should remain independent and that the Turkish community was not to be reduced from the point of view of legal arrangements to the status of a mere minority, but that the state, in some sense, was to be recognised as being bicommunal, the task of the two negotiators became one of setting up a system of internal government that was appropriate to the *needs* and *realities* of Cyprus, and which would conduce to the prosperity of the island as a whole. The system proposed by the Turkish side was clearly unsatisfactory against the background of the functional and operational criteria that the Greek side had in mind, the Greek Cypriot negotiator asserted. It was 'unworkable, cumbersome and would lead to friction between the communities'. It was expensive because, as envisaged by Mr Denktash, separate civil services and separate establishments would have to be created. Effectively, there would be three governments, one for the Greek Cypriots, one for the Turkish Cypriots and one for Greeks and Turks alike, 'and the expense for this triplication would in effect absorb the biggest part of the financial resources of the republic in paying salaries to civil servants for doing unnecessarily the same work', whereas, as logic and common sense alike dictated, the resources of the country should be devoted to its development. The Turkish proposals, moreover, both in the complexity and prolixity of their provisions and in the rigid institutional separation they envisaged, would either make 'effective planning for the development of the island' completely impossible or at best put it into slow motion. 'We all have experience of separate institutions making their own development plans and then trying through the means of a coordination committee to coordinate the development of the country. The simplest matter would take months before it is resolved with the result that the economy of the island would suffer a serious set back'. In fact, communalism, the Greek Cypriot representative believed, could not possibly provide any acceptable criterion for the restructuring of the republic. If a system of local administration, for instance, was introduced and organised along communal criteria with a limited right on the part of some villages to opt out, the government of the country 'would in fact be based, not on objective criteria or principles, but on communal criteria and the whims of the villagers in the various areas, and would not present a uniform pattern applying to the whole of Cyprus'. There would be 'a chaotic situation'.

Cyprus should remain a unitary state with, among other things, complete security for the Turkish Cypriots. This was the article of faith of the Greek Cypriot side and its basic approach throughout the negotiations. Turkish Cypriot security and rights were to be achieved and protected by a variety of safeguards. There would thus be balanced participation of the Turkish Cypriot community in the central government, adequate local government based partly on communal criteria would be recognised, the police in areas inhabited almost exclusively by Turkish Cypriots would consist exclusively of Turkish Cypriots and in areas predominantly inhabited by Turkish Cypriots would consist predominantly of Turkish

Cypriots, and all other arrangements necessary for absolutely securing the Turkish Cypriot community and its interests would likewise be made, including international guarantees and safeguards. But it could not be accepted that the Cyprus State should become a fully bicommunal one, or that the 'partnership principle' could be recognised or made the juridical basis of the restructured republic. The state that should emerge from the negotiations should be a unitary one with balanced bicommunal participation. There was clearly, in the Greek Cypriot view, a very important difference between a bicommunal state and a unitary state with balanced bicommunal participation. It was not a mere matter of words. The first expression denoted an arrangement in which the two communities were of equal political importance and where political and governmental power would 'belong' to the two communities and be shared between them, whereas the second one indicated that what was to be brought into existence would be a unitary, sovereign and integral state where, however, for various reasons, the principle of majority rule could not be allowed universal scope; instead, one group, the Turkish Cypriots, would be able under the new governmental arrangements to exercise separately 'their political rights' and would be accorded powers and responsibilities not normally given to minorities. Or, to put it differently, as Mr Clerides said, there were to be arrangements in which the Greeks and the Turks of Cyprus, at the insistence of the latter, would exercise political rights and power 'separately as communities', but since the two groups were of substantially unequal size, the state could not be a bicommunal one. Similarly, as regards the related partnership principle so eagerly promoted by the Turkish Cypriot side, namely that political and governmental power both in the sense of theoretical entitlement and in the sense of actual participation should in general be vested in the two communities on a basis of equality, no such proposition could be accepted. Of course, all Cypriots, Greeks and Turks alike, would have the same political rights. But when what was being discussed was in effect the political power of the two communities, could one disregard the force of numbers? After all, the Turks were only 18 per cent of the total population of Cyprus. Surely, majorities had their rights as well. Nor could Mr Clerides and the Greek Cypriot side agree with the other meaning attributed to the partnership theory by Mr Denktash, namely that both communities had 'won' the independence of Cyprus and that therefore such independence was 'owned' by them both. In fact these two issues, how the independence of Cyprus had come about in the first place and what the significance of this was for the restructuring of the constitution, were not really dealt with by the Greek Cypriot negotiator, and clearly advisedly so. The theories of the parties on such primarily historical points were bound to differ widely and no useful purpose could be served by rediscovering old issues and allowing them to interrupt the search for a solution. But what the Greek Cypriot side believed on these issues, as expressed elsewhere, was that independence had come about in consequence of the liberation struggle waged between 1955 and 1959 by the Greek Cypriots against the British colonial government. It was of course true that the original goal of the armed struggle was union with Greece and not independence, but this did not matter. For whatever the original objective of the the 1955 revolt, liberation and political freedom had also been sought and to a considerable extent realised; and the indisputable fact was that the Turkish Cypriots, far from fighting against the British, had in fact sided with the colonial administration and had for most of the time opposed any change in the status quo. How then could it be said that independence had been won and should therefore be shared on a basis of equality by both communities? But in any case all this was history and quite irrelevant to what the two sides were engaged in at the time. Cyprus and Cypriot independence belonged to all Cypriots, Greeks and Turks alike, and it was time that communal considerations gave way to the more general interests of the people of Cyprus. The task facing the negotiators was to set up a fair constitution and construct a satisfactory system of government for Cyprus unburdened by past animosities, though naturally the tragic experiences of the past could neither be ignored nor forgotten. The lessons of the past had to be learned, not disregarded, and this could only be done if communalism was at last subordinated to policies predicated upon the need for unity and cooperation among Cypriots of both communities.

The real distance that divided the two sides on the matters discussed above, namely basic approach, conception of Cyprus and of themselves, and vision of the future, can therefore be seen to have been fundamental at most times. Naturally, statements and formulations expressing this difference appeared in a great number of forms, and the gap dividing the parties was made to vary (or appeared to vary) accordingly. However this might be, the clear lesson of the first round of talks (1968–71) was that once the parties abandoned 'negotiation' and embarked on attempts to articulate their 'conception' of Cyprus, of themselves and of their task, as happened during 1971, they would cease effectively to speak the same language. This is the most obvious danger in situations where diplomacy and negotiation have to function in an environment that is heavily charged with suspicion and mistrust, and where the parties' 'real' views and 'ideal' objectives sharply diverge. For unless restraint is exercised and unless pursuit of narrow self-interest is subordinated to the pragmatic art of the possible, diplomats and negotiators will still meet but will be unable either to persuade or to resolve difficulties; and before long negotiating sessions will become nothing but elaborate stage plays occupied not with the adjustment of differences but with the repetition of diametrically opposed 'initial' positions and endless accusations of bad faith. Eventually, the very sterility of these efforts will drain the negotiating process of all substance, and at the end of the day the parties are likely to find themselves both more deeply entrenched in their positions and more oppressively shackled by their respective slogans.

This was the danger confronting the Cyprus negotiations at the end of 1971. Discussion had been skilfully generalised by Mr Denktash who chose on 27 April 1971 and in subsequent communications to abandon what might be called efforts to arrive at a pragmatic resolution of difficulties and had abruptly brought up issues of purely theoretical interest and past grievances that could only make the task of finding an agreed solution more difficult, confounding in this way the until then apparent negotiating themes and effectively causing the collapse of the talks. What was obvious was that if the talks were to resume, there should this time be, first, a careful avoidance of theoretical generalisation and counterproductive historical digression, secondly, basic acceptance of at least a general framework of negotiation, and, thirdly, determined efforts on the part of both sides to adjust differences – and not attempts to settle a priori the nature of the state and its constitution. In fact, the second prerequisite already existed by acceptance of the UN formula whereby the parties were negotiating on the basis of an independent, integral and unitary state based on the balanced participation of the two communities in governmental organs and a degree of local government not incompatible with the notion of state unity. But it remained to be seen whether it would also be possible, in the event of a resumption of the talks, to develop a new and more pragmatic conception of negotiations, utilise the positive results of 1968 – 71, and concentrate with a greater sense of urgency on the remaining issues.

4

The Expanded Talks and the 1974 Model

1. The reactivation of the talks

The breakdown of the intercommunal talks in 1971 was fraught with danger and therefore, almost immediately, UN authorities intervened in order to have the talks reactivated.[1] The Secretary-General himself made various soundings with all the interested parties, particularly with Greece and Turkey, and conveyed his impressions of their attitudes to the two Cypriot sides. As reported by him,[2] these can be set out as follows:

Turkish attitudes

(1) Turkey was adamant against enosis, which she would oppose by all means, including intervention in Cyprus and even risking a war with Greece.

(2) The Turkish government firmly maintained the validity of the treaties which ruled out both partition and enosis. Partition, however, would be an unavoidable reaction to any attempt to bring about enosis.

(3) The future of Cyprus resided in the cooperation of two autonomous communities, through a balanced partnership, including the full participation of the Turkish Cypriots in the economic life of the island.

(4) The Turkish Cypriots were not a minority; they were a distinct community, and their security, under the circumstances, demanded military preparedness in order to avoid any attempt by the Greek Cypriots to impose a fait accompli. This precluded even balanced reduction of the Turkish armed contingent present in Cyprus. In this connection, Turkey emphasised the complete mistrust of the Turkish Cypriots regarding the intentions of the Greek Cypriots. The Turkish government fully shared this mistrust.

(5) Turkey was in favour of the reactivation of the intercommunal talks and thought that they provided the most suitable framework for finding a solution to the Cyprus problem.

[1] Unless it is otherwise indicated, all quotations come from the documents of the intercommunal files (see Preface).

[2] My account of this matter is based on confidential documents and memoranda prepared by the Secretary General and circulated to the interested parties.

(6) Turkey wished to avoid war or any military confrontation with Greece. The Turkish government thought that there should be cooperation between the two countries regarding Cyprus.

(7) Turkey thought that the basic approach of the intercommunal discussions, i.e. through the recognition and establishment of local governmental autonomy, was correct. Basically, the Turkish community should become autonomous. This would of course necessitate drastic revision of the constitutional framework of the republic. Since Archbishop Makarios should realise that enosis was not feasible, he should, the Turkish government thought, accept the treaties as a legal framework, make a declaration to this effect, and use the reactivated intercommunal talks for a revision of the constitution in a way agreeable to the two communities.

Greek attitudes

(1) The Greek government realised the impracticability of achieving enosis. It therefore supported an independent, sovereign, unitary state of Cyprus, recognised and safeguarded as such.

(2) Greece (at this stage) believed that a settlement of the Cyprus question was only possible through the efforts of President Makarios via the procedure of the intercommunal talks which would be facilitated by improved relations between Greece and Turkey. The Greek government knew well that Archbishop Makarios expressed the views of the overwhelming majority of the people of Cyprus and that his policies represented their wishes.

(3) Greece was realistic about the Turkish position. It felt that the intercommunal talks should begin without delay and that they could start at the point where they had stopped. What was needed was to fill the gaps in the agreements previously achieved through formulas developed by constitutional experts that Greece and Turkey would send to the negotiations as assistants to the two interlocutors.

(4) The Greek government was still apprehensive about the long-term plans of Turkey and the Turkish Cypriots. It feared that their aim was to create an infrastructure for partition. Indeed, there was already on the Turkish side a de facto partition, whereas, on the other hand, there were no signs that the Greek side was moving towards enosis.

(5) Greece believed that the basic principle of the Zurich agreement and the associated treaties which ruled out both partition and enosis should be maintained. Article 185 of the 1960 constitution which prohibited 'the integral or partial union of Cyprus with any other state' or any 'separatist independence' should therefore be included in a new constitution. But separate declarations on enosis and partition might be attended by psychological difficulties and should if possible be avoided.

(6) The Greek government believed that the Turkish Cypriots should show more cooperation with the government of the republic in measures of deconfrontation and in improving relations between the communities so as to enhance the possibilities of success of the intercommunal talks. There was no need to wait for a complete settlement to be arrived at; considerable progress could be achieved in the meantime through goodwill and an easing of tension. In fact both sides, the Greek government suggested, should agree to further reciprocal concessions and gestures so that a favourable atmosphere for the local talks could be created.

(7) The Cyprus problem, the Greek government finally believed, could and should be settled without impinging on the wider interests of either Greece or Turkey.

In consequence of his soundings and consultations the Secretary-General circulated an aide-memoire on 18 October 1971 which paved the way for the reactivation of the talks. In this U Thant submitted to the governments of Cyprus, Greece and Turkey a suggestion designed to reactivate and make more effective the intercommunal talks. The suggestion was that 'with a view to facilitating the future conduct of the intercommunal talks, his special representative in Cyprus, Mr B. F. Ozorio Tafall, should, in the exercise of the Secretary-General's good offices, take part in the talks between the representatives of the two communities'. It was also suggested that the governments of Greece and Turkey should each make available a constitutional expert who would attend the talks in an advisory capacity.

Upon assuming office in January 1972 Dr Waldheim asked Mr Roberto E. Guyer, Under-Secretary-General for Special Political Affairs, to visit Nicosia, Athens and Ankara in order to convey to all concerned the Secretary-General's earnest wish that the suggestion for the reactivation of the talks should be fully accepted by all concerned. Mr Guyer visited the three capitals between 30 January and 5 February 1972. His conversations there resulted in agreement in principle for the reactivation of the intercommunal talks on the basis of the aide-memoire of 18 October 1971 and under a UN formula applicable to all concerned, namely that participation in the reactivated talks pursuant to the suggestion of the Secretary-General should not prejudice the well-known legal and political positions of all concerned. Finally, the reactivated intercommunal discussions, attended now, in addition to Messrs Clerides and Denktash, by the Secretary-General's special representative in Cyprus, Mr Tafall, and the Greek and Turkish experts, Messrs Dekleris and Aldiçasti, were inaugurated on 8 June 1972. The Secretary-General attended this first meeting and made some remarks with regard to the negotiations that were once more under way. He reminded the parties that the UN had been involved in the problem of Cyprus for more than 8 years and had 'a strong interest in seeing its peacekeeping function progress into the phase of peaceseeking, and, hopefully, of peacemaking'. Many difficulties lay ahead, the Secretary-General pointed out; and the difficulty of the task of finding a peaceful solution should not be underestimated. He was profoundly convinced that what was needed more than anything else was a mutual willingness to understand and preserve the vital interests of all sides, 'a spirit of forward-looking conciliation, a readiness to compromise, and a clear realisation that any agreed, peaceful, lasting and just settlement is not only feasible but essential to the welfare of all concerned'.

2. *Constitutional developments*

It will be recalled that even though the basic premises and approach of the intercommunal talks had effectively been settled during the first round, namely that there would be an exchange of Turkish Cypriot prerogatives at governmental level for some measure of local autonomy, serious disagreements had remained in the areas of the legislature (but here to a lesser extent than elsewhere), the executive, the judiciary and, particularly, that of local government. Between 1972 and 1974 intensive negotiation and bargaining took place on all these, and it was eventually found possible to bridge many previously acutely felt differences. One of the main reasons for this was that greater flexibility was now shown in the tactics used. Thus, no longer was there almost exclusive emphasis on direct exchanges between the two interlocutors, but instead increasing reliance was placed on a great number and variety of negotiating methods, including the use of what might be called techniques of 'two-stage negotiation', whereby the mediator (who was now assuming a more active role) would first hold talks with the two sides separately; determined efforts would then be made by him both to narrow outstanding differences and isolate particularly troublesome points, preparing at the same time alternative formulae for the attention of the parties regarding their possible resolution; and finally (and not before adequate preparatory work had been done) direct and face-to-face meetings would be held between the parties for a final thrashing of the issues that had already been identified and discussed. Indeed within the broad rubric of 'two-stage negotiation with the active participation of the mediator' (that might be a good description of the general course of the reactivated intercommunal talks, as opposed to 'the direct negotiations or exchanges' of the first round of talks) two distinct methods were tried between 1972 and 1974, depending either upon the precise issue or upon which side was expected to prove more troublesome. At times there was 'a process of simultaneous running conversations by the middlem(an) with both sides',[3] the UN mediator transmitting statements from one to the other and aiming in this way to bring them closer to agreement, at least on some issues, only sanctioning direct meetings when initial positions had either been abandoned or sufficiently modified. On other occasions the mediator, Dr Tafall, would first conduct detailed discussions with one side on an issue on which that side either entertained particularly strong views or on which it had in the past taken a more or less uncompromising position, making an effort both to convince the recalcitrant party that its position was not a realistic one and to produce a statement of that party's modified position and (if possible) a draft agreement that would provide the basis for meaningful negotiation with the other side; consultations would then be held by the mediator with the other side, and if prospects appeared promising, then the final step would be to get the two sides to meet face-to-face so that any remaining differences could (hopefully) be overcome. Further, for the most part of the reactivated intercommunal discussions, there was careful avoidance of useless theoretical discussions and digressions into the past, and this too was significant in making it possible for the parties to retreat from some of the positions that had been assumed previously.[4]

In any case considerable progress was swiftly achieved in most of the areas pertaining to the organisation of central government. It will be remembered that agreement as regards the legislature had been within sight ever since the opening exchanges in 1968–9, and, true to form, all outstanding issues in this area were satisfactorily resolved during the early stages of the reactivated dialogue. It was thus agreed that the 1960 House of Representatives would basically be retained, that the two communal chambers would be abolished, and that their functions under the new constitutional arrangements would be transferred to two branches of the House consisting of the Greek and Turkish representatives respectively. These two branches, as will be seen shortly, were also intended to exercise various regional functions, mainly on the basis of standard laws to be enacted by the House as a whole. It was also accepted that the House

---

[3] Campbell, *Successful Negotiation: Trieste 1954* (1976), at 150 et seq.

[4] Another welcome development during the early stages of the expanded talks was the Greek Cypriot side's abandonment of its prior insistence that the 1960 constitution did not provide the framework for the intercommunal talks. The Greek Cypriot side made no explicit admission on this matter but the way the discussions proceeded confirmed what was surely implicit even in the earlier exchanges, namely that what the two sides were engaged on was the substantial restructuring of the 1960 constitution in the directions indicated by their respective interests, namely simplification and liberalisation of governmental procedures and structures on the one hand and increased protection and security on the other. In exchange for this 'concession' the Turkish side, through its constitutional expert, acknowledged that the 1960 constitution was substantially defective and in need of thorough-going reform.

should consist of 75 members, of whom 60 would be Greek and 15 Turkish, that in this way the proportion of Turkish to Greek members would be 20 : 80, that the Greek and Turkish members would continue to be elected on separate electoral rolls, that the President should be a Greek and should be elected by the House as a whole, and that there should be two Deputy Speakers or Deputy Presidents, one of whom should be a Turk and the other a Greek (each of the two Deputy Presidents to preside over his community's branch of the House and in the case of the temporary absence of the President or in similar circumstances the Presidency to be assumed by the two Deputy Presidents by rotation). The Turkish side also accepted the abolition of the 1960 separate majorities and that decisions of the House should be taken by majority vote, except in the cases of the electoral law and any amendment thereof, of amendments of constitutional clauses, and of the organic law incorporating the provisions of local government. In these cases a specially reinforced majority of the House would be required, including a specified number of Turkish representatives.

Potentially thornier problems lurked in the reorganisation of the judiciary, as appears from the early exchanges. The two most important issues here were the composition of the Supreme Court and the types of criteria that would determine jurisdiction. On these matters (principally the constitution and functions of the Supreme Court) the reactivated talks may be said to fall into two stages. To begin with, what looked like a complete agreement was not late in materialising. It was thus agreed by late 1972 that the judiciary should consist of the Supreme Court, the Assize Courts, the District Courts and other such subordinate courts as might be agreed upon; that the Supreme Court should exercise the functions of both the Supreme Constitutional Court and the High Court of Justice, the two 1960 Superior Courts in this way to be amalgamated; and that the Supreme Court should consist of six Greek Cypriot judges and three Turkish Cypriot judges, all appointments to be made by the President of the republic but the President to appoint as Turkish judges the candidates for whom the Vice-President had expressed a preference. As regards jurisdiction it was at this same time agreed that Article 159 of the 1960 constitution which provided for communal criteria should be made optional, in the sense that orthodox jurisdictional criteria would prevail unless the particular litigant or litigants invoked its provisions and asked that the case be heard by a judge or judges belonging to the same community; and it was finally accepted by both sides, first that there would be local magistrates to try cases arising from the regulations, bye-laws and orders of local authorities, and secondly that these should be appointed by the Supreme Council of Judicature which, the two sides had already agreed, would be in charge of all judicial appointments with the exception of those to the Supreme Court. In this way the Turkish side accepted the

Greek-Cypriot proposal that the local magistrates should be a part not of the (partly communal) structure of local administration but of the state judicial system. It therefore appeared as if a complete agreement on the judiciary would soon be possible. But during the course of the reactivated talks, and contrary to what had clearly been agreed upon between Messrs Clerides and Denktash earlier, Mr Aldiçasti, the Turkish constitutional expert, suddenly brought up again the question of the reconstitution of the 1960 Supreme Constitutional Court. The Turkish side, he indicated, was not convinced of the future impartiality of the proposed Supreme Court and would therefore reconsider its acceptance of the amalgamation of the two 1960 superior courts. The Greek Cypriot side in its turn was not willing to accept either the reestablishment of the Supreme Constitutional Court or any suggestion concerning equality of judicial representation for Greek and Turkish Cypriots on the Supreme Court.

Three distinct schemes regarding the resolution of the difficult problems that would inevitably be presented by an unequally composed Supreme Court (whose decisions were bound, at least initially, to be viewed with suspicion by the Turkish Cypriots) were canvassed. It was first suggested that the President of the International Court of Justice should be entrusted with authority to give advisory opinions on matters pertaining to the constitution of Cyprus, particularly in those cases where strong judicial disagreement had manifested itself. Though seemingly novel, especially in view of the fact that the constitution of Cyprus could only be domestic and not international law, this idea was nevertheless strongly supported, among other considerations, by the very nature of the Cyprus intercommunal conflict and the particular conditions and characteristics of its precipitation and development into a major international problem. In addition, the advisory role proposed for the President of the International Court would be predicated on the trust of the two communities in the UN and other international organs in both peace-keeping and peace-making and would in this way represent the culmination of supranational efforts for the promotion of a peaceful solution to the Cyprus problem. It was envisaged that this international procedure (which could, conceivably, be of some future use) would be structured in the following way: It would be provided that, for a transitional period, any decision of the Supreme Court on any question as to whether any law or decision of the House of Representatives or its branches was repugnant to or inconsistent with any provision of the constitution would be subject to revision, as follows: The interested party would first petition the Supreme Court to revise its judgment, if this was a majority one; in such cases the President of the Supreme Court would request the President of the International Court for an advisory opinion; if the opinion given by the President of the International Court was in agreement with the decision already given by the Supreme Court, the petition for revision would be dismissed; but if the opinion given by the President of the International Court was contrary to the decision of the Supreme Court, the Supreme Court would accept the petition and revise its judgment accordingly.

Two other compromise formulae on this matter that were apparently also examined during the talks were, first, to set up a 'branch' of the Supreme Court consisting of an equal number of Greek and Turkish judges and vest such branch or sub-Court with sole power of adjudication over the constitutionality of legislative enactments, and, secondly, to adopt, mainly in conjunction with the establishment of a branch of the Supreme Court, as above, some way of returning, in cases of acute and equal judicial disagreement, disputed laws and decisions of the House for reconsideration in the light of the discussions, arguments and judgments of the members of the Supreme Court who had touched upon the matter. Finally, it seems that the solution on this issue that gradually gained ground with both sides was a procedure whereby elements of international adjudication would be combined with the setting up of a distinct branch within the Supreme Court. In this way, for a transitional period of between 7 to 10 years, there would operate within the Supreme Court a special judicial body or branch consisting of two Greeks and two Turkish judges who would exercise exclusive jurisdiction over the constitutionality of laws or decisions of the House or its branches. This body was to be presided over by the President of the Supreme Court and not by Greek and Turkish judges in rotation as had been originally insisted. If now there was a 2:2 disagreement within this body, recourse would be had to the 'advisory' opinion of the President of an International Court.

Even greater difficulties were encountered in discussions on the executive set-up of the state. Here the crucial issues, as both sides saw them, pertained not only to the powers that would be vested in the various executive organs but also to the 'executive' appearance of the state, so vital for symbolic purposes. On some matters agreement was easier to achieve than on others. Thus, by the middle of 1973, it had been agreed after much elaboration of earlier exchanges and fresh discussion that the regime would continue to be a presidential one (with a Greek Cypriot President and a Turkish Cypriot Vice-President), that there would be a Council of Ministers composed of Greek and Turkish Cypriots in proportion to population (which meant that the Turkish side had accepted a decrease in its participation to 20 per cent), that there would be a substantial reduction of the separate executive responsibilities of the Vice-President, and that both the presidential and the vice-presidential vetoes would be abolished. The Turkish side also indicated readiness to recognise some additional presidential functions and convert into exclusively presidential powers and rights what had once been the joint preserve of President and Vice-

President. But two particularly troublesome problems remained, first, the emanation and derivation of executive power in general, and, secondly, the particular mode of appointment of ministers. On the former, the Turkish Cypriot side initially insisted on the retention of the 1960 set-up, particularly the principle that executive power should be jointly 'ensured' by the President and the Vice-President, whereas the early position of the Greek Cypriot side was that under the new constitutional arrangements executive power should not belong to the President and the Vice-President jointly but should rather derive from and be exercised by the President of the republic through the Council of Ministers. During the reactivated talks these initial positions were gradually abandoned and finally both the Greek and Turkish Cypriot sides expressed satisfaction with a formula to the effect that 'executive power would derive from and be exercised by the executive organs of the state', namely the President, the Vice-President and the Council of Ministers, 'according to the specific and detailed provisions of the constitution'. The issue of the appointment of ministers, primarily if not exclusively of symbolic significance, defied resolution almost until the end. The Turkish side demanded either that all ministers should be appointed by the President and the Vice-President jointly, as with the 1960 constitution, or that Greek ministers should be appointed by the President and Turkish ministers by the Turkish Vice-President. The Greek Cypriot side in its turn insisted that all ministers should be appointed by the President of the republic, the President being constitutionally obliged to appoint as Turkish ministers those Turks for whom the Turkish Vice-President had expressed a preference or whom the Vice-President had nominated. Finally, by mid-74, a compromise solution on the issue of appointment seems to have appealed first to the two constitutional experts and then to the negotiators. On this compromise solution the President would sign the instruments of appointment of all ministers (i.e. perform the legal act of appointment) but (i) he would be obliged constitutionally to sign instruments of appointment for those Turkish Cypriots who had been designated by the Vice-President and (ii) the 'countersignature' of the Turkish Vice-President would also be required in their case, this countersignature being not a 'joint signature' but simply a signature indicating 'concurrence'. In this way almost all outstanding issues in the area of the executive were satisfactorily resolved.

The basic constitutional issue throughout the intercommunal discussions was the question of local government,[5] and the most acute disagreement that had already manifested itself in this regard was whether there should

[5] Many papers and proposals were exchanged by the two sides on local government. Particularly important are: *Greek Proposals on the Organic Law of Local Government* (14.12.73); and *Turkish Cypriot Proposals on Regional Autonomy* (21.12.73).

be central authorities, one Greek and the other Turkish. The Turkish side had declared itself absolutely committed to two such central authorities and had suggested that preferably appropriate local governmental functions should be added to the functions of the two communal chambers existing under the 1960 constitution. The Greek Cypriot side until about late 1972 continued to express stiff opposition to this and any other Turkish proposals envisaging two central communal organs, whether for communal or regional affairs. But after sustained UN 'persuasion' the Greek Cypriot side decided that if it wished the negotiations to continue it had no choice but to agree provisionally to the recognition of two branches of the House of Representatives, one consisting of the Greek and the other of the Turkish members of the House, and also that coordination and supervision of agreed local affairs in Greek and Turkish villages and other units of local government would be their responsibility. This compromise formula was first introduced by Mr Tafall, the UN mediator, and at first the Greek Cypriot negotiator expressed interest without finally committing himself. Conditional acceptance, contingent upon agreement being reached on the powers of the two branches and the way they would operate within the state, came shortly thereafter. In effect, the Greek Cypriot side declared itself willing to recognise two separate bodies and authorities for Greek and Turkish local governmental affairs, and vest in them delegated power to issue regulations with regard to any matters recognised as local (under existing legislation) and any other matters that were to be agreed upon between the parties. In addition to this subsidiary rule-making authority, which, the Greek Cypriot negotiator insisted, should only be exercisable on the basis of the existing laws and those to be enacted by the House of Representatives, the two branches could be given some carefully defined executive responsibilities and be allowed to set up their own establishments or bureaus. Of course, the Greek Cypriot side made it clear, there would have to be integration of regional arrangements within the state, and satisfactory controls and governmental supervision should also be set up.

Attention now shifted to the related issues of the juridical origin of the powers to be vested in the two branches of the House and of the exact functions and responsibilities that would be exercised both by them and by the various other regional organs. On the first issue the Turkish side's initial insistence that original power directly deriving from the constitution should be given to these two central establishments so that they would enact separate legislation on matters of local government, with the result that the House of Representatives would be incapable of enacting any legislation or of exercising any control whatsoever in this area, was soon modified once the Greek Cypriot side accepted that there could be central authorities for local government and also abandoned its earlier (related) proposals, first that all local government authorities, including the two (communal) branches of the House, should be set up by an ordinary law of the House (any amendment of which would require an increased majority including an adequate proportion of the votes of the Turkish members), and secondly that the House itself should be able to legislate on all matters of local administration (delegating authority to the local authorities to make regulations and bye-laws on matters falling within their jurisdiction). The key to the problem, Mr Clerides now suggested, lay in a reasonable differentiation and classification of those powers and functions that would be designated as local or regional ones. It seemed to him that even in terms of Turkish Cypriot interests it would be a serious mistake first to incorporate in the constitution itself all those essentially local powers and responsibilities (most of which were minor ones and as to which it was not anticipated that there would be any problems) that would eventually be vested in the branches of the House or other regional organs, secondly to allow all such powers to be exercised by the various local organs on a completely independent and autonomous basis and without reference to overall standards, and finally to immunise them from any kind of substantive state supervision. The Greek Cypriot negotiator was supported in this line of argument by the UN mediator, and Mr Denktash finally admitted that it was indeed an oversimplification to group all 'local' powers together and demand both juridical independence in their origin and complete autonomy in their exercise. This marked a very important point in the intercommunal talks. In any case, discussion now centred not on the issue of the organisation of the separate authorities for local administration, as had been the case in the past, but on a quite different one, namely the classification of state and governmental powers, particularly local or regional ones, and the light which this might throw on the overall system of local government. In this connection a determined effort was made to differentiate between state affairs and local ones, and in this exercise the list of the functions of local authorities that appeared in existing legislation dating back to the colonial years proved very useful. In the course of many meetings Mr Clerides further developed the thesis that, in most matters, whatever the eventual structure to be agreed upon, there should be common standards on the basis of which the local authorities would then proceed to make regulations. Many problems would arise if this was not the case. There would be dissimilarity of regulation and the viability of the local authorities themselves would suffer. As a result and as a general rule, it was neither possible nor desirable to vest original legislative power in either local authorities or any other organs that would exercise local functions. Common standards and their enactment should, in this way, be the preserve and responsibility of a common legislative body, with local organs only possessing secondary regulation-issuing power. Mr

Clerides then proceeded to examine the various powers and responsibilities that would, in all probability, be vested in local authorities. The inescapable conclusion of this examination (and Mr Denktash agreed with this) was that in the case of most uniformity in enactment and regulation was imperative. What this meant was that as regards most local authority functions it was necessary to have general legislation that would be enacted by the House of Representatives setting out common standards on the basis of which local organs would then issue subsidiary regulations. As to certain other local functions the independence of the regional organs could be more pronounced. Almost complete autonomy should be ceded in this area, the Greek Cypriot side intimated, but even here, Mr Clerides suggested and the Turkish Cypriot side now accepted, there had to be provisions ensuring coordination and some limited supervision.

In turn, realisation that powers and functions that it was desirable to vest in regional organs were neither of the same juridical order nor for that matter of the same importance facilitated a resolution of the twin problems of the precise origin of such powers and of the way they would be exercised. In view of the objectives and premises of the parties, and in the context of what had already been agreed between them, what was needed was a legal regime that would not demand the incorporation of agreed local powers and functions in the constitution itself but which at the same time would not relegate them (at least those functions of supervision and coordination that were to be vested in the two branches of the House) to the rather fragile protection of ordinary legislative enactment. After much negotiation this compromise was achieved by the expedient of the proposed adoption of an organic law falling in between ordinary municipal legislation on the one hand and the constitution itself on the other. The emerging formula as regards both the envisaged structure as well as the related distribution of powers and functions looked as follows: There were to be two branches of the House which would have competence in relation to their respective communities on those matters that were provided for by Article 87 of the 1960 constitution, namely communal matters. In addition to the provisions of Article 87, the branches were to exercise, in relation to their respective communities, such powers and functions in respect of local government as were to be provided for by a constitutional law, an organic law, which would be enacted and only be capable of amendment by a two-thirds majority of the House that would also include one third of the Turkish votes. This constitutional law was to be enacted as soon as the House convened following the first general elections to be held under the new constitutional arrangements. In this way legislative power would belong to the House as a whole, whilst communal affairs together with regional supervisory functions would be vested in the two branches, ultimately deriving from a quasi-constitutional law well protected from what the Turkish Cypriots regarded as the infirmities of ordinary legislation. Similarly, achievement of compromise on the issues of the existence of central authorities and the derivation of regional supervisory powers paved the way for complete accord on the issue of 'functions' regarding both the various local authorities and the branches themselves. Thus, functions to be exercised by local authorities at village level by village councils and the like were to be those defined by laws in force before December 1963, and, similarly, functions to be exercised by any other authorities at municipal level were to be those provided for by the law before December 1963. There was at first less agreement on the issue of the 'local' powers and responsibilities of the branches of the House, but after many exchanges the Greek Cypriot side proposed and the Turkish Cypriot side accepted, first that the organic law would delegate power to the respective branches to regulate the internal organisation of their bureaus and other such matters, and secondly that, subject to the provisions of the organic law and on the basis of the existing laws and those to be enacted by the House of Representatives, the branches were to issue regulations on a variety of recognisably 'local' matters, including, most important of all, 'the coordination, control and supervision of the exercise by the village authorities of all the powers and functions conferred on them by the organic law or any other law in force for the time being'. Many other local matters were included, and eventually an agreed list of all these was drawn up.

The only remaining problem after complete agreement was reached on both structure and functions was that of state control over the discharge of regional powers. Mr Denktash again insisted that there could only be minimal supervision and control over the branches in the exercise of local functions and responsibilities. The concept of autonomy, he said, was incompatible with anything but ex post facto judicial review and a minimum of parliamentary supervision. This approach was staunchly resisted by the Greek Cypriot side. Traditional concepts of local government were once more invoked. Local government free of all central controls and restraints was bound to develop into a state within a state; nor was the concept of autonomy incompatible with any but judicial intervention. Autonomy could be otherwise safeguarded. As a rule, the Greek Cypriot side insisted, local governmental organs in almost all countries are subject to three kinds of control, parliamentary, administrative and judicial. Since the Turkish side did not resist judicial control or parliamentary supervision, the latter through the establishment of common standards in agreed areas and control by means of the branches, the only remaining issue was (preliminary) state administrative supervision for the purpose of ensuring the compliance of the various 'local' regulations with the organic law and the specified standards. The basic Greek Cypriot argument developed as follows: The central administration, in order to ensure that there would be no conflict between the discharge of the regional supervisory functions that were to be vested in the two branches and the basic law of the country, should be entitled to challenge at an early stage regulations or decisions of both the local units and all other regional organs which it considered to be ultra vires, 'irregular', 'illegal', or contrary to the national interest. And to accommodate the accepted primacy of central state authority with the interests of the autonomous local units, it was proposed that all 'legislation' and regulations passed by the branches of the House should be submitted for preliminary scrutiny to some central governmental body or authority which would then have the right to challenge their validity before the constitutional chamber of the Supreme Court within a prescribed period, without this or any other central organ having itself the right to annul or declare void the rules or regulations of the branches. The Supreme Court would then be authorised to annul or suspend any law or regulation found to be contrary to law, against the national interest or outside the sphere of autonomous power of the local units. If the annulment were not made within a certain period of time, the local legislation or regulation would be valid and could be put into effect. This basic procedure, combining preliminary or provisional administrative control/challenge with the finality of a conclusive adjudication by the Supreme Court within a prescribed period of time and constituting in essence a hybrid form of supervision straddling the boundaries of the separation of powers, held out the promise that it would serve more or less efficaciously in ensuring that local bodies enjoyed full discretion in the regulation and administration of local affairs subject to provisional central governmental inspection intended eventually to secure a definitive and speedy judicial determination of the disputed matter; appeared to be the only way to narrow the hitherto unbridgeable gulf between Greek Cypriot insistence on full a priori state control of local government (fortified with the power of unilateral invalidation) and Turkish Cypriot intransigence anchored obstinately to the untenable doctrine that there should be no central control at all except for minimal judicial investigation after final promulgation; and by March 1974 was declared to be acceptable in principle by all parties. Various detailed formulae were then exchanged between the two sides; some of these were very similar to the Greek Cypriot proposals set out here; and it seems very likely, as has also been confirmed by the Greek Cypriot negotiator, that if it was not for the coup of July complete agreement on this seemingly intractable problem would have been reached by August 1974.

3. Political developments

But already, despite this remarkable progress on constitutional matters, events both within the Greek Cypriot community and in the relations between the governments of Greece and Cyprus were casting a long and ominous shadow on the talks. These events can be grouped and considered under three headings, that of terrorist activity within the Greek Cypriot community, that of the ecclesiastical crisis within the Church of Cyprus, and that of the growing rift between the Greek junta and the government of Archbishop Makarios.

To begin with, a determined political and terrorist campaign by people professing faith in enosis and implacable opposition to Archbishop Makarios and his policies had begun. Initially opposition to Makarios and advocacy of enosis took a political form, but after the crushing defeat of the enosist candidate, Dr Evdokas, at the presidential election of 1968, where he only obtained a derisory 2 per cent of the vote as against Makarios' 98 per cent, a number of terrorist organisations appeared campaigning for enosis and backing their campaign with explosions and other acts of sabotage and violence. The most vociferous of these organisations was the National Front, an extremist right-wing movement consisting mainly of fanatics and malcontents embittered towards the Makarios government for not giving them positions of authority in the post-independence administration of the island and animated by naive loyalty to the concept of enosis, which, both with increasing prosperity at home and with Greece being ruled by a group of military dictators, was becoming less and less popular. At first, despite Mr Clerides' warning that the situation needed drastic action and that internal violence, if unchecked, would jeopardise the intercommunal talks, Archbishop Makarios was apparently not unduly perturbed, but seems instead to have taken the view that with time irrational emotionalism would evaporate, that without support from Greece (the government of which took an early stand against the activities of the militant elements in Cyprus) the National Front would before long be disbanded, and that strong governmental action might be counterproductive in that it would tend to make martyrs of arrested terrorists. It is now only too clear that President Makarios' failure to smash the extremists, born no doubt of his perennial unwillingness to shed and replace even for a short while his archepiscopal vestments and pectoral cross with a decisive assertion of state power, was a serious error. At this time the available evidence supports the view that the Greek regime and Colonel Papadopoulos in particular were alarmed by the outbreak of violence in Cyprus, took measures to discourage the extremists and were not supporting the National Front or other nationalist organisations. This, despite the junta's dislike of Makarios, is hardly surprising, because it seems that during this period what the Greek regime wanted to avoid most of all was 'the curse of a fresh Cyprus crisis'.[6] Thus, the withdrawal of the Greek troops from the island in January 1968 (which of course meant that any conflict between Greece and Turkey over Cyprus could no longer be contained within the island), the shaky state of the Greek economy, and other serious internal problems as well as international hostility made the Athens regime most reluctant to encourage or find itself involved in a new Cypriot internal conflict that, as the events of November 1967 showed, could easily escalate into a Graeco-Turkish war and an international crisis which this time would almost certainly bring it down. President Makarios himself was apparently satisfied by the Greek Prime Minister's assurance after talks in Athens in January 1970 that the Greek government, as opposed to certain officers of the National Guard, was neither supporting nor encouraging the terrorists or the National Front, and was at that stage not aiming to overthrow him and instal in his place a puppet regime. According to the communiqué issued after these talks both sides strongly condemned terrorism in Cyprus and expressed the hope that, despite any difficulties, 'the intercommunal negotiations would be pursued to their successful outcome'.

On 8 March 1970 there was an attempt to assassinate Archbishop Makarios when his helicopter which had just taken off from the courtyard of the archbishopric came under fire from the roof of the Pancyprian Gymnasium, a school just across the road. Although very seriously wounded, the pilot managed to land; President Makarios escaped unscathed. There was immediately little doubt among informed observers that the attempted assassination was the work of the National Front, and recent disclosures make it clear that the whole operation was masterminded by Colonel Papapostolou, an officer with the National Guard, a close friend of Colonel Papadopoulos and a strong supporter of the junta. But it is not thought that Papadopoulos either knew of the assassination attempt or had a hand in planning it. Another person widely suspected of complicity in the attack was Polykarpos Georkadjis, a former Minister of the Interior and a close associate of Makarios, who had fallen out of favour with the Archbishop some time earlier and who had himself been implicated in an earlier assassination attempt against Colonel Papadopoulos. Makarios himself was in no doubt that Georkadjis was involved in the attempt on his life, but just before he could be arrested and only days after the earlier assassination attempt Georkadjis himself was murdered. For a long time the mysteries surrounding these events remained unsolved but now the picture is clearer. Three factions with different motives and contradictory objectives appear to have collaborated in the attempted

[6] *The Economist*, 24 January 1970, at 26.

assassination of Makarios: first, Papapostolou and certain other officers who were probably acting in collusion with the extreme members of the junta like Colonels Ioannides and Ladas (as opposed to the 'moderates' like Colonels Papadopoulos and Makarezos) and who simply wanted to assassinate the Cypriot leader to pave the way for a new government that would repudiate independence and readopt enosis; secondly, the terrorist organisation, the National Front, some members of which, like Papapostolou, considered the Archbishop's abandonment of union in favour 'of what was feasible' to be treason, while others in addition to this may also have been opponents of the Greek regime who wished at any cost to foment an upheaval in the island as the only way of provoking a new international crisis and overthrowing Papadopoulos; and thirdly Georkadjis who was basically animated by personal ambition, believing that if the Archbishop was killed he would be called upon to replace him. After the assassination attempt failed Georkadjis became desperate and was on the verge of revealing all. At that point Papapostolou lured him to a side road four miles east of Nicosia and killed him. Even though Makarios himself did not believe Papadopoulos to be implicated in the attempt on his life there was substantial evidence which he did not then make public about the involvement of members of the National Guard instigated and supported by the junta hardliners; not surprisingly the result was a sudden rise in tension between Nicosia and Athens in March and April 1970. In the months that followed numerous more bombings, attacks upon police stations and other terrorist acts took place, and it was during this period when it was becoming increasingly obvious that the new violent enosist movement was no passing phenomenon that Makarios decided to take stronger action, for as he himself put it in May 1970 in what proved a prophetic warning, if the National Front carried on, the result would be not enosis but partition. More people suspected of terrorism were rounded up, including several policemen, and a special detention law was introduced. But still the Archbishop failed to take really decisive action to save the situation. The enemy, as he himself observed more in sorrow than in anger, was already within the walls.

To say that much confusion surrounds the events of this period is a considerable understatement. Most Cypriots were baffled by much of what was happening, and to many international observers Churchill's famous aphorism about the situation in Russia, that it was a riddle wrapped in a mystery inside an enigma, sounded like a brilliant flash of elucidation when compared to the mysteries enveloping the events described above.[7] But what could not be doubted was that deep divisions between sections of the Greek Cypriot community had surfaced, and it was clear that these,

[7] *The Economist*, 21 March 1970, at 26.

despite the fact that the government of Archbishop Makarios and its policies (predicated upon the maintenance of an independent Cyprus) continued to enjoy overwhelming popular support, constituted a new explosive element in an already precarious situation endangering the continuation of the intercommunal talks and putting in serious doubt prospects for early or even ultimate success. These dangers were exacerbated by the secret return to the island in early September 1971 of General Grivas who had organised guerrilla warfare against the British between 1955 and 1959 and who now promptly set up a new terrorist movement, called EOKA B, modelled closely on the lines of his anti-British EOKA organisation of the 1950s. What was not at all clear was the precise objective of General Grivas and his armed followers, assuming they had one, whether, that is, they aimed to bring about union with Greece, which of course would have meant first a coup d'etat against the Makarios government and then almost certainly a Turkish invasion, or whether they merely wished to frustrate the intercommunal discussions and in this way prevent a constitutional settlement barring enosis. Equally uncertain was the exact relationship between General Grivas and the Greek dictator, Colonel Papadopoulos. Did General Grivas return to the island as Papadopoulos' man, as many supporters of Makarios claimed, or as an independent agent, as the Greek regime alleged, or was the true explanation a different one, namely that Papadopoulos knew of the General's plans and simply let him implement them, in the expectation that the presence and activities of Grivas would put pressure on Archbishop Makarios? Whatever the correct explanation, in the period that followed General Grivas and his supporters engaged in numerous acts of political terrorism, blowing up police stations, kidnapping prominent supporters of Makarios, taking away weapons, and the like, and even though the Grivas guerrillas were not many, what mattered was first that they enjoyed the support of many Greek officers serving with the Cypriot National Guard (the Greek Cypriot army) and secondly that there had been extensive infiltration of the police and the Cypriot security forces whose loyalty in this way could no longer be relied upon by the government.

Not surprisingly, as a result of these events, Turkish attitudes hardened. The situation among the Greeks, Mr Denktash is reported to have said, was such that the general demands of the Turkish Cypriot side on the issue of local government, as formulated during preceding stages of the intercommunal dialogue, were not enough. Greater independence and increased autonomy should be granted to the Turkish Cypriots. Total security should be guaranteed, and this was only possible through fully equipped communal police forces. Other issues also had to be reopened, particularly in the areas of the executive and the judiciary. The Greek Cypriot official line was naturally that the conflict within the Greek

Cypriot community was an internal matter, that it did not concern the Turkish Cypriot side, and that it did not affect the intercommunal negotiations which, as before, should continue on the basis of a unitary, independent, sovereign state. There was, Mr Clerides often told Mr Denktash, and should be, no relationship between the internal difficulties of the Greek Cypriot community and the progress of the local constitutional talks. Indeed, the Greek Cypriot negotiator complained, the Turkish side had only taken advantage of a convenient pretext in order to prevent an agreement and strengthen further its 'territorial' position. On the other hand, as was also generally admitted by political observers and by the Greek Cypriot side in private, both the political climate in which the talks were being held and the attitudes of the Turkish side could not but be influenced by the violence within the Greek Cypriot community.

Intimately connected with agitation for enosis and the intensification of the terrorist campaign against the government was the eruption of open conflict within the Church of Cyprus, with the three other Cypriot bishops, members of the Holy Synod of the Greek Cypriot Church, turning against Archbishop Makarios and challenging his until then undisputed ecclesiastical authority, for many the source of his political charisma. What of course was apparent to all was that the motives of the rebel bishops were not ecclesiastical but political. Contemporaneously with political agitation for enosis they began making statements, both in sermons and elsewhere, expressing discontent with the political and ecclesiastical stewardship of Makarios, complaining that he had abandoned the struggle for enosis and settled for independence, and calling upon him to modify his policies and revert once more to the old uncompromising nationalist line that the only goal should be union with Greece and nothing but that. Finally, on 2 March 1972, Archbishop Makarios was asked by the three bishops to resign as President of the republic, the office he had held throughout the twelve and a half years of the island's independence, on the ground, rather belatedly discovered, that according to the laws of the Orthodox Church temporal power and ecclesiastical authority were incompatible. Efforts were made behind the scenes to heal the breach, but to no avail. In March 1973 the three bishops decided to depose Archbishop Makarios for allegedly violating canon law by continuing to hold the secular office of President, and gave him thirty days in which to appeal. He ignored them and on 13 April they met again and completed their action by announcing that their previous decision to unfrock Archbishop Makarios had now become 'definitive and final'. They also issued a communiqué stating that the 'deposed' Primate of the Orthodox Church of Cyprus had been reduced to the rank of layman and should henceforth be known as Michael Mouskos. Archbishop Makarios immediately denounced the bishops' action as 'null, void and unconstitutional', and promised to take decisive steps to rectify the ecclesiastical order which, in his view, had been seriously disturbed. Meanwhile the decision of the three bishops to unfrock Makarios was greeted on the one hand with evident satisfaction on the part of General Grivas, who had indeed at an earlier stage taken them under his wing and strongly encouraged their efforts to compel Archbishop Makarios to abdicate, but on the other with expressions of serious concern in some Greek circles. Thus, the Greek Deputy Foreign Minister said that the Greek regime was 'watching with great concern developments which, by increasing dissension among Greek Cypriots, could harm (the) great national issue', and voiced the hope that 'any action likely to aggravate the situation would be avoided' and that all concerned would exercise 'self-restraint and show good sense'. Further, on the purely ecclesiastical aspects, Archbishop Ieronymos, the Primate of the Orthodox Church of Greece, obviously acting after consultations with the Greek regime, questioned the validity of the bishops' decision, stating that ecclesiastical law did not allow the trial of a bishop (the more so of a primate) by fewer than 12 of his peers. 'Any other action taken by anyone, in any other manner or for any other reason, would be contrary to the holy canons,' he announced. In July 1973 Makarios once more took the initiative by convening a Synod of Eastern Orthodox Churches. The synod first ruled that the attempt to unseat Archbishop Makarios was contrary to canon law (which authorised only the Archbishop to convene a synod of the Cyprus Church) and was therefore irregular, null and void, and then proceeded to find the rebel bishops guilty of schism by provoking disunity, by holding secret meetings in disobedience to canon law, and by conspiring against the Archbishop. For these reasons they were unfrocked and deprived of all clerical power and authority. On the question of the dual role of Archbishop Makarios as Head of the Orthodox Church of Cyprus and Head of State on which the three bishops had based their case the Synod ruled that the assumption of the Presidency by Makarios had been in response to the people's demand and wishes and therefore constituted 'a duty which was not contrary to the true spirit of the Holy Scripture and canon law'. So what appeared to many observers to be a byzantine tangle ended with yet another comprehensive victory for Archbishop Makarios, with the three bishops finding themselves unfrocked and outside the Church. At the same time, and despite the overwhelming popularity the Archbishop continued to enjoy, the schism in the Cyprus Church, to some extent reflecting the political schism within the Greek Cypriot community, was now complete and irrevocable, and could not but complicate further the task of reaching a negotiated internal settlement of the Cyprus problem.

Even more significant was a sharp (and public) deterioration in the relations between the Greek junta and the government of Archbishop Makarios that took place in the early part of 1972. It has been observed[8] that from the very beginning of the intercommunal dialogue an acute contradiction existed in the relationship between Athens and Nicosia, in that now democratic Cyprus, where there was a strong Communist party and whose government was aggressively pursuing in international affairs a non-aligned policy, depended for military and political support on Greece, since April 1967 under the rule of an extreme right-wing dictatorship fanatically opposed to Communism and a faithful supporter of United States foreign policy. Only five months after coming to power, Colonel Papadopoulos, without prior consultation with Makarios, met with the then Turkish Prime Minister, Suleyman Demirel, and proposed that Turkey should accept Cyprus' union with Greece in exchange for territorial concessions in Thrace and elsewhere. Apparently the Turkish Premier ridiculed the Greek proposal and declared it completely unacceptable, indicating that Turkey would only accept partition; but what could not have been lost on the Turkish government was the new Greek regime's apparent willingness to negotiate directly with them, and indeed against Makarios' declared policy, something which they would in future use to bring pressure to bear upon and weaken the authority of the Cypriot leader. After the ignominious collapse of his diplomatic initiative and the humiliating withdrawal of the Greek troops from Cyprus in the wake of the events of November 1967 Papadopoulos seems to have decided that for the time being the Cyprus problem should be left to Makarios and his government but that at the same time the National Guard, without becoming involved in useless and counterproductive acts of terrorist violence that might possibly lead to yet another direct confrontation with Turkey, should continue to be controlled by the Greek government through Greek officers who would be sent from Greece ostensibly to train the Cypriot recruits. Frequent declarations that a harmonious working relationship existed between Athens and Nicosia continued to emanate with steady regularity from both governments in the years following the opening of the intercommunal talks, and it has been seen in an earlier chapter that there is evidence that this procedure in its early stages was positively favoured and supported by the Greek military regime or at least some members of it, including in all likelihood Colonel Papadopoulos himself. But unmistakable tension nonetheless persisted, things taking a turn for the worse, first, with the assassination attempt against Makarios in 1970 in which high-ranking Greek officers of the National Guard were implicated, and, secondly, with revelations that a

---

[8] Markides, *The Rise and Fall of the Cyprus Republic* (1977), at 132 et seq.

secret plan had been drawn up in Greece by certain members of the junta and possibly with the consent and knowledge of Papadopoulos himself envisaging a possible overthrow of Archbishop Makarios and the assumption of power by the National Guard.

Finally, on 11 February 1972, an open crisis broke out between the Cyprus and Greek governments. On that day the Greek government issued a virtual ultimatum to President Makarios demanding, first, that a quantity of arms which the government of the republic had imported from Czechoslovakia for use by the security forces against General Grivas and his terrorists should be surrendered to the National Guard whose officers were Greek and under the direct orders of the junta; secondly, that Makarios should reshuffle his cabinet and dismiss some ministers considered hostile to the Greek regime; and, thirdly, that there should in future be compliance on the part of Makarios and his government with the policies laid down by the Athenian junta. These demands were included in a note which was delivered to the Cypriot President by Mr C. Panayotakos, the Greek Foreign Under-Secretary, one of the junta's closest collaborators, who, apparently, acting on the orders of Colonel Papadopoulos, also formulated verbally two other demands, first that Makarios should leave Cyprus and retire to Athens as a sort of elder stateman, and secondly that in any case drastic action should be taken to eliminate what the Greek dictator viewed as widespread communist penetration of the Cypriot government. Apparently a further message was sent from the Greek government to Archbishop Makarios on 3 March in which the junta reiterated its previous demands, particularly that Makarios should form 'a government of national unity composed of all the segments of nationalist Cypriot Hellenism' and that he should from then on unqualifiedly accept the policies formulated in Athens, but this time no mention was made of the Cypriot leader's desired resignation and departure from the island. In any case President Makarios made clear to the junta's emissary that he took the strongest exception both to the tone of the note and to the demand that he should reshuffle his administration and form a so-called government of 'national unity', and emphasised that neither he nor his government would accede to crude Greek pressure or willingly tolerate interference in Cypriot internal affairs. Further, there was deep suspicion in Nicosia as to the motives and timing of the Greek ultimatum, and President Makarios himself apparently formed the view that the most likely explanation of the unprecedented publicity which the Greek regime (previously an avid practitioner of secret diplomacy) gave to the Athens-Nicosia crisis was that the Greek and Turkish governments must have entered into a secret agreement or understanding, first to eliminate him from the scene or at least weaken his authority, and secondly to resolve the Cyprus problem itself either by federation or partition. The fear among many Greek Cypriots that the Greek regime was indeed prepared to abandon diplomacy and 'persuasion' and if necessary use force in order to impose its will on the Cyprus government was strengthened in the weeks that followed by numerous events and incidents, mainly by growing evidence that many of the Greek officers of the National Guard were guilty of collaboration with the terrorist groups under General Grivas and by a significant declaration on the part of Mr C. Panayotakos, the junta's messenger, that 'Greece would intervene in the island's affairs if her interests demanded it'. It was widely noticed by political observers not only that this was the first time that a Greek government official had asserted rights of military intervention *against* Cyprus but also that this could not but cause immense pleasure to Turkish strategists who had consistently been claiming such rights ever since the Zurich agreement had been signed between Greece and Turkey. Finally President Makarios, in an effort to resolve the crisis, surrendered control of the arms consignment from Czechoslovakia to the UN peace force. But even though the elimination of this particular issue helped defuse the situation, it was obvious that the seemingly abrupt deterioration in the relations between Athens and Nicosia could no longer be repaired. Three things which also became clear as a result of the crisis of February – March 1972 were, first that the Greek government's clumsy efforts and stratagems either to remove Archbishop Makarios from the scene or to give him a less preponderant role had failed and in the absence of crude military force were likely to continue doing so, secondly that the Cypriot leader ultimately served not the interests of mainland Greece or the so-called aspirations of Hellenism but rather the independence of Cyprus and the interests of its people (mainly the Greek Cypriots), and thirdly that the Archbishop had become singularly skilful in preserving that independence against the manifold external and internal pressures that were threatening to engulf the island.

In late November 1973 Colonel Papadopoulos himself, by now President of Greece, was swept away swiftly and bloodlessly by another set of army officers. The two things that became immediately apparent were, first that the real power behind the new order was Brigadier Ioannides, the chief of the military police and a man known both for his fiery anti-communism and his intense hatred of Archbishop Makarios, and secondly that the new regime was to be considerably more authoritarian than its predecessor. What were the intentions of the new junta towards Cyprus? These were not made clear but what was only too obvious in view of Brigadier Ioannides' undisguised hostility both to the concept of an independent Cyprus and to Archbishop Makarios personally was that additional support would now be given to terrorist groups agitating for enosis and that any attempt by the Cyprus government to come to a final agreement with the

Turkish side would meet with stiff Greek opposition, culminating perhaps in a military coup. This was confirmed by what happened on General Grivas' death in late January 1974. Immediately there were reports of dissension within EOKA B's ranks. Apparently, shortly before his death, Grivas named a former officer in the Greek army, Colonel George Karousos, as his successor to the leadership of EOKA, but it seems that Karousos, realising the futility of terrorist activity and the serious danger of Turkish military intervention if the conflict within the Greek Cypriot community was allowed to degenerate into civil war, was opposed to the continuation of guerrilla operations against the Makarios government. His 'moderation' was resisted by other members of the organisation on the direct orders of the junta, and it was not long before Karousos was forced by Brigadier Ioannides and his agents in Cyprus to leave the island. Arguably Grivas' death left Makarios in sole control of the Greek Cypriots' political future, and indeed the pious hope was expressed in some quarters that, without Grivas' threat in the background, it would become possible for the Cyprus government to show greater flexibility in the intercommunal talks and possibly make some further concessions to the Turks which with Grivas alive may have been politically impossible. But it may be that General Grivas' death narrowed even further the already severely restricted room for manoeuvre Archbishop Makarios possessed. There is some evidence that during his last months Grivas himself was becoming increasingly disillusioned and indeed alarmed with the policies of Ioannides and his associates and may have been exerting some effort to restrain his wilder and more extreme followers. Whatever the truth, without his discipline violence in the months that followed increased, and his terrorist organisation came under the complete control of Ioannides and the hardliners in Athens.

How did all these events affect the formulation of Greek Cypriot policies and in particular the way the Greek Cypriot side pursued the intercommunal negotiations? The only thing that was clear was that developments both within the Greek Cypriot community and in the context of the relationship between Cyprus and Greece put Archbishop Makarios and his government in a particularly invidious position and confronted them with a painful dilemma. In one sense constitutional agreement and political settlement were more urgent than ever before, for not only would further intensification of strife among the Greek Cypriots be used by the Turkish Cypriot side as an argument for even wider powers at the local and communal levels but also Turkey could well take advantage of a new outbreak of violence in order to intervene militarily and effect partition. But in another sense, as both Makarios and some of his leading supporters realised, the conclusion of a final agreement with the

Turkish Cypriot side, unavoidably entailing exclusion of enosis, would be fraught with serious dangers, in that then the Archbishop would be denounced as a traitor, both within sections of his own community and by at least some of the military rulers in Greece, and moves, instigated from Athens, almost certainly be made to topple him, in this way giving Turkey the opportunity to invade. It may be that the best course for Makarios, as he himself subsequently acknowledged, was to play a waiting game and try to come to a complete internal accommodation with the Turkish Cypriots but without either giving away too much in terms of local (communal) autonomy, since given the Turkish Cypriots' reliance on Turkey that would in effect bring about a Turkish military presence in the island, or officially concluding an agreement with the Turkish side, since in that case there would be an attempt to overthrow him that would in all probability trigger off an invasion. Meanwhile it was to be hoped that the Greek junta would fall, or that there would be a decisive turn in American policy in the direction of active support for the intercommunal talks, or that terrorism in the island would be eliminated.

4. *The Papadopoulos policy and the Graeco-Turkish 'understanding'*[9]

Adequate and satisfactory evidence on the complex events and almost indecipherable political developments of the years between 1971 and 1974 has not come to light, but it is possible to piece together the following account, first of the policy towards the Cyprus problem followed for the most part during these years by Colonel Papadopoulos and his regime, and secondly of efforts to bring about a Graeco-Turkish understanding as to how best to deal with this and other matters. The basic doctrine of Papadopoulos' approach to the Cyprus problem was strong and calculating determination to solve it in a way that would be acceptable to the American government and NATO, and therefore Turkey as well. Papadopoulos knew that though American policy makers might ultimately favour double union or partition they would in the near future be most reluctant either to sanction an overt joint Graeco-Turkish political or military operation against the popular and well-established government of Makarios, or for that matter to look with favour upon unilateral Greek military adventurism in Cyprus. At the same time the American

---

[9] Information on these matters was derived from a number of sources and documents, most of them confidential. On the contacts between Greek and Turkish officials at Lisbon and Vienna I had access, among other documents, to 'secret' internal memoranda of the Greek Foreign Ministry. It was encouraging to find that my conclusions (first tentatively set out in Polyviou, *Cyprus, In Search of a Constitution* (1976)) are confirmed by Stern, *The Wrong Horse: The Politics of Intervention and the Failure of American Diplomacy* (1977), 90 et seq.

Government was impatient with the apparent stalemate in the inter-communal talks, was apprehensive about what it viewed as Makarios' flirtations with the eastern bloc and the non-aligned, and was not averse to having some pressure brought upon him, provided it was not implicated in this directly, particularly if the result would be to speed up a political settlement that did not jeopardise western interests. What therefore seems to have happened is that the Papadopoulos junta, almost completely isolated internationally and desperately needing American support, accepted in principle, in response to American and NATO pressure, that the Cyprus problem should be solved without delay and that strongarm tactics, if need be, were to be used in order to exact concessions from Makarios and his government. But it was not at this time intended that Makarios should be overthrown or that there should be a radical alteration in the international status of Cyprus as an independent and sovereign state. The main objective of the Greek junta under Papadopoulos was that the political authority of Archbishop Makarios should be weakened, that he should explicitly recognise that 'national' policy would be formulated in Athens and not in Nicosia, and that his government should be reconstituted so that it would be more amenable to Greek pressure. General Grivas himself was allowed to come to Cyprus in order to weaken the position of the Archbishop and make him more dependent on Athens and therefore more susceptible to Greek pressure, and it was clearly for the same reason that the three bishops and other Cypriots were encouraged by Greek officials to launch their movement for enosis. The broad theory behind the whole affair was that the Archbishop, with the presence of General Grivas in Cyprus and with the launching of an aggressive enosis movement, would feel his position threatened and would have to rely on support from the mainland. That support, in order to be given, would require the recognition that Greece had the main say on the Cyprus problem. It does not seem likely that Colonel Papadopoulos or the Greek government of that time had intended General Grivas to take any action to oust the Archbishop or to provoke Turkey; and it is probable that, at first, Colonel Papadopoulos, a master of espionage, had seen to it that General Grivas was under Greek control, though the General himself did not realise it and seems to have been acting throughout in the belief that the Greek government had no hand in his arrival and activities in Cyprus.

The culmination of the Papadopoulos policy is the reaching of a secret agreement or understanding with Turkey regarding, among other things, the resolution of the Cyprus problem. This agreement or understanding was mainly worked out during the first part of 1971 and seems to have had as a starting point the acknowledgement by the Greek government of the validity of the Zurich and London agreements and of the related external guarantees, and, in addition, to have been based on acceptance by Greece of (a) basic partnership principles in the constitutional reconstruction of Cyprus and (b) the extension and recognition of substantial local autonomy for the Turkish Cypriots. In exchange for this Turkey apparently agreed that it would not unilaterally invade Cyprus, or that it would only do so after consultations with the Greek government. Moreover, there are indications that the Graeco-Turkish understanding outlined above was not limited to broad and general matters of principle but also extended to more specific issues and points of difficulty. It seems likely, for instance, that Graeco-Turkish contacts during this time covered the controversial issue of the organs through which Turkish Cypriot autonomy in local affairs would be expressed and that various ideas in this direction were canvassed. More significantly, there is substantial evidence that the accord between Greece and Turkey outlined above was due in great measure to NATO mediation. Thus, at the 1971 NATO Foreign Ministers' Conference and at subsequent meetings, both Greece and Turkey were seriously warned to avoid any action towards a *forcible* solution of the Cyprus problem because, in the evaluation of NATO, in any such event there would be a serious risk of Soviet military involvement. At about this time NATO countries formed the view which they then communicated to the Greek and Turkish governments that, although Archbishop Makarios would not like Soviet involvement in Cyprus, he might not have any alternative but to ask for it, particularly if an attempt was made to impose a solution. It was further pointed out that even if an attempt was made to remove the Archbishop from office by force, not only could there be unforeseeable complications between Greece and Turkey but also the Soviet Union might not recognise his forcible removal and still intervene. It was in this connection recommended to the two governments that, should the intercommunal talks fail, the best solution from the point of view of NATO would be the 'freezing' of the situation as at that time with, perhaps, mutual efforts at military deconfrontation. But Turkey's reaction to the ideas of freezing the situation and military deconfrontation was apparently unfavourable. The Turkish government instead proposed that in the event of a deadlock in the talks, Greece, Turkey and the UK, or Greece and Turkey jointly, should exercise their rights under the treaty of guarantee and intervene militarily. Greece resisted this, and apparently the Turkish suggestion concerning a joint and official intervention by the guarantors found no appeal in NATO.

Developments in Graeco-Turkish relations after this can only be sketched out in the broadest outline. As appears from confidential documents of this period, after the Lisbon Conference and right until the time he was overthrown in November 1973 Colonel Papadopoulos' *basic* perception of the Cyprus question continued to be that it was primarily a thorny issue in Graeco-Turkish relations and had to be tackled as such. The government of Greece was well aware that it could not allow Greece to be involved in a war with Turkey. It also knew that Turkey would not allow the Cyprus problem to drag on indefinitely. If Greece had to choose between a war with Turkey and forcing developments in Cyprus in its favour, including a coup, then Greece would choose the second course, and it had the necessary force in Cyprus to do it. But Papadopoulos hoped that events would not develop in this way, since any attempted overthrow of Makarios would meet with serious local resistance and with widespread international condemnation. Besides, the Greek dictator does not appear to have trusted the Turkish government or, unlike his successors, to have believed that the American government in the event of a coup against Makarios would prevent Turkey from invading. It was therefore necessary to weaken the Archbishop, maintain some control over his internal opponents, and, most important of all, not allow any differences with Turkey to provoke a wider confrontation that could jeopardise America's 'constructive' and friendly attitude. The best way to achieve this last objective was by the continuation and streamlining of Lisbon-type high-level contacts between the two governments. Any progress achieved there would then be implemented by pressure that would be brought to bear on the Greek and Turkish Cypriots. The latter were never a problem, as the Turkish community of Cyprus was totally dependent on Ankara. Archbishop Makarios and his government were however another matter. It would not be easy to curb Makarios and force him back into the Greek camp, Papadopoulos informed the Turkish government, and would in any case require some time. Throughout 1972 and early 1973 the Turkish government seemed willing to go along with the intricate Papadopoulos plots and machinations, but it eventually lost patience. At the last meeting in the series of high-level contacts between Greece and Turkey (which took place in Vienna in May 1973) the Turkish government appeared quite aggressive and expressed grave displeasure with what was happening in Cyprus. It made two principal points, first that it could not wait indefinitely but that a solution to the Cyprus problem *had* to be found, either in the context of the intercommunal talks or by separate agreement between Greece and Turkey, and secondly that a solution, in order to be acceptable to it, had to be based on ingredients, including territorial arrangements, that in the event of a crisis could easily be transformed into partition. The matter was of the utmost urgency, the Turkish representative continued, and the Greek government had to assume its 'responsibilities'. If it was not prepared to do so Turkey itself would have to take action. The Greek representative apparently stayed silent during all this, and only asked how long Turkey was willing to wait. The answer was that Turkey could not wait longer than a few months.

There is some evidence that after the Vienna meeting the Greek regime reconsidered its policy in the light of the Turkish ultimatum and now decided that the only way to settle the Cyprus problem once and for all was by overthrowing Makarios and having him replaced by someone who would be more amenable to their 'suggestions'. This decision was apparently communicated to the American government which 'approved' of the conciliatory attitude of the Papadopoulos regime towards the Turkish government but 'discouraged' any incidents that might lead to bloodshed and possibly a Graeco-Turkish confrontation as well.

Colonel Papadopoulos' overthrow by a more extreme junta marks the beginning of the last phase in the relations between the Greek dictatorship and the Cyprus government. From this point onwards the nationalist terrorist organisation EOKA B receives almost undisguised support from official Greek circles, and the National Guard, openly now, declares its hostility to Makarios and his policies.

5. *New Turkish demands*

As has been seen above, despite political violence within the Greek Cypriot community and the growing conflict between Athens and Nicosia, the intercommunal negotiations continued in a more or less uninterrupted way between 1972 and 1974, and by early 1974 a comprehensive settlement with regard to the internal constitutional problem had almost been reached. Effectively no problems in the area of the central government remained and a full agreement on local administration was also emerging. Then the Turkish side brought up another demand, namely that the Cyprus government should publicly declare that it was forever excluding enosis. It was pointed out to the Turkish Cypriot negotiator, first, that the terms of reference within which the talks were being conducted provided for an independent and sovereign state, and that this necessarily excluded both union with Greece and partition, and, secondly, that if the Turkish side wanted more by way of assurances that enosis and partition had been buried forever, there was nothing to stop Turkey and Greece from coming to a separate agreement not to pursue policies leading to solutions inconsistent with the status of sovereign independence. This was not acceptable to either Greece or Turkey, the Turkish side persisted in its demand that there now had to be specific (and public) assurances from the government of Cyprus itself and Archbishop Makarios personally that enosis had been firmly abandoned and would never again be sought, and even Mr Clerides, the Greek Cypriot negotiator, felt, and so told Makarios, that a formula had to be devised whereby enosis would be excluded to the satisfaction of the Turkish side (even though all internal constitutional issues had not yet been fully resolved) without at the same time endangering the Cypriot government. After much hard bargaining even this was achieved by an ingenious agreement that for the time being no politically hazardous public renunciations would be insisted upon but that on the successful conclusion of the intercommunal talks both sides would affirm and in effect readopt in an unqualified and irrevocable manner those articles and provisions of the 1960 constitution enshrining the status of sovereign independence and the island's territorial integrity and forbidding any other incompatible solution, including of course both enosis and partition.

Despite this, in the early months of 1974, the newly installed Turkish government, in a series of formal statements both in Ankara and in the UN, announced a fundamental change of policy over Cyprus. Thus, Mr Ecevit, the Turkish Prime Minister, made repeated declarations during the early months of 1974 to the effect that the best solution of the Cyprus problem was a federal one. These declarations culminated with a statement after he had held talks in Ankara with Mr Denktash that Turkey was prepared and was going to exert every effort to secure by peaceful means a federal solution of the Cyprus question. And Mr Olcay, Turkey's Permanent Representative at the UN, during the meeting of the Security Council of 29 May 1974 stated that the official Turkish line was now that the intercommunal talks were not based on any particular principle; that statements by the Secretary-General in his various reports to the Security Council regarding 'a lasting and agreed solution based on the concept of an independent, sovereign, unitary state' should not have contained the term 'unitary state', but that even though this term was contained, it represented nothing but the views of the Secretary-General and did not bind the parties concerned; that the constitution of 1960 on the basis of which the parties were negotiating actually provided for a federal system of government or at least a functional federative system; and that, partly because of that and partly because of the new realities on the island, the new Turkish government of Mr Ecevit favoured a federation for Cyprus. Of particular importance was also a statement by Mr Gunes, the Turkish Foreign Secretary, made at about the same time. The basis of Turkish policy in Cyprus, he stated, was the establishment of a federative system. This was not a question of details or of particular issues of constitutional reconstruction, but a fundamental tenet of political philosophy, and no agreement could ever be accepted unless it clearly reflected this 'federal' philosophy. The official Turkish goal therefore once more became some sort of federative order.[10]

[10] Mr Denktash's argument after these Turkish statements that no substantial change was intended in as much as the 'unitary state formula' had never really been accepted by the Turkish government is not correct. Study of Security Council debates and the reports of the UN Secretary General between 1968–1973 that were not objected to by the Turkish side

The explanation for this seemingly abrupt shift in policy is not difficult to find. The Turkish government realised that the relations between Archbishop Makarios and the Greek junta had entered a critical stage of hostility and confrontation, and that an attempt to overthrow the Cyprus government would not be long in coming. This would give Turkey a plausible excuse justifying military intervention that would settle the problem once and for all. A military solution had become inevitable, Turkish strategists now knew, and the sooner it came the better.

On 15 July 1974 a coup was staged against the Makarios government by the National Guard led by Greek army officers. The Cypriot President narrowly escaped assassination and sought refuge abroad. On 20 July 1974 Turkey, alleging a breach of the treaty of guarantee, invaded Cyprus militarily and by 16 August 1974 had occupied 40 per cent of the territory of the republic. The realities of power changed decisively; a new stage of the intercommunal conflict was reached; and six years of arduous intercommunal negotiations and any progress achieved there were completely overtaken by events.

---

makes it abundantly clear not only that there was a consensus concerning the framework of a unitary state but also that this had been deliberately adopted by Turkey and the Turkish Cypriot leadership, in deference, it may be, to the views of the UN Secretary General. A good example is the statement of the Secretary General of 2 December 1970 that *'the two sides have indicated* that a settlement can be worked out on the basis of an independent, sovereign and unitary state of Cyprus in which the two communities participate', an unambiguous passage that was subsequently referred to by the Permanent Representative of Turkey in the course of a Security Council debate in terms of full approval. (See also numerous UN documents, mainly S/9814, 1 June 1970, para. 70; S/10005, para. 120; S/10199, para. 83; S/10401, para. 101; S/10842, para. 80; S/11137, para. 80).

5

The Intercommunal Discussions: an Evaluation

Some additional comments can now be made on the intercommunal negotiations, both as an exercise in political negotiation and as an attempt at constitutional reconstruction. Some of the main questions which are raised by what has been said above are: given the situation the parties were confronted with, what were the options available to them, and were they wise to proceed as they did? In view of the 'real' objectives of the parties as these unmistakably emerge from a description of their philosophies and attitudes, how did the type of state that was taking shape in their negotiations compare with what they desired at the opening and during the initial stages of the intercommunal discussions? Naturally the most important question concerns the reasons why the talks failed.

1. *Political options*

What was the situation that the two sides were faced with at the beginning and during the period of the intercommunal discussions? The Zurich constitution which, whatever its exact juridical designation, had set up a 'partnership' state or a unitary state with bicommunal participation institutionalised on a rigid pattern broke down functionally as a result of the events of 1963. The Turks, faced with the collapse of a constitution which had favoured them and forced by the crisis, followed a policy of self-segregation and a proportion of them withdrew into several enclaves scattered within the territory of the republic, where they set up their own organisation outside the provisions of the constitution. Originally only a rudimentary military-political administrative structure was established without a differentiation between military and political functions, this structure being apparently characterised by the clear predominance of military elements and organs over political ones. After the 1967 crisis the fragmentation of the state and the consequent separation of the communities became more distinct. Signs of permanence gradually appeared. Thus, in December 1967, at a meeting of leading members of the Turkish community, the 'basic provisions of the provisional Turkish Cypriot administration' were adopted. These basic provisions, purporting to create within certain defined areas a structure of separate administration to be carried on by newly ad hoc created organs, were followed by a gradual differentiation of political from military functions and responsibilities. During the following years there was steady development of the various Turkish Cypriot administrative structures, and such stabilisation and development, made possible by steady and regular subsidies from Turkey, were expressed by and reflected in the enactment of a more definite charter of government and administration for the Turkish areas. The Turkish administration was no longer called 'provisional', and in effect between 1967 and 1974 a state within a state, not recognised internationally and existing in contravention of the constitution which by Article 185 had expressly declared the indivisibility of the republic and had prohibited any separatist independence, functioned within its territory. The Greek Cypriots, on their part, ignoring the constitutional limitations and invoking the doctrine of necessity, namely that the government of the republic had to continue functioning in view of societal needs, took over the entire governmental and administrative machinery. This splitting up of the state produced a continuous political crisis with on the one hand sporadic incidents of violence varying in magnitude and significance but always seriously endangering the peace, and on the other many extreme declarations and what would be called crisis language on the part of both communities rekindling mutual fears and suspicions and effectively reducing communication between them to a minimum.

It is obvious that one option that could have been chosen by the parties would have been to do nothing but to continue in their ambivalent situation. But, as is equally apparent, the continuation of the status quo would have presented considerable dangers to peace and would have perpetuated intercommunal tension. Moreover, as the Greek Cypriot side realised, the Turkish administration would with time tighten its grip over the areas under its control, organise more effectively its political and administrative structures, and thereby inevitably reinforce its claim to international recognition on account of its permanence and durability; the stage might thus be set for an eventual geographical federation of the island, based on the fact that there had come into existence two territorial entities, however unequal or irregular these might be, which should now link up in a new form of political association. Equally, the Turkish Cypriots, in a completely unregulated situation, might fear either some kind of surprise attack, or that the prevailing impression of Cyprus as an island governed entirely by the Greek Cypriot community, with the Turkish Cypriots a small and recalcitrant minority excluded from the economic advantages of prosperity by their own intransigence, would before long displace and eventually obliterate what some might regard as the current reality of two communal administrations functioning separately in the island. Some kind of 'agreement' was therefore essential for both Cypriot sides, and because of international and internal factors both enosis and partition or any of their permutations were outside its purview. Consistently with this the common ground discovered by means of the early soundings of the Secretary-General was predicated upon the two communities' mutual decision to restore 'cooperation' and reestablish political integration within a common independent state. But how was this objective to be achieved, and what distinctive character would 'integration' and 'cooperation' assume?

A number of distinct political models offered themselves to the two sides and their representatives. The first was some kind of legalisation of the status quo, or some kind of official and formal recognition of the existing state of affairs. On this model, efforts would be made to establish a modus vivendi between the two communities on the basis of their existing arrangements and institutions. Any such solution would be expressly declared to be a temporary one, e.g. for a period of five years, and would be adopted by the parties without prejudice to their interests and 'rights'. Meanwhile, some coordinating mechanisms and procedures would be set up, and common and acute problems would be dealt with by the two sides acting together. This, with time, might lead to a normalisation of relations and in this way facilitate a later determined effort to negotiate an overall constitutional agreement. Indeed, Mr Tafall, the Secretary-General's representative in Cyprus, investigated the possibility of this temporary solution, which was strongly favoured by Turkey and the Turkish Cypriot side. But this was not acceptable to the Greek Cypriots, both because it would inevitably entail, whatever the legal phraseology in which it was disguised, some recognition of what they regarded as an illegal Turkish Cypriot rebellion and secession, and because, as they feared, any such halfway procedures might speed up a cantonisation or federation of the island. Geographical federation, after all, the Greek Cypriot side believed, was the ultimate aim of the Turkish side, and their suggestion 'to freeze the situation' could therefore be seen as a devious way in which that same objective could be achieved.

The second possibility, not very dissimilar in appearance from the first model but substantially different in political and legal implications, was the following: At an early date and as a first step a mutually satisfactory modus vivendi between the two communities could have been agreed upon, enabling them to resume their normal relations and making it possible for Cypriots of both communities to go about their normal daily occupations anywhere in the island in freedom and security. This would also have permitted the whole of the population to benefit from the economic development of the island, thus narrowing the gap in the economic levels of the two ethnic groups. With luck such an accommodation could become a springboard for the subsequent resolution of outstanding issues which in turn might open the way for a full constitutional settlement. With this model the existing situation would neither be legalised nor officially 'frozen', as would be the case with the previous one. Instead, there would be a regulated stage-by-stage advance towards a full constitutional settlement. Thus, as a first step, there would be (a) military deconfrontation, (b) a return of Turkish civil servants to their posts, (c) the opening up of the Turkish enclaves, and (d) the re-establishment of freedom of movement and conditions of normality in all parts of the island. Simultaneously, constitutional negotiations would take place and those agreements on specific issues that were successfully concluded (as with the legislature where, it will be recalled, complete accord had been reached by 1971) would forthwith be implemented. Eventually, a complete settlement might become possible, facilitated both by the restoration of everyday contacts between members of the two communities and by the hopefully successful operation of those parts of the new constitutional arrangements that had been put in motion. Such procedures aimed at normalisation had been proposed by Mr Clerides at a very early stage of the discussions but had been declared completely unacceptable by the Turkish side which throughout insisted on a complete constitutional settlement. The Turkish side might possibly have been willing to return to the 1960 constitution, at a later stage proceeding to an agreed modification of existing arrangements on the basis of this model, but even this is not clear. They would, it is clear, have accepted a return to the 1960 constitution with a restoration of all Turkish civil servants to their posts *plus the maintenance of the enclaves*, but this last point was naturally completely unacceptable to the Greek Cypriot side. Equally, it is not clear whether a return to the Zurich arrangements, even on a temporary basis and as an interim measure, would have been accepted by the Greek Cypriot side which had declared as early as 1963 its lack of confidence in their fairness and workability. Some other variations on this model may well have deserved serious study, but there is no evidence that they were actually considered. But what, for instance, if there was an immediate return to the non-contentious parts of the 1960 constitution plus the implementation of some reforms that had already been cheerfully accepted by the Turkish side, such as the reduction of their participation in the public service from 30 per cent to 20 per cent, to be followed by military deconfrontation, full re-establishment of communal relations and the holding of further constitutional talks for a complete overhauling of the 1960 constitution? This compromise course seems to combine elements that would have appealed to both sides without unduly jeopardising the long-term interests of either. But it may well have been thought that it was too complex and risky, and that in the troubled circumstances of Cyprus it could not be put into successful operation without great difficulty.

A third possibility, often suggested by the Greek Cypriot side, was a partial constitutional settlement. On this view, since some issues were not likely to cause difficulties and had not in the past proved unduly troublesome, why not come to 'agreement' on those issues and proceed with their 'piecemeal implementation' without prejudice as regards outstanding matters? Side by side with this procedure, there could be reciprocal gestures on the part of both communities that would bring about an easing of tension and would permit the negotiators to continue their talks in a better climate. But this approach too was rejected by the Turkish Cypriots who consistently declared themselves interested either in the implementation of a package deal incorporating agreement on all issues (including the question of guarantees) or alternatively in some kind of continuation (and legitimation) of the status quo. This clearly left only one option, namely negotiating and arriving at a complete constitutional and political agreement; and the 1968–1974 negotiations were accordingly directed to that end.

As regards the procedure and forum of the discussions, from 1963 onwards Archbishop Makarios had expressed strong opposition to the holding of multilateral talks among all the 'interested parties', namely the three guarantors and the two Cypriot sides, and this remained throughout fundamental Greek Cypriot doctrine. Insistence that the future of the island was an internal question, Greek Cypriot spokesmen were quick to point out, did not deny the 'international aspects' of the problem, primarily in the sense that vitally important principles of international law and of the UN charter were involved on the basis of which a solution should ideally be sought, but this was very different from accepting the Turkish position that a settlement should be determined by the guarantors or any other foreign states; and as concerns any concrete constitutional talks, the people of Cyprus and the legal government of the republic were the only ones who had a legitimate and direct interest and a consequential right of participation. On the other hand, as Archbishop Makarios had indicated to the UN mediator as early as 1965, he did not reject but accepted in principle bilateral talks with qualified representatives of the Turkish Cypriot minority but, as the Cypriot President had also stated on several occasions, these discussions should be limited to the question of minority rights, the principles of a unitary state and majority rule not being negotiable. Moreover, any negotiations to be undertaken would end abruptly if the Turkish Cypriots brought up proposals for partition or federation. The initial position of the Turkish Cypriots on the question of negotiations, as this was formulated after 1963, was substantially different.

The Turkish Cypriot community favoured constitutional talks among *all the parties* concerned for the purpose of discussing and settling the Cyprus problem. In his memorandum to the UN mediator of 22 February 1965 Vice-President Kutchuk stated that the Turkish Cypriot community was convinced that the Cyprus problem should be settled by peaceful means through negotiations among the interested parties, namely the Greek and Turkish communities and the three guarantor powers, and that it had neither refused to hold talks with those parties nor put forward any conditions before accepting to participate in them. As to bilateral talks between the two communities, the Turkish Cypriot leaders indicated to the UN mediator that they were willing to meet with the Greek Cypriots to discuss the day-to-day administration of the island but insisted that certain conditions should be met before such talks could be held. As a first precondition, they indicated that the constitutional order which had been disturbed should be restored and that any bilateral talks should take place in the institutions provided by the 1960 constitution, such as the Council of Ministers. Another precondition was that the balance of power prevailing before the December 1963 events should be re-established by the removal of the armed forces created and brought into the island by the Greek and Greek Cypriot sides since, as they stated, the Turkish Cypriots would refuse to negotiate under duress. Dr Kutchuk further stated that he had called upon the Greek Cypriot leaders to meet with their Turkish Cypriot counterparts in order to deal with the many day-to-day problems pending the finding of an agreed political solution, but the Greek Cypriot leaders had failed to respond to his appeals. In fact, Dr Kutchuk complained, the Greek Cypriot leaders were only prepared to meet with the Turkish Cypriot leadership as representatives of a minority, and this was completely unacceptable to them. The Turkish Cypriots, he concluded, could not be expected to abandon their 'status' and their 'rights' before sitting at the conference table.

It can now be seen that the holding of the talks in the format that was eventually chosen, namely direct negotiations between Greek and Turkish Cypriots on how to arrive at an agreed restructuring of the constitutional arrangements of Cyprus, with the assistance in the later stages of legal experts from Greece and Turkey, was a rough and at times uneasy but generally fair political compromise that departed from the initial doctrinal positions of both sides without irrevocably jeopardising the interests of either. Thus, as regards the Greek Cypriots, even though the Turks had for one reason or another departed from the constitutionally constituted organs of state and were in consequence looked upon as 'rebels', still, under the 1960 constitution, whose continued validity and existence were not in doubt, they were in the position of a distinct community, and negotiations with them, particularly in the framework of an independent, sovereign and unitary state, could not be construed either as an abdication of governmental responsibility or as recognition of the 'Turkish Cypriot administration' established in 1967. As regards the Turkish Cypriot side, it was true that the constitutional discussions were not taking place either in the context of the executive and legislative organs set up by the 1960 constitution or after a restoration of the governmental prerogatives they had previously enjoyed; but at the same time the intercommunal dialogue was conducted with the Greek Cypriots more or less on a basis of 'equality', its subject matter was not confined to the question of minority rights as wished by the Greek Cypriots, and most important of all the Turkish leadership had not been forced to dismantle the administrative structures they had organised after the 1963 events before negotiations could begin.

2. The 1974 model[1]

Despite the many complications and difficulties, very substantial constitutional progress was achieved at the intercommunal talks. This was of two kinds, progress with regard to the many particular and specific issues, and progress at the theoretical level. The former may best be gauged if a brief general survey is made of the most prominent features of the constitutional settlement that was emerging from the talks, particularly as compared with those features of the 1960 constitutional arrangements which they were intended to replace.

Under the proposed 1974 model legislative power would continue to be exercised by the House of Representatives which this time would be composed of Greek and Turkish representatives in proportion to their communities' respective populations. The representatives, unavoidably, would continue to be elected on separate electoral rolls but all three officers of the House would now be elected by all the members of the House jointly. The communal chambers would be abolished and all communal affairs (together with the supervision and coordination of agreed local affairs on the basis of standard laws to be enacted by the House as a whole) would be transferred to the two branches of the House. As regards the exercise of legislative power, the 'separate majorities' provisions of the 1960 constitution would be abolished. Instead, simple majority vote would reign supreme except for some cases where a special majority would be required, which, in very special circumstances, would have to include a specified number of Turkish members. If one compares

[1] In my book *Cyprus, In Search of a Constitution* (1976) I spoke of the 1973 model, but since, even though much of the constitutional progress was achieved during 1973, it was only in early 1974 that an actual agreement was almost finalised by the resolution of the last thorny problems in the area of local government, it seemed better to me in this book to speak of the 1974 model.

these arrangements with the 1960 provisions, it is demonstrable that great progress had been made in the direction of the simplification and liberalisation of legislative procedures. In particular, the exercise of legislative power was placed on a more rational footing, the element of bicommunalism, which previously had been the sole criterion of legislative composition and organisation, was considerably curbed, and the discharge of legislative authority would no longer be disfigured by the need for separate majorities or by the separate existence of wholly independent communal chambers. It goes without saying that the 1974 legislative model was still predicated to a substantial extent on communal criteria, but politically it could hardly have been otherwise; and, in important respects, the communal image of the state was significantly dented. Most important of all, there were no longer to be three independent legislative assemblies, i.e. the House and the two communal chambers, an arrangement that stood for communal partnership and divided loyalties, and represented a dualistic splintering of legislative power, or five assemblies, the three 1960 bodies plus two central authorities for local affairs, as originally proposed by the Turkish side. Instead, all legislative power would be exercised by one single assembly, even though this would have to separate into its Greek and Turkish parts when specific matters came up; and the House itself and the branches were now to be structured in such a way that in effect, both in appearance and in reality, the latter would be integral parts of the former. Thus, they would be presided over by the two Vice-Presidents, and, in the crucial area of local affairs, discharge of regulatory and supervisory powers could only be effected on the basis of general and uniform standard laws. Further, the fact that under the new arrangements all officers would be elected by the House as a whole should not be underestimated, as this was well calculated to promote and reinforce the unitary image of the legislature and make in the long run for a body of representatives conscious not exclusively or even primarily of narrow communal concerns but of the broader interests of the country as well.

Great progress was also visible in the restructuring of the executive. As has been seen, under the 1974 model executive power would belong to and be exercised by the President of the Republic, the Turkish Vice-President, and a Council of Ministers composed in proportion to population; the executive powers and functions of the President were to be considerably increased, those of the Vice-President correspondingly decreased, and their joint responsibilities so symbolic of principles of communal partnership similarly significantly curtailed; and as a result of these and other changes the main repository of executive power under the new regime was to be the Council of Ministers. These features of the 1974 model and the related proposed modifications of the 1960 constitution would have considerably improved the executive set-up of the state and facilitated the efficient discharge of executive functions, ensuring at the same time proper Turkish Cypriot participation on all executive organs.

A similar simplification and rationalisation is evident in the judiciary. The 1960 Supreme Constitutional Court and the High Court would have been abolished, and the Supreme Court that was to replace them was to be a unified court with adequate Turkish Cypriot participation and sufficient safeguards regarding the impartiality of its judgment. It was of course agreed that local (communal) magistrates would be added to state judicial organs, but it was finally accepted that they would be appointed not by the local authorities themselves but by the Supreme Council of Judicature. Another surely welcome result of a successful implementation of the 1974 model would have been a considerable strengthening of neutral jurisdictional criteria, and with time Article 159, providing for communal criteria, might well have fallen into complete disuse.

Local government was of course the main difference between the 1960 constitution and the 1974 model. As finally emerging, local government was neither the conventional decentralisation of authority that the Greek side initially proposed nor the completely autonomous and independent communal system that the Turkish side had at times insisted on. Both sides made considerable concessions. The Greek side accepted organisation of local government partly on communal criteria, the existence of two central organs of local administration, and adequate powers at local level. The Turkish side abandoned its idea of cohesive Turkish geographical areas, accepted that the two central organs should be constituent parts of the House of Representatives, resigned itself to the existence of substantial central controls on the discharge of local functions, and conceded that, in general, local legislative powers would be exercised on the basis of standard laws to be enacted by the state legislature as a whole. This scheme of local administration appears to be structurally sound, a fair political compromise between the parties, and a suitable response to the then realities of Cyprus.

But the progress achieved during the intercommunal talks was not limited to particular issues and matters of constitutional reconstruction. General progress was also achieved, in the sense that the views of the two sides on the overall settlement they were aiming at, or had resigned themselves to, had by 1973–4 come much closer to each other. It has been seen above that the demands and proposals of both sides underwent considerable changes and shifts of emphasis as their talks progressed, and it is equally true that the two negotiators did not at any time expressly take stock of what conceptual rapprochement had been effected as a result of specific constitutional advances, or of how much the theoretical gap in the Greek and Turkish Cypriot conceptions of the constitutional problem had narrowed. Nevertheless, both parties, perhaps without realising it at the time, moved considerably from their initial theoretical stands. Thus, the Greek Cypriot side, from insistence on a completely unitary state, both in appearance and substance, with, at most, proportional representation for the minority and a very limited degree of local government, came, by the end of the intercommunal dialogue, to adopt the principle of a unitary state with bicommunal participation and a very generous measure of communal local autonomy. Equally, the Turkish leadership, having abandoned or temporarily shelved the idea of a geographical federation which could only be brought about by a compulsory population exchange, embarked upon the negotiations with the objective of securing, or retaining, as much political autonomy for their community as possible. The two communities, according to these plans, would be given the right to organise themselves politically, something that would be effected by the addition of local governmental autonomy to their already entrenched communal status, and would, in addition to their own arrangements, be represented in a central government in proportion to their numerical strength. This would be a partnership state, or, as Mr Denktash called it during the third phase of the talks, 'a functional federative state'. There was, on all accounts, a substantial modification of Turkish views by, at the latest, early 1973. A functional federation was no longer insisted upon or even envisaged, the Turkish constitutional expert at the expanded discussions expressly told his Greek colleague. What was sought was 'a bicommunal state with adequate protection of communal rights'; and on other occasions it was apparently acknowledged that the state that was emerging and which the Turkish side was prepared to accept was 'a unitary bicommunal one with full recognition of communal autonomy'. Thus, during 1973, the views of the two sides on the nature of the state and the type of governmental system they were negotiating on and were ready to adopt came considerably closer to each other than at any other stage. 'A unitary state with bicommunal participation and adequate local government organised partly on communal criteria but compatible with state unity' was the Greek Cypriot basic principle upon which their later efforts were predicated. As to the Turkish Cypriot side, 'a unitary bicommunal state with communal and local autonomy' seems capable of adequately summarising their later views. It should be repeated that this conceptual rapprochement was mainly due to the impact on the general character of the emerging state of the many specific points of agreement and the noticeable narrowing of particular differences with regard to concrete issues of constitutional structuring rather than through a conscious attempt at a narrowing of the theoretical gap. Important differences of course remained almost at all times; yet the progress achieved should neither be denied nor belittled.

The general verdict can be no other. The 1974 model was constitutionally, both in its particular dispositions and arrangements and in its overall effect, much superior to the 1960 constitution. A settlement along these lines would have favoured, both constitutionally and politically, Greek and Turkish Cypriots alike. The Greek Cypriot side would have satisfied its demands, first expressed in 1963, for simplification and liberalisation of constitutional structures and procedures. It would have been able to point to a more unitary governmental structure and a more rational state appearance, and could have claimed with considerable justification that what had finally emerged from the negotiations of the preceding seven years was a workable and viable constitutional settlement based on the principles of an integral and unitary state with proportionate participation in government and an adequate degree of communal local administration integrated within the state and not incompatible with its unity and sovereignty. Likewise, in the event of a finalisation and implementation of the 1974 model, the Turkish side would have considerably improved its general constitutional position. As has been seen, the Turkish leadership had early on, even before the intercommunal dialogue, resigned itself to the inevitable abandonment of many of its 1960 super-privileges. The main problem, as they saw it, related to the way they would be replaced in the balance of power. Based to a considerable extent on communal criteria and held together by the supervisory and coordinating functions of the Greek and Turkish branches of the House of Representatives, local government seemed to be the most appropriate answer to the Turkish Cypriots' acknowledged needs for security and some independent and separate development. Thus, the Turkish side would no longer have to rely on the ineffective negative safeguards of the 1960 constitution, which had provoked the Greek side without affording the needed security, but, within the limits of the organic law and on the basis of standard laws to be enacted by the state legislature, would now be allowed to make regulations on a substantial number of recognisably local matters. Whether of course the new political and constitutional system would have worked would have depended, like all constitutions, on the goodwill of those who were to operate it and on the general political climate, both local and international. But what at least can be said in comparing the 1960 constitution with the 1974 model is that the latter stood a far better chance both to operate satisfactorily and to obtain the governmental cooperation of the two communities, in this way achieving their all-important political interaction.

3. *Why did the talks fail?*

Why did the intercommunal talks fail? It must first be pointed out that the word 'fail' must be used with qualification. The talks did not simply fail but were rather interrupted first by the Greek coup against the Cypriot government and then by the Turkish invasion. Further, as both the Greek Cypriot negotiator and the UN authorities have since made clear, if it was not for the events of July and August 1974 a complete constitutional settlement would before long have emerged. Yet in a sense the intercommunal dialogue did fail, and was not simply interrupted by events or frustrated by extraneous forces, in that agreement at that late stage had not yet been reached, and in that many opportunities for accord had been missed, despite the considerable narrowing of differences between the Greek and Turkish Cypriot sides. One can therefore legitimately talk of 'failure', in which case an investigation of its causes becomes necessary. It is possible of course to spend much time studying and analysing a political event or a diplomatic episode without ever fully locating the factors responsible for success or failure, or the proportions in which admitted factors operated and among which responsibility must be apportioned. 'It is hardly possible to measure in any precise way how much the ultimate outcome of any negotiation is attributable to general conditions, methods of negotiation, the initiatives or influence of third parties, or the flexibility of the governments directly involved.'[2] But it is none the less worthwhile to consider the record.[3]

The causes for the failure of the talks can be grouped under three headings, first the reluctance and insufficient motivation of the two Cypriot sides themselves, secondly the policies of the Greek and Turkish governments, which for the most part were inimical to a speedy agreement between the two Cyprus communities, and thirdly insufficient international support. To begin with, it has been observed above that both the Greek and the Turkish Cypriots had reasons for wishing the intercommunal negotiations to succeed and the constitutional conflict to be resolved. This in a sense is true. The Turkish Cypriots themselves had seriously suffered after the breakdown of the 1960 constitution and their withdrawal into the enclaves. Their prosperity had markedly declined between 1963 and 1968, in contrast to remarkable Greek Cypriot economic development, many young Turkish Cypriots were emigrating to Turkey, and it was furthermore clear that it would only be through some kind of political reintegration that their security could be permanently assured. The Greek Cypriots too were in favour of a constitutional settlement and political normalisation. Without them not only could economic prosperity itself prove ephemeral but also there would be a continuing danger of either Turkish intervention or a Greek coup. Yet at

[2] Campbell, *Successful Negotiation: Trieste 1954* (1976), at 145.
[3] See Polyviou, *Cyprus, In Search of a Constitution* (1976), 257–64.

the same time both the Greek and Turkish Cypriots thought that they had secured important gains in the aftermath of the 1963 constitutional breakdown as compared with the previously existing situation, which made it necessary both that any proposed constitutional arrangements could not be uncritically accepted but had to be looked at carefully and that these should in a way enshrine some of the 'gains' they now enjoyed. The Turkish Cypriots, whatever their loss of central governmental prerogatives, now lived in their 'own' areas and were 'in charge' of their 'own' affairs, as Mr Denktash often reminded Mr Clerides. A system of local administration should therefore be organised which would not only ensure that they would not again be completely dominated by the Greek Cypriots but also allow them to remain 'in control' of some areas of the island. Two other factors made the Turkish Cypriot leadership unwilling to compromise and inflexible in its demands, first the close proximity of Turkey, which promised speedy military assistance in the event of a new crisis, and secondly the increasing divisions within the Greek Cypriot side and in the relations between the Greek junta and the Makarios government, which made it increasingly likely that one day the Greek side would give the Turks what they really wanted – that is, the opportunity to invade and partition the island – on 'a silver plate'.[4]

The Greek Cypriot side too was not as flexible in its conduct of the intercommunal negotiations as might have been wished. This is due to five principal factors.[5] First, the Cypriot government, as Archbishop Makarios subsequently declared, was acutely aware that the Greek military regime was supporting subversive activities in Cyprus and would probably stage a military coup once an accommodation with the Turkish Cypriot side forever excluding union with Greece was reached. Direct and permanent renunciation of enosis, the Cypriot leadership believed, would spark off violent internal dissension, as a result of which either Greece or Turkey might intervene. Secondly, the Greek Cypriot side, ever since 1963, was in total control of the machinery of government, the republic of which it was now in sole charge was still recognised internationally, whereas the withdrawal of the Turkish Cypriots was widely looked upon as a rebellion against the legitimate state instigated by Turkey, and the inequitable 1960 constitution had in practice if not in theory been substantially modified. Its remarkable prosperity was for the Greek Cypriot side additional proof that without governmental or political fragmentation social and economic progress would be swift. It was therefore vital that the outcome of the intercommunal negotiations should be a unitary state with any system of

---

[4] This is what Ismet Inonu, the Turkish Premier, is reported to have told the UN mediator, Dr Plaza: see Markides, *The Rise and Fall of the Cyprus Republic* (1977), at 144.

[5] Markides, supra n.4, at 145 et seq.

local administration that would be recognised being compatible with this all-important unity. Thirdly, there was a strong Greek-Cypriot fear that if the Turkish side was allowed 'to govern' particular areas of the island, whether under a regime of reinforced local administration or under a system of communal autonomy, this would ensure a continuing Turkish military presence in the island, allowing Turkey to invade at will if future conditions allowed. This made the Greek Cypriot side suspicious of any proposal that was likely to result in Turkish Cypriots exercising any kind of territorial jurisdiction. Fourthly, it has already been seen how deep were the divisions within the Greek Cypriot community over the conduct of the talks and the goals of the Greek Cypriot side. At one extreme was the reactionary right still supporting enosis and for whom the very concept of an independent Cyprus was illegitimate. At the other extreme were those who argued that genuine non-aligned independence was incompatible with the concessions the Greek Cypriot side was making, that it was improper to conduct talks on the future of Cyprus in secrecy, and that not only the Turks but also Clerides himself who was considered too friendly to the West should not be trusted. This undermined the authority of the Greek Cypriot negotiator who on occasion would offer his resignation which he would then withdraw at Makarios' insistence. Other political parties took from time to time different positions on the intercommunal negotiations, sometimes supporting them and at other times expressing serious reservations. What of course all these divisions meant was that there could be no political consensus among the Greek Cypriots as to how best to approach the problem and therefore no agreed policy. Finally there was President Makarios' and the Cypriot government's rather equivocal and enigmatic stance. The official policy which indeed Makarios had brought in in 1968 over strong nationalist objections was that enosis was no longer feasible and could not therefore be pursued; but occasionally during the following years high-ranking government officials would make declarations reaffirming ultimate loyalty in enosis; and Makarios himself, as has been seen, refused to make a categorical statement forever ruling it out. Not surprisingly, the Turkish Cypriots regarded the official line of independence with suspicion, and at times argued that the talks could not continue, or at any rate succeed, unless enosis was ruled out in the most absolute fashion. One view is indeed that Makarios should have taken a more decisive line, that since he was the only one with the political power and charisma to break the impasse his statements to the effect that independence was now the goal were not enough, and that he should instead have made a forthright denunciation of enosis, taking at the same time effective measures to crush the disloyal opposition. On the other side it might be argued that, whatever Turkish Cypriot suspicions to the contrary, it was quite generally obvious that the Greek Cypriots, in view of the undeniable advantages of independent statehood and the demonstrable disadvantages of merger with Greece, had in fact definitely abandoned enosis, that since the agreed framework of the intercommunal talks was in fact sovereign independence yet another statement to the same effect would be meaningless, that a direct affirmation concerning enosis emanating from Makarios would be not only embarrassing but also fraught with serious political dangers both to him personally and to his government and would therefore in its likely internal disruption cause more harm to the negotiating process than if it were not made, that some equivocation on the part of Makarios was not only inevitable but in fact necessary if the complex edifice of domestic Greek Cypriot politics was to be held together, and that since the Cypriot leadership had no objections to Greece and Turkey renewing in the most explicit fashion 'the self-denying ordinance to which they put their hand when they signed the Treaty of Guarantee',[6] namely to support independence and never seek any other arrangement, no more could fairly or sensibly be asked of it. President Makarios' political problems and his apprehension, not entirely unfounded, that the Greek junta would attempt to overthrow him if he came to an accommodation with the Turkish side entailing permanent and explicit renunciation of enosis should not be underestimated. At the same time what cannot be denied is that, partly because of internal political problems and partly because of Makarios' perhaps inevitable (but in any case characteristic) equivocation, the intercommunal talks never obtained local support, and this in many international quarters cast doubt as to whether the policy the government was pursuing had passed the preliminary but essential hurdle of domestic acceptance.

Much has already been said about Greek political subversion and Turkish intransigence, and their adverse impact on the course of the intercommunal negotiations. The Greek junta was throughout hostile to Archbishop Makarios and did its best to undermine his authority, even in the early stages when its aim was not enosis but accommodation with Turkey under American auspices. Despite the issuing of routine proclamations supporting the procedure of the intercommunal talks, the Greek colonels were never in favour of a genuinely independent and sovereign republic, particularly if it was to remain under the Archbishop's rule, but much preferred either a weak partnership state or even a solution of outright partition that would destroy Makarios' authority and eliminate alleged communist infiltration and power in the island. Turkey too never saw the problem either as an ethnic conflict or as a constitutional crisis between Greek and Turkish Cypriots, but rather in the broader context of Graeco-Turkish relations and in terms of the wider regional balance of

[6] Kedourie. *The Cyprus Problem and its Solution* (1973) (An International Seminar Report), at 18.

power that made it vital, first that there should be no enosis, secondly that there should be a Turkish military presence in the island, and thirdly that any settlement finally emerging from the intercommunal dialogue should neither be inimical to Turkish strategic interests nor make impossible a future military invasion of the island. It was therefore important from the Turkish point of view both that the talks should continue, particularly since this aggravated further relations between the Cyprus and Greek governments, and that the military option should remain open, which in turn meant that the enforced separation of the two communities should continue and would only be allowed to break up if what appeared to be a 'satisfactory' system of reinforced local and communal autonomy ensuring and legitimising that very separation could be devised and put in its place. This was why Mr Denktash and the Turkish Cypriot leadership on the instructions of Ankara refused at all times to consider either an issue-by-issue implementation of the constitutional agreement, i.e. implementation of those items on which agreement had been reached without prejudice as to the rest, or a normalisation of relations by permitting freedom of movement and allowing Turkish Cypriots to engage in everyday relations with Greek Cypriots, steps that would have eased tension and facilitated an eventual settlement.

Something else that cannot be ignored in any survey of the causes and reasons why the intercommunal talks did not succeed is the fact that insufficient international support and assistance were extended to the negotiating efforts of the two communities. Instead of bona fide attempts to mediate between the two sides and assist their discussions with positive and constructive diplomatic initiatives, interested foreign powers either spasmodically attempted to impose pressure upon one side or the other to moderate its positions or make concessions, and more often than not this was the Greek Cypriot side, or schemed and engaged in behind the scenes contacts that in their overall effect exacerbated rather than reduced tension and made genuine compromise and accommodation even more difficult.

In this connection particularly important throughout were the policies pursued by Anglo-American circles. These favoured in principle the procedure of the intercommunal discussions, especially in the early stages when they seemed the only alternative to continuing confrontation and the eruption of open conflict, but did very little to assist positively in their successful conclusion. The basic reason for this was that the local talks were never regarded, particularly by successive American administrations, as the most promising procedure for the resolution of the Cyprus problem, which in terms of western strategic interests was viewed as a primarily bilateral issue that could only be 'settled' finally if Greece and Turkey reached a mutually satisfactory accommodation. American attitudes towards the intercommunal talks will be understood better when placed in the general context of the broad objectives of American and western policy-makers with regard to Cyprus, which, as stated earlier, are to ensure, first that the British military bases are not endangered and that the island does not come under communist domination, secondly that the communal conflict is contained and does not degenerate into a Graeco-Turkish war, and thirdly that any settlement that is reached is not inimical to their long-term interests. But American policy over Cyprus has been neither uniform nor monolithic. It can instead be viewed as falling into four distinct phases.[7] To begin with, between 1963 and 1967, American policy was based on two related elements, distrust of Archbishop Makarios for his alleged flirtations with the eastern bloc and the non-aligned, and adherence to the view that the best solution in terms of western interests in the eastern Mediterranean would be the elimination of independent Cyprus and either union with Greece, attended by territorial concessions to Turkey and the recognition of a Turkish military presence in the island, or some form of partition whereby the island would be divided between Greece and Turkey; and it was in pursuit of this broad policy that a number of unsuccessful diplomatic initiatives, such as the Acheson plan, aiming at the dissolution of the republic and its partition between Greece and Turkey were either initiated or encouraged, and that it was sought to establish some form of 'friendly' military presence in the island, first by proposing in 1963 and 1964 that US troops should be sent to Cyprus as part of a NATO peacekeeping force, which the Cypriot President unceremoniously rejected, and then by encouraging the despatch of Greek troops to the island which could one day either forcibly impose enosis or alternatively join with the Turks in toppling the Cyprus government and effecting partition. The crisis of November-December 1967 seems to have ushered in a new phase of American policy towards Cyprus. The State Department realised that the situation was still precarious, that it would be much more difficult if not impossible in the event of a new eruption of intercommunal violence in the island to avert a Graeco-Turkish war, that it was highly unlikely that Greece and Turkey would in the near future be able to come to an accommodation, that President Makarios, even though still 'difficult' and 'unreliable', was someone who had secured considerable international support and who therefore had to 'be lived with', and that for the time being at least it was best to discourage unilateral Greek and Turkish attempts to disturb the status quo and support both an independent Cyprus and the United Nations procedure of the intercommunal talks. But in late

---

[7] See Van Coufoudakis, 'United States foreign policy and the Cyprus question: a case study in Cold War diplomacy', in Couloumbis and Hicks, eds., *U.S. Foreign Policy Toward Greece and Cyprus: The Clash of Principle and Pragmatism* (Washington D.C.: The Center for Mediterranean Studies, 1975).

1970 and 1971 there was once more a shift back to older proposals envisaging a bilateral Graeco-Turkish understanding over Cyprus, which was to be reached in the absence of Makarios and his government, and an eventual partitioning of the island. Three considerations seem to have prompted this reappraisal, first the slow pace with which the inter-communal talks were proceeding and the view held by some American officials that the Greek Cypriot side was not sufficiently conciliatory over the issue of local autonomy, secondly continuing and indeed increasing suspicion of President Makarios and his links with the non-aligned, and thirdly the obvious fact that both the Greek junta and the Turkish government seemed equally impatient with the Archbishop and might therefore be 'favourably disposed' towards some kind of double enosis.[8] But American and NATO officials also realised that it was important to be cautious and not commit themselves directly and openly to what might be regarded as attempts 'to impose' a solution on Cyprus. It was not certain whether Greece and Turkey would be able to find enough common ground for an eventual compromise agreement, the Cyprus government and its mercurial leader were not to be underestimated, and if formal talks between Greece and Turkey were sanctioned and these failed the dangers of a new crisis would be increased. This was the thinking that led to the Lisbon meeting of June 1971 and subsequent informal contacts between Greek and Turkish officials. Even though there was no final agreement between the two sides United States policy makers were encouraged by the fact that some common ground was found; they therefore wanted direct Graeco-Turkish talks to continue. Makarios, it was now decided, should be left to Greece, and if he proved difficult or unaccommodating, it was the Greek government that should undertake to 'discipline' him.[9] But he was not to be overthrown. At the same time it would be desirable that it should be made clear to him (again by the Greek officials) that he should curb his non-aligned and 'pro-communist' activities and purge his administration of elements considered hostile to the west. In February 1972, as has been seen, Colonel Papadopoulos decided to show the American and Turkish governments that he could be trusted to assert control over Makarios; but his ultimatum was calmly defused by the Cypriot leader, the Greek junta was exposed as weak and clumsy, and it was again demonstrated that no settlement of the Cyprus problem would be possible without Makarios' approval. Once more the American State Department reverted to its 1968–1970 policy of grudging respect for the Archbishop and support for the intercommunal talks. But it was still widely believed that the intercommunal discussions would not of themselves yield a 'satisfactory' solution to the Cyprus

[8] Ibid.
[9] Ibid.

problem and that it was therefore important to encourage direct contacts between Greece and Turkey that might be particularly helpful in the event of a new crisis. Hence American intelligence operatives stationed in both Athens and Nicosia continued to maintain their own contacts with the junta, particularly with the change of the Greek regime in November 1973. During the early part of 1974 the gap between façade and reality in American policy widened further. In public the State Department still supported the efforts of the two communities to settle their differences via the intercommunal dialogue; moreover certain officials in the American government were strongly opposed to any attempt instigated from Athens to overthrow the Cyprus government, and tried to communicate their anxiety to the Secretary of State, Dr Kissinger, and, through the US Ambassador in Athens, to the Greek military regime. But these efforts failed, partly because of indifference, partly because of Dr Kissinger's preoccupation with other 'more pressing' matters, and partly because of unwillingness to antagonize the Greek junta, which the United States continued to support even more strongly during the second Nixon term. The two things which emerge are these: first, American policy over Cyprus fluctuated between the ideal and the practical,[10] the ideal being a comprehensive political accommodation that would eliminate independent Cyprus, effect partition and in this way irrevocably 'link the island to the western alliance'[11], while pursuit of the practical for most of this period indicated the need to come to terms with the reality of an independent Cyprus and the considerable international prestige and diplomatic dexterity of President Makarios, both of which precluded separatist solutions and demanded abstention from open intervention; and secondly, the inevitable result of the establishment, alongside the sanctioned procedure of the local talks, of an informal but direct Graeco-Turkish channel of communication under American auspices was that the intercommunal dialogue was exposed to the danger of becoming at best a temporary expedient intended to occupy the two sides until a comprehensive solution was found elsewhere and at worst a meaningless exercise in futility.

If it cannot be said that the attitude of the eastern bloc was more helpful, it was certainly less disruptive. Throughout this period high-sounding but characteristically vacuous declarations concerning the need to maintain inviolate the independence, sovereignty and non-alignment of the republic of Cyprus, and resolutely to protect its security and integrity from the machinations of Anglo-American and NATO circles, emanated with steady regularity from the Kremlin and its satellites. This attitude of course was so general and non-committal on all important points as to be

[10] Ibid.
[11] Mackenzie, *Cyprus: The Ideological Crucible* (Conflict Studies) (1972), at 19.

practically useless. The real interest of the Soviet Union during the period of the intercommunal discussions centred on the maintenance of Cypriot independence and the frustration of any plan that would, by destroying Cyprus' independence and annexing the island either to Greece or Turkey or both, bring Cyprus within the orbit of NATO and direct American influence. Russia never exhibited any interest in the substantive problems of constitutional planning and reconstruction provided that the constitutional negotiations and any other related discussions held under the auspices of the United Nations continued to be conducted within the broad framework of 'an independent and non-aligned Cyprus'.

Two conclusions emerge from what has just been said about the failure of the intercommunal talks. First, in view of the numerous problems which beset the intercommunal discussions and militated against their successful conclusion, particularly the fundamental divergence in the two communities' conception of Cyprus and its problem, the absence of any coherent theoretical framework of discussion, inadequate identification and analysis of some issues, insufficient encouragement and support from abroad, the suspicion and distrust in which the two sides were negotiating, the major complications represented by the intransigence of Turkey on the one hand and the continuous efforts of the Greek junta to subvert the Cyprus government on the other, and much else besides, it is nothing short of remarkable that there was what can only be described as an amazing narrowing of differences on virtually every issue which in its turn makes it almost certain that had it not been for the Greek coup and the Turkish invasion of July 1974 a complete agreement would have been concluded before long. This suggests that in involved situations such as the Cypriot one, heavily charged with ethnic suspicion and additionally complicated by big power politics and related strategic considerations, substantial progress can still be made not only (or even mainly) by tackling first principles or by trying to balance external influences but also by pragmatically attending to the arid details of constitutional reconstruction. If that more limited task is attended by success, and constitutional government can again operate more or less satisfactorily, then, despite continuing disagreement on first principles or unresolved tension in the broader strategic and international aspects of the problem, 'the pacificatory and calming influence of common economic endeavour' and 'ordinary social intercourse' may once more be made possible and facilitated,[12] with consequent beneficial results both in terms of the restoration of the body politic and in terms of an ultimate resolution of the underlying problems themselves, whether they be ethnic, social or political.

[12] Kedourie, supra, n.6, at 25.

But, and this is the second lesson of the failure of the intercommunal talks, it will be rare for this type of pragmatic exercise to succeed, particularly if the general political climate is not favourable to a negotiated settlement. In the ultimate analysis it is impossible either to consider (as a scholar) or to attempt to deal (as a statesman) with a particular dispute in isolation from its broader political and international context. It is of course very important to devise appropriate negotiating techniques, and then use them skilfully and with flexibility. But only if the general international conditions and the particular political circumstances are favourable can there be genuine success in the quest for a durable negotiated settlement.[13]

[13] Campbell, supra, n.2, at 158.

6

The Geneva Conference

1. *Coup and invasion*

It appears that sometime in June 1974 Brigadier Ioannides, the Greek junta leader, took a firm decision to assassinate Archbishop Makarios and overthrow his government, instal a puppet regime in its place, and then move by direct negotiation with the Turkish government (and as he no doubt hoped with American encouragement and approval) towards either union of Cyprus with Greece (with important concessions, possibly in the form of a military base, being made to Turkey) or a geographically federated Cyprus that would with time be partitioned between Greece and Turkey.[1] The news was apparently communicated to officials of the American government, misgivings were expressed in some circles of the State Department, but it does not appear that serious measures were taken to prevent what could easily be seen to be a potentially disastrous military operation against the Cyprus government. In any case Cyprus in June and July of 1974 was filled with rumours of an impending coup, terrorist activity in the island obviously supported by Greek officers intensified, and in addition evidence was now accumulating that Turkish and Turkish Cypriot forces were being put on a military alert, in expectation no doubt of what in many quarters was now regarded as an inevitable attempt by the Greek regime to overthrow Makarios that would at last provide Turkey with the long-awaited opportunity to invade the island. Finally on 2 July Archbishop Makarios decided to take the initiative by issuing a direct challenge to the Greek dictators. He wrote an open and extraordinarily audacious letter (which he made public on 6 July) to General Ghizikis, the Greek President, setting out in detail Greek subversive activity in Cyprus, accusing the Greek government of responsibility for the resulting situation, and demanding that Greek officers serving with the Cypriot National Guard should without delay be withdrawn from the island.

What prompted Archbishop Makarios to write this letter? One can only speculate. It may be that he made the cardinal mistake of assuming that the junta leaders possessed some rationality and that they would not attempt to

[1] See Stern, *The Wrong Horse: The Politics of Intervention and the Failure of American Diplomacy* (1977), 92–109; Polyviou, *Cyprus: In Search of a Constitution* (1976), 319 et seq.; Markides, *The Rise and Fall of the Cyprus Republic* (1977), 173 et seq.

overthrow him since a coup or even an attempt on his life would almost certainly be seized upon by the Turks as providing them with a reason for military intervention under the treaty of guarantee. On this theory, Makarios thought that when the junta received his letter they would either withdraw all Greek officers and sever diplomatic relations with him, or refuse to withdraw their officers and openly accuse him of being a traitor, or make no answer at all and intensify terrorist activity against him but without attempting a coup. Meanwhile he would gain time, expose the moral bankruptcy and criminal activities of the junta, and assume sole stewardship of efforts for a solution of the Cyprus problem. Alternatively, Archbishop Makarios wrote the letter precisely because he regarded a coup against him as inevitable and therefore wanted to alert international opinion and in particular draw the American government's attention to the imminence of a disastrous Greek military expedition, if possible enlisting their help and support in stopping it. According to this version the Cypriot President knew that some sections at least of the American government were becoming more and more embarrassed by the policies of the junta, and therefore wanted to bring matters to a head in a way that could well, or so he hoped, precipitate an open crisis in the relations between Athens and Washington. The Americans, he thought, would know if any coup against him was being planned and would almost certainly do their best to try and prevent it since if constitutional government in Cyprus were disturbed Turkey would be bound to invade, with catastrophic consequences for NATO and American strategic interests in the area. And if then the junta refused to fall into line, American support would be withdrawn and the Greek regime would not survive. Yet another explanation for the Makarios letter and its publication was that His Beatitude had information about serious disagreements and ever deepening discord among the members of the junta itself and therefore hoped, by forcing an open confrontation, to speed up its disintegration from within. It may therefore be that what Archbishop Makarios was aiming to do was to set in motion events that would provoke some members of the Greek government to take action against him; any rash action that would then be initiated by them would be resisted by others, with the result that there would be a power struggle within Greek military circles; and in any case any overt military move against him was certain to be stopped by the Americans who could surely anticipate the dangers to their own interests if that happened.

Whatever the true explanation of Makarios' action, there can be no doubt that it was a risky move, fraught with danger, and ultimately based on unsubstantiated assumptions, particularly about the rationality of the Greek junta and the likely response of American foreign policy first to an attempted Greek coup against him and secondly to a Turkish invasion of

Cyprus aiming to partition the island (an outcome that whatever its short-term problems might appeal as an ultimate solution to American strategists, as indeed it had done in the past).

On Monday morning, 15 July, troops and tanks under the direction of Greek military officers stormed the presidential palace. Archbishop Makarios escaped and sought temporary refuge abroad. The National Guard on the directions of the junta proceeded to announce the formation of a puppet government which, it was immediately apparent, did not enjoy any chance of international recognition, except possibly from the American government, even though it managed temporarily and through brutal force to liquidate open resistance and establish military control over the island. The Greek military coup met with universal condemnation, with the remarkable exception of the American government. In contrast to the strong declarations of support both for Archbishop Makarios and for the legitimate governmental order of Cyprus that were immediately issued by both European and other governments the American State Department first greeted the dramatic events of the coup and the reported assassination of Makarios with unseemly silence and then denied that there had actually been outside intervention in Cyprus, making an effort to present the Greek coup as a purely internal affair. On the day after the coup the State Department's press spokesman declared that, 'as of the moment', the question of recognition did not arise and indeed in response to a further question refused to acknowledge that Archbishop Makarios was still the legal President of Cyprus. The overall situation, it was also announced, was still being evaluated, and a decision as to which regime to accord recognition to would only be made when clearer reports arrived from the American embassy. At the same time it was widely reported in the press that the American administration was only too happy at the departure of Archbishop Makarios and would soon recognise the puppet government installed in his place. It is not clear why the American government and Dr Kissinger in particular behaved so irresponsibly during the early stages of the Cyprus conflict. Explanations range from essentially undocumented United States complicity in the attempted ousting of Makarios to a hardly plausible decision on the part of the Secretary of State that only through a passive American role could a Turkish invasion be averted. A more likely explanation may instead be that Dr Kissinger concluded immediately after the coup, if indeed not before it, that a Turkish invasion was inevitable and that any American pressure that was brought to bear on the Turks would be counterproductive in terms of wider American strategic interests. What is abundantly clear is that the early equivocation and hesitation of the American administration were interpreted by the Turkish government as signs that recognition of the new Cyprus regime was imminent, and that unless immediate military action was taken the stage might be set for eventual union of Cyprus with Greece. Turkish officials began to speak of military invasion and a geographical partitioning of Cyprus.

Meanwhile the American Under Secretary of State, Joseph Sisco, was sent to both Athens and Ankara in a futile effort to persuade the Greek and Turkish governments to begin some kind of dialogue. But it was made clear by the American government that it was not ready to exert pressure on either side.[2] In a note to the United Kingdom Turkey called for joint British-Turkish action under the treaty of guarantee, announcing that if this did not take place she would proceed unilaterally. Inconclusive conversations followed in London on 18 July between the Turkish Prime Minister and the British Foreign Secretary at which apparently Mr Callaghan pointed out that the Cypriot puppet regime could not survive but would inevitably fall from power (perhaps together with the Greek junta itself) and therefore asked Turkey not to embark on any military expedition against Cyprus that would exacerbate the already precarious situation and indeed almost certainly lead to a deterioration of the position of both Cypriot communities.

On 20 July 1974 Turkey invaded Cyprus, acting purportedly under the treaty of guarantee. It has been argued elsewhere and quite generally accepted that this treaty did not give such rights to Turkey, that Turkey was never motivated by a desire to re-establish constitutional legitimacy, and that in any case Turkish military operations in Cyprus, particularly as they subsequently unfolded, were in direct and flagrant violation both of the expressly declared purposes of the treaty and of applicable principles of international law.[3] Soon after the Turkish invasion of Cyprus the Greek junta and its Cyprus offshoot fell from power, and the Presidency of Cyprus was assumed by Mr Clerides, President of the House of Representatives, as Archbishop Makarios' constitutional successor under the 1960 constitution in the case of the latter's temporary absence.

On 22 July a ceasefire was negotiated between the two sides under UN auspices, but this was almost immediately disobeyed by the Turkish military forces which continued their operations. As a result the area under their control was considerably extended in the days that followed until on 30 July it essentially consisted of a rough triangle lying between the northern part of Nicosia and the Kyrenia coast, approximately six miles west and six miles east of the town.

On the invasion of Cyprus the Security Council, by its various resolutions and particularly by Resolution 353, 'deeply deploring the outbreak of violence and continued bloodshed, gravely concerned about the situation which led to a serious threat to international peace' and

[2] Stern, supra n.1, 116–24.

[3] See Polyviou, *Cyprus: The Tragedy and the Challenge* (1975), 55–94, and the *Report of the Commission of the Council of Europe on Human Rights in Cyprus 1974.*

'equally concerned about the necessity to restore the constitutional structure of the republic of Cyprus established and guaranteed by international agreements', called upon all states to respect the sovereignty, independence and territorial integrity of Cyprus; called upon all parties to cease all firing; demanded an immediate end to foreign military intervention; requested the withdrawal without delay from the republic of Cyprus of foreign military personnel, present otherwise than under the authority of international agreements; and called on Greece, Turkey and the UK 'to enter into negotiations without delay for the restoration of peace in the area and constitutional government in Cyprus'. In purported compliance with the last request, and 'having regard to the international agreements signed at Nicosia on 16 August 1960', the Foreign Ministers of Greece, Turkey, and the UK, 'deeply conscious of their responsibilities as regards the maintenance of the independence, territorial integrity and security of the republic of Cyprus', held discussions in Geneva from 25 to 30 July 1974. The result of their deliberations was the Geneva declaration which, briefly, provided the following: first, the ceasefire that had already been negotiated should be observed, hostile or offensive activities should cease, and the areas in the republic of Cyprus controlled by opposing armed forces on 30 July 1974 should not be extended; secondly, some urgent pacification and regularisation measures, namely the determination of a security zone, the evacuation of Turkish enclaves occupied by Greek or Greek Cypriot forces and the exchange of military personnel and civilians detained as a result of the recent hostilities, should be put into immediate effect; and, thirdly, further negotiations, as provided for in Resolution 353 of the Security Council (which itself was to be implemented in the shortest possible time), should be carried on with the least possible delay to secure '(a) the restoration of peace in the area, and (b) the reestablishment of constitutional government in Cyprus' (para.5). These further talks, the three Foreign Ministers concluded, should begin on 8 August 1974 at Geneva and should be attended, in addition to themselves, by representatives of the Greek Cypriot and Turkish Cypriot communities. Among the constitutional questions to be discussed was to be 'that of an immediate return to constitutional legitimacy, the Vice-President assuming the functions provided for under the 1960 constitution'. As a final observation the ministers noted the existence in practice in the republic of Cyprus of two autonomous administrations, that of the Greek Cypriot community and that of the Turkish Cypriot community, and, 'without any prejudice', agreed to consider 'the problems raised by their existence at their next meeting'.

Following this, the second Geneva conference was duly called. But meanwhile the Turkish armed forces in Cyprus continued to flout the original ceasefire which had been confirmed by the Geneva declaration, and this resulted in more and more territory coming under the control of the Turkish army. Further advances took place during the first week of August, important Greek Cypriot villages were first shelled and then occupied, all their inhabitants being made homeless, and already Turkish leaders were making bellicose statements, refusing to withdraw their forces despite the restoration of constitutional legitimacy and leaving no doubt that what they were really after was a geographical federal settlement based on the principle of complete political and governmental autonomy for both communities. Turkey's invasion forces were on the island with the rights and authority of a guarantor power, declared the Turkish Prime Minister on 28 July, and therefore their right both to remain there indefinitely and to receive additional reinforcements could not be questioned until 'the final and legitimate status for Cyprus was decided upon in a way satisfactory to Turkey'. Moreover time was running out and what the Turks envisaged as that 'final and legitimate status' had to be acceded to by the Greek Cypriots without delay. In the meantime, Mr Ecevit also made clear, Turkey would continue amassing troops and armaments in the northern part of the island and would take all necessary steps to secure her troops from the possibility of a surprise attack from the Greeks, including extending and reinforcing further the Kyrenia bridge-head. What was obviously happening, as political observers were pointing out, was that the Turkish government felt that the longer any talks or consultations went on the weaker its bargaining position would become as delay would give the new Greek government and the Greek Cypriot side time to recuperate diplomatically and militarily. Already the balance of international opinion was decisively swinging against Turkey – so blatant and undisguised had been her violations of the ceasefire and so excessive and needless the brutality of her troops – and calls were being made upon her to withdraw if not all at least the bulk of her troops from the island, allow the many thousands of refugees to go back, and moderate her demands at the forthcoming Geneva conference.[4] But all this had little effect. Only one day before the conference was due to begin the Turkish Foreign Secretary issued a veiled threat against Greece and the Greek Cypriots, saying that if the Geneva talks were not brought to a speedy and satisfactory conclusion 'Turkey would not be the one to suffer'. It was in these circumstances that the various delegations departed for Geneva.

2. *Preliminary consultations*

The two issues on which, it could easily be anticipated, the initial stages of the conference would revolve were, first, the implementation of the

[4] See *The Times* (London), 5 August 1974 (leading article).

Geneva declaration and the continuing violations of the ceasefire by the Turkish military forces, and, secondly, the basic approach of the conference, something that in turn was intimately connected both with the jurisdictional competence the conference would be recognised as having and with the substantive objectives of the interested parties, mainly the Turkish government and the Greek Cypriot side. As regards the former, the Turkish Foreign Secretary, despite the fact that on universal admission his side had refused to observe the ceasefire and had continued to occupy more territory, complained that the Greek Cypriots had refused to implement that section of the Geneva declaration which had demanded the evacuation of the Turkish enclaves occupied by Greek Cypriot forces and indicated that unless this took place immediately and without further consultations and unless Turkish and Turkish Cypriot security forces were allowed to return to these enclaves, wherever they might be, the Turkish government would forthwith withdraw from the conference and military operations would once more be resumed. The position the Greek Cypriot side took on this was that the Geneva declaration was not a one-sided document but had imposed reciprocal duties and obligations. Turkey herself had observed no part of her obligations, whether under the Geneva declaration or under the treaty of guarantee, military aggression was continuing, more and more Greek Cypriots were being expelled from their homes every day and being taken to Turkey as prisoners of war, and indeed those other measures which that very same section of the declaration had singled out as necessary for the maintenance of peace had not yet been effectuated as a result of Turkish unwillingness to do so. In those circumstances, how could it be demanded that it should be the Greek Cypriot side alone that should comply with the Geneva declaration? Further, it was obvious that 'return' of 'Turkish Cypriot security forces' which, by the way, was nowhere in so many words sanctioned in the declaration, might be used as the vehicle for the transportation to the various Turkish Cypriot areas of regular Turkish troops. Something else that worried the Greek Cypriots related to the safeguards, if any, concerning the security of Greek Cypriot villages adjacent to or near the Turkish enclaves whose evacuation was being demanded. Considerable intermingling of Greek and Turkish villages and other settlements was the standard pattern, and unless the UN peacekeeping force was allowed to play a full part, something which again the Turkish government was resisting, the uncontrolled return of 'Turkish Cypriot security forces' would pose grave danger to the Greek Cypriots of those areas. Finally, what was the meaning of the word 'enclaves'? The Greek Cypriot thesis was that 'enclaves' had a more or less settled meaning and that it referred to a number of Turkish Cypriot areas which became heavily populated after the 1963 events and had since been fortified by the Turkish Cypriot leadership. Not every Turkish village was an 'enclave'. This interpretation was disputed by the Turkish side, and in the provisional lists they gave of Turkish Cypriot enclaves they wanted evacuated a great number of ordinary Turkish villages were mentioned and it was demanded that the provisions of the Geneva declaration, as interpreted by the Turkish side, should apply to all. But, as events unfolded, the issue of the non-implementation of the Geneva declaration had no perceptible impact on the course of the conference as the Greek Cypriot side soon gave in and ordered the evacuation of most of the Turkish villages and areas the Turkish side insisted upon.

On the second issue, that of the general approach of the conference, the policy of the Greek Cypriot side, as this was communicated on arrival at Geneva both to the British Foreign Secretary, Mr Callaghan, and to the UN Secretary-General, Dr Waldheim, can be set out as follows: The essential thing was to take all necessary steps so that peace and order could return to the island. Constitutional legitimacy, which had admittedly been disturbed by the Greek coup, had already been restored by Mr Clerides' assumption of power in accordance with the provisions of the 1960 constitution. Furthermore, it was essential to return fully and immediately to the constitutional order of the 1960 settlement, the Vice-President, as was also provided by the Geneva declaration, assuming his functions thereunder. Thereafter, Mr Clerides told Mr Callaghan at their meeting of 9 August, he would begin (or rather continue) holding intercommunal discussions with Mr Denktash for the purpose of amending the 1960 constitution. This course was fully in line not only with the spirit and letter of the Geneva declaration but also with the 1960 constitution itself and in particular with the rights claimed by Turkey as a guarantor. Turkey, as a guarantor power, together with the other guarantors, could at the highest only claim the right to intervene in Cyprus in order to reestablish the political and legal order under the 1960 constitution but it could claim no right whatsoever of administration of any part of the area of the republic. In this respect the Greek Cypriot leader indicated the willingness of his side to accept (a) a time-limit within which to report on the progress of the intercommunal talks, and (b) UN or other supervision to ensure that the rights and security of the Turkish community were meanwhile protected and fully observed. Both Dr Waldheim and Mr Callaghan were in broad agreement with Mr Clerides and regarded his suggestions as constructive. Privately the Greek Cypriot side realised that the Turkish government would hardly accept such a course of action, not with the type of military presence they now had on the island, but the view was none the less taken that this had to be the opening negotiating position until further developments unfolded and international opinion was, it was hoped, given a chance to influence Turkish policy.

Particularly interesting was a further conversation between members of the Greek Cypriot delegation and the British Foreign Secretary. Captured Turkish military documents which had only reached Mr Clerides at Geneva made it obvious that the Turkish government had no intention of conducting serious negotiations but had already decided that unless its geographical plans were immediately accepted by the Greek Cypriots military operations would once more begin, such plans being thus implemented by force of arms. The British Foreign Secretary was taken aback with this revelation, admitted that he was by now totally exasperated with Turkish intransigence and bad faith, and told Mr Clerides that he would do what he could to help. He pointed out however that Britain was no longer a superpower, that it could not afford another Suez, and that therefore no 'dynamic' action on the part of the United Kingdom could be contemplated otherwise than in the context of either the UN or a general American initiative. This was a point he stressed repeatedly, even though he said that the British forces in Cyprus would be reinforced and put on alert. He also said that he was in constant communication with Dr Kissinger who was in close contact with Mr Ecevit, the Turkish Prime Minister, and that both he and the American Secretary of State would exert all possible diplomatic efforts to save the conference.

But this was already becoming increasingly doubtful in view of frequent Turkish and Turkish Cypriot statements, both before the Geneva conference and during its first days, that what the Turks were after was a political settlement on the basis of which they would secure a substantial Turkish Cypriot area under effective Turkish military control. Turkish and Turkish Cypriot leaders were already talking of the necessity for a rigidly defined federal structure, and even though it was unclear what precisely this meant, it seemed likely that what they had in mind was a totally separate geographical area from which Greek Cypriots would be forcibly excluded and into which Turkish Cypriots would be moved.

3. First session of the plenary conference (Saturday, 10 August)

First to speak at the plenary conference was the British Foreign Secretary, Mr Callaghan, who indicated the general nature of the problem and the issues to be dealt with. There were first various humanitarian questions, as to which no serious difficulty was anticipated, and secondly the constitutional one – namely, whether the conference could come up with an agreed declaration of principles as to the constitutional future of Cyprus.

Next to speak was the Turkish Foreign Secretary, Mr Gunes, whose opening statement was a short one. Cyprus, he said, was 'in need of a constitution', and it was for the Geneva conference to provide the constitution needed. The Acting President of Cyprus, Mr Clerides, disagreed but was none the less willing to deal with both possible lines of argument on the issue raised by Mr Gunes. He would first assume hypothetically that the Turkish Foreign Secretary was correct and that Cyprus indeed had no constitution. If so, one had to be set up. And how was one to go about this? The answer, in his view, was provided by the Geneva declaration. This in more than one place contained references to the 1960 constitution and the international agreements signed at Nicosia on 16 August 1960. Indeed, para. 5 contemplated an immediate return to constitutional legitimacy, 'the Vice-President assuming the functions provided for under the 1960 constitution'. So, on the hypothesis that Cyprus had no constitution, the Geneva declaration provided for a return to the 1960 one. As to the second issue mentioned in para. 5, namely 'the restoration of peace in the area', this, Mr Clerides continued, was primarily the duty of the constitutional government to be 'reestablished' under the declaration of Geneva. The constitutional government mentioned could only be one in the context of the 1960 constitution and should therefore be composed of Greeks and Turks, with a Greek President and a Turkish Vice-President, the latter having all his rights on foreign affairs and security, and it was this government which should have the primary responsibility of immediately undertaking to restore peace and order in the island. It was only when this was done that the question of a new constitutional settlement could be considered. But Mr Clerides was not prepared to accept that Cyprus had no constitution. In his view the 1960 constitution was still legally valid, and should immediately and fully be put into effect. He declared his readiness to return immediately to this constitution and set up a government with Mr Denktash, Mr Denktash assuming all his powers – including the power of veto. Thereafter he would hold negotiations with him for the purpose of revising the island's constitutional structure. This indeed was Turkey's only justification for the invasion of Cyprus; for, if the invasion was, as it was alleged, perpetrated under the treaty of guarantee, the restoration of the 1960 constitution was the only legitimate course. If Turkey did not accept this analysis, an effort was being made to impose a constitution on the people of Cyprus. This was beyond the powers of the guarantors, and would be strongly resisted by him. He was not prepared to negotiate at gun-point, and he would not give way before threats or intimidation.

Mr Callaghan then said that basically he agreed with what Mr Clerides had said. 'We have to be a little careful here because speaking for myself and the U.K. I do not think that we are entitled to propose amendments to the 1960 constitution. The republic of Cyprus is an independent republic; it is also a member of the Commonwealth, and although we were parties to the 1960 settlement, we do not dare or presume on that score to propose changes to the 1960 constitution.' It had been said that their task under the relevant Security Council Resolution and the Geneva declaration was to reestablish constitutional government in Cyprus. His own position on this could be expressed as follows: first, there was only one Cyprus constitution he knew of, the 1960 constitution, and, secondly, it was not for him to propose changes to this constitution. Full agreement therefore was expressed by Mr Callaghan with Mr Clerides' basic position. There had to be a return to the 1960 constitution and only then could talks begin with regard to amendments and an agreed revision of the republic's constitutional structure.

Mr Denktash spoke next. The position of Mr Clerides seemed to him untenable. For many years the Greeks had tried to destroy the 1960 constitution. There had been widespread harassment of the Turks and continuous efforts to unite the island with Greece. Underground organisations had been set up with the aim of destroying the Cyprus republic, and a coup had just been staged by the Greek junta with the same objective. 'Having done all the above', the Turkish Cypriot leader remarked, 'all that the Greek side could now think of was a return to the 1960 constitution'. This could not be accepted. If the only thing that the conference could do was the restoration of the 1960 constitution, nothing would be accomplished. Instead the game of enosis would continue being played, much time would be lost discussing amendments, and meanwhile discrimination against the Turks would continue. He had had enough of this game. The clock could not be turned back. Return to the 1960 constitution was impossible. This constitution had been shown to be ineffective in the past. In any case, why had it not been implemented before? It was too late to do so now. He himself took para. 5 of the Geneva declaration to be an invitation to the President and Vice-President of Cyprus, the constitutional government of which had been suffering for 11 years now and which had been functioning 'in its Greek and Turkish compartments', to come to a new agreed settlement. 'But we cannot go back to the 1960 constitution because the 1960 constitution has not protected us.' The problem of Cyprus was security, Mr Denktash said. This problem had not been solved in the past despite the arduous efforts of the two communities through the intercommunal negotiations. That problem had to be solved now. Further, the guarantor powers were there and they were involved in the Cyprus problem. Help was expected from them in finding a solution. And this solution had to be a geographic one. Two separate areas had to be demarcated where the two communities would be in charge of their own security. 'The two communities are the components of Cyprus. Both had co-founded Cyprus. Each would now feel safe and secure in its own area.'

Mr Clerides then spoke briefly of the suffering inflicted upon the Greek Cypriot community by the Turkish invasion. But he was not going to dwell for long on that. His purpose was not to play or recount tragedy. He was there to make suggestions and present his case; and his case was that there should be a return to the 1960 constitution consistently both with the constitution itself and the related international agreements under which Turkey had purportedly acted. The 1960 constitution, of course, as he would be the first to admit, did not satisfy in many respects. It was in important aspects not workable, and it should be amended and modified. But his position was not legalistic, as alleged by Mr Denktash. It rested on a most fundamental point. Were the guarantor powers going to assume a new role for themselves, the role of giving a new constitution to an independent and sovereign country? This is what Mr Denktash had invited them to do. He himself could not accept this. Had this been the purpose of the Geneva conference he would not have come to Geneva. He was of course not present when the Geneva declaration had been signed, but this was a document produced by the three guarantor powers pursuant to their right and duty to reestablish the Cypriot constitutional order. Constitutional order in Cyprus could only be reestablished by a return to the 1960 constitution. If this constitution did not give the necessary protection to the Turkish Cypriots, he was prepared to discuss this problem, but not at the Geneva conference. Any talks concerning amendments to this constitution had to be held between the two Cypriot sides themselves, and not the guarantors. But before he finished there was another matter he wanted to deal with. Mr Denktash had alleged that Greek Cypriot policy all along had been the destruction of the Cyprus state. The correct position, however, was that the intercommunal negotiations were taking place on the basis of an independent state and that the Greek Cypriot side had expressed willingness to have Cyprus' independence secured and guaranteed to the satisfaction of Turkey. It was of course a fact that could not be denied that certain elements of the Greek population had agitated for enosis and that these elements had even turned against the lawful government of the republic for the purpose of bringing this about, but, on the other hand, it was also common knowledge that secret organisations existed on the Turkish side for the purpose of producing partition. And if Mr Denktash accused Greek army officers of being implicated in the attempt of those unruly Greek Cypriot elements to bring about enosis, there were also clear examples of Turkish officers who had acted in a similar manner with the aim of partitioning the island and who had even spoken of Cyprus as already a part of Turkey. The position therefore was that there were elements in both communities which were pro-union with Greece and pro-union with Turkey. Neither Mr Denktash could deny what he had said about the Turks nor could he deny what had been said about the Greeks. A return now to the 1960 constitution would be the first step towards reestablishing the independence and sovereignty of Cyprus. From there on they could go on and consider what amendments were necessary to the Cyprus constitution so that both Mr Denktash could be happy about the security of his community and he could be happy about the security of the Greek Cypriots. But it could not be allowed for the Geneva conference to undertake the role of giving a constitution to the republic of Cyprus. This conference could only reestablish the 1960 constitutional order, any further discussions regarding constitutional reconstruction to take place between Greek and Turkish Cypriots. How these latter talks would be conducted could of course be discussed and settled at Geneva. He himself would be willing to have a time-limit put on these negotiations so that they would not drag on forever, and observers from the guarantor powers could attend, if they so wished, to ensure that a reasonable effort was being made to find a solution. But that the Geneva conference should decide the principles on which the Cyprus constitution was to be based was an untenable proposition, would signify an unjustified extension of the rights of the guarantors, and was therefore not acceptable to him.

Mr Gunes strongly objected to the suggestion of Mr Clerides concerning a return to the 1960 constitution. He did not think that this constitution existed. It was therefore impossible to return to it. The phrases used in the Geneva declaration, 'constitutional government' and 'constitutional legitimacy', signified something quite different, namely the independence, integrity and security of the republic of Cyprus as well as the existence of two autonomous communities. This, in his view, was the 'intent' of the Geneva declaration where it had been noted that there were two autonomous administrations in the island. What had to be discussed, therefore, was quite clear. This was a return to constitutional legitimacy and a reestablishment of constitutional government, not the restoration of the 1960 constitution. What was now the role of the three guarantor powers? It might be theoretically correct to say that the guarantors could not impose a constitution upon the republic of Cyprus. But it was important to avoid excessive legalism. Both the guarantors and the leaders of the two communities found themselves together at Geneva and it was vital that this opportunity should not be missed. The guarantors, Mr Gunes continued, were there to see whether agreement could be reached within the essential principles outlined above, namely the independence, integrity and security of the island as well as the existence of the two communities. The situation, once again, was as follows: 'The 1960 constitution does not exist. Secondly, the two communities should be able to agree with each other on a formula for the application of the principles concerning the legitimacy of Cyprus.' This might very well have to be some kind of geographical settlement. What was not possible was a restoration of the 1960 constitutional order.

Mr Clerides could not leave the above unanswered. The Foreign Minister of Turkey had expounded a long thesis to the effect that the 1960 constitution did not exist. He could not agree. This constitution existed because neither the Greek Cypriot side nor the Turkish Cypriots had abrogated it. It was true of course that it had not been implemented fully in the past because of abnormal political circumstances but partial implementation was not the same as abrogation. Another surely significant fact was that in the past the 1960 constitution had been accepted by all as valid and existing and all the negotiations that had been carried on until then had proceeded on the basis that amendments would be sought to that existing constitution. In any case, if the constitutional arrangements in issue did not exist for one reason or another, how could Turkey possibly justify her invasion which had allegedly taken place under the treaty of guarantee, an inseparable part of those very arrangements? As to the second point of Mr Gunes, that the declaration of Geneva did not intend a restoration of the 1960 constitution, Mr Clerides again could not agree. Para. 5(b) provided for the reestablishment of constitutional government in Cyprus. How else could one establish a constitutional government otherwise than on the basis of a constitution? And, in the case of Cyprus, what else was there other than the 1960 constitution? Reestablishment of constitutional government meant and presupposed the restoration of the 1960 constitution. Further, Mr Clerides observed, the way the position of the Vice-President and his specific powers, including the veto, were mentioned in the Geneva declaration was a clear intimation that what was envisaged was nothing but a full return to the 1960 constitutional order. Mr Denktash had made two additional points in opposition to his proposal. The Greek side, it was alleged, might drag on the negotiations. Well, he himself had proposed, and was proposing again, concrete ways of seeing that that did not happen. Time-limits, for instance, and a related duty to report could be adopted in this respect. The second issue raised by Mr Denktash concerned the security of the Turkish Cypriots. How could that be ensured, particularly during the course of any future constitutional negotiations? The 1960 constitutional order itself, Mr Clerides said, included a very important provision which went some way towards answering this. It was provided in Article 132 that in areas inhabited exclusively by members of one community all police duties would be discharged by officers of that community. 'If, therefore, we accept the principle that every Turkish village and every Greek village will be policed by police officers of the community to which the village belongs, and if we also accept that in the quarters of the towns inhabited exclusively by members of one community the same principle will apply, the security of both communities will be safeguarded to a great extent.' He was willing to enter into any other arrangements the guarantors viewed as essential for extending added protection to the Turkish Cypriots. .

Mr Mavros, the Greek Foreign Secretary, then presented to the conference the views of his government. He thought it was very important to clarify what was the legal basis of their presence there. Was it in their capacity as representatives of the guarantor states or was it in consequence of the use of force which they had witnessed in Cyprus? It was not the latter; nor was he there for the purpose of accepting the conditions and terms of a victorious commander. Neither he nor Greece were called upon to surrender. 'We must not forget that under the treaty of guarantee the guarantor powers have the right and even the duty to concern themselves only with the reestablishment of the constitutional order of Cyprus'. This could only be the 1960 constitution. He further knew that this was not perfect and that it had given considerable trouble in the past ten years. 'But it exists.' The guarantors could not impose upon or dictate to the republic of Cyprus either a specific constitutional settlement or even the holding of particular 'constitutional talks'. In his view, any revision of the constitutional order of Cyprus presupposed power as well as (a) revision procedures and (b) criteria for the revision to be undertaken. As regards revisional power, the guarantors had none. Exclusive power in this regard belonged to the two communities, the people of Cyprus. What about procedures for the necessary revision? Until recently intercommunal talks had been going on and these had yielded considerable progress. Did Turkey think that she could disregard this simply by invading? Mr Mavros, for his part, was ready to declare that the Greek government would gladly accept all the points on which agreement had been reached between Messrs Clerides and Denktash during the intercommunal discussions. If the revisional procedures had not worked satisfactorily in all respects, appropriate modifications could and should be made. And some initiatives from the guarantors might well be useful here, provided they were exercised in the proper manner and did not amount to imposition or dictation. As to the problem of the criteria for the constitutional revision that should be undertaken or continued, Mr Mavros was of the view that these were essentially two, 'first, the restoration of harmonious relations between the two communities, and, secondly, the sound functioning of the administration of the State'. Mr Mavros wanted to make himself clear. 'We cannot accept that the Turkish fait accompli should be the basis on which the problems of Cyprus are to be solved; especially, we cannot accept that the occupation of one part of the territory of a sovereign state should be included among the criteria that should influence the solution of the constitutional problem. The fundamental rule of the international order lays down that the revision of agreed solutions should only be accomplished through new agreements freely negotiated. We are ready to proceed in this manner and to give our full cooperation to the consideration of the constitutional problem along the lines I have just outlined'. The questions which therefore arose and could properly be dealt with by the conference were: (a) clarification of the question of the revision of the constitution and (b) the establishment of the procedures and the elucidation of the criteria that should be followed in this connection.

Mr Denktash would have none of the above. Many factors made return to the 1960 constitution impossible. As a result it was to the Geneva declaration that one had to look for guidance. This, the Turkish Cypriot leader went on, spoke of reestablishing constitutional government in Cyprus and of two autonomous administrations. So, probably, what was meant was that the meaning and import of 'reestablishing constitutional government' should be sought in the recognition it accorded to the two autonomous administrations. What about the offer of Mr Mavros to accept immediately and endorse all the results of the intercommunal talks? Things were different now, and therefore the Greek offer could not be accepted. When he and Mr Clerides had embarked on the intercommunal discussions, the 1967 crisis had just taken place and it seemed to him then that the Greek Cypriot leadership had for ever abandoned enosis. It had therefore been agreed that the Turks would give up their rights at governmental level in exchange for local autonomy. 'We were then situated all over Cyprus', Mr Denktash observed, 'and we had not sought a geographical basis to our existence because I thought that the 1967 crisis had proved to the Greek leadership that enosis was completely out of the question'. That belief, Mr Denktash now said, had proved erroneous. Enosis had not been abandoned. There were many statements on the part of many Greek leaders and the recent coup to prove it. Previous proposals and procedures had as a result been overtaken by events and what was now necessary was a fresh approach – a geographical approach. There was need for security and this security could only be provided by the creation of two geographic zones, one for the Greek community and the other for the Turkish. It was unrealistic to go back to the 1960 constitution. It was true that when the intercommunal talks had started, that constitution had been taken as the basis of the attempted constitutional reconstruction. But the problem now was full security for the Turkish Cypriot community. Only a geographical federation could guarantee that. 'I therefore say that a geographical basis must be put to our existence so that we may know that the security of that area is our responsibility.'

Mr Callaghan, at this point, tried to turn the discussion back to fundamentals. The main problem, it was agreed, was security. It seemed to him from what Mr Denktash had said that the main danger to security had come from adventurous Greek officers. These officers were now to be removed from the island. Further, there was readiness on the part of Mr Clerides to enter into any other arrangements that would achieve better security for the Turkish Cypriots. Why then have a geographical division? 'Or is there something I do not understand?'

Mr Denktash replied that it had not been only the adventurers from Greece who had endangered Turkish Cypriot security. It was the policy of the Greek Cypriot administration, he alleged, to harass Turkish Cypriots and deny them their rights. The Turks had been made to feel unwanted in Cyprus. It was not only the Greek officers but the Makarios government itself, Mr Denktash said, that worked for enosis; and this was a fanatical policy that had imperilled the Turkish community. But if this attitude was indeed fanatical, Mr Callaghan insisted, why did the Turkish Cypriot leadership believe that a geographical settlement of the type insisted upon would ensure greater security? It seemed to him that in the long run it would not. 'Fanaticism takes no notice of geographical considerations. Let us even suppose that you have your own armed forces. The Greek Cypriots would also have their own armed forces. Will one earn security that way?'

Mr Denktash answered that if the two communities had their own geographical areas, the Greek side would be unlikely to declare enosis for fear that the Turkish side might also declare partition. Further, it was only by the recognition of a cohesive Turkish zone in Cyprus that the two communities would become fully and irrevocably 'equal'.

In his final statement Mr Clerides first refuted Turkish allegations that Turkish Cypriots had in the past been harassed by the Cyprus government and driven from their villages, and then emphasised that he was not prepared to accept the creation of a 'purely Turkish area' because the aim behind this on the part of Turkey could not be other than the partitioning of Cyprus and the eventual annexation of that area to Turkey. Mr Denktash, Mr Clerides concluded, had spoken of 'security' for the Turkish Cypriots. What about security for the Greek Cypriots? The true position was that whereas Greek Cypriots were a majority on the island they were a small and defenceless minority in the strategically relevant area given Turkey's geographical proximity and military might. 'So, when one considers the general position of the area, it is clear that it is we who need protection from a territorial division of the island.'

Mr Callaghan once again turned to Mr Denktash and Mr Gunes. Was it not the case, he said, that what the Turkish side was in effect proposing was the creation of two different states within the island of Cyprus and, further, that this would turn the island into a refugee camp?

Mr Gunes retorted that it was not the Turkish intention to impose solutions on Cyprus; they only wanted to make some proposals and put forth certain views. He himself was of the opinion that the only solution would be the establishment of two regions for the two communities. Everything else had been tried, negotiations, conferences, talks. There had been nothing but crises. The time had come for a definite geographical solution to the Cyprus problem.

4. Plans and mediation

After the end of the first session of the conference a number of meetings and consultations took place between the various delegations in an effort to break the stalemate and see whether there could be some agreement on a declaration of principles concerning the political and constitutional reconstruction of Cyprus.

On the morning of Monday 12 August, at a meeting between Mr Clerides and the British Foreign Secretary, Mr Callaghan produced a draft proposal embodying the British views on the basis of which, he hoped, the conference could be adjourned. This proposal emphasised the need for 'a fundamental revision of the system of government of the republic of Cyprus' and stressed the necessity for ensuring 'conditions in which the Greek Cypriot and Turkish Cypriot communities can live together in the republic in peace with mutual trust and in full confidence that the security of each is safeguarded'. The English proposal went on to say that 'this revision should result in the establishment of a system based on the existence of two autonomous administrations within suitable boundaries, united under a central government'. The British Foreign Secretary made it clear that if agreement was reached on 'the matter of principle', then he would press for assurances regarding the orderly withdrawal of the Turkish forces from the island. Mr Callaghan indicated clearly that if the Greek Cypriot side accepted his proposal, then the Greek Cypriot delegation could count on the wholehearted support of Great Britain, and that all efforts would be made to ensure a return to peace and to safeguard the integrity of the republic. But, of course, he could not give any guarantees about Turkey's conduct. Mr Clerides took the view that this proposal was unacceptable. It was not possible to approve of a proposal which provided for 'two autonomous administrations within suitable boundaries'. 'Boundaries', despite its somewhat vague connotations, could only refer to a geographical division of the island and he had already made it clear that no such plan could be accepted. Was there a possibility however of producing something acceptable on the basis of an 'autonomy' clause? Autonomy itself was a peculiarly amorphous concept, but it was tentatively agreed that the objections of the Greek Cypriot side to the proposed British Declaration would be removed if, instead of 'two autonomous administrations within suitable boundaries', there was provision for 'a system of autonomy on certain matters' or some phrase concerning an integral state with bicommunal participation and adequate local government within administrative areas. The British Foreign Secretary expressed particular interest in this last idea. Would formulations such as 'a bicommunal integral state with provision for regional administration' or 'an integral state with provision for bicommunal regional government' be acceptable to the Greek Cypriot side? Mr Clerides made it clear that such formulations which did not envisage a geographical carving up of Cyprus could be considered seriously. What about the ideas of 'groupings of villages' and of 'areas'? These had been brought up during the intercommunal talks when they had not been regarded with favour by the Greek Cypriot side. But circumstances had now changed. If such concepts, Mr Clerides observed, were divested of the element of geographical cohesion that held out the spectre of partition, and if, further, provision was made for a distinction between regional/communal and state matters (only the former being within the jurisdiction of the communal administrations), the basis could be laid for a compromise approach to the problem that would go some way towards satisfying all concerned. Mr Callaghan was evidently impressed with this, and intimated that efforts would be made by the British side to produce a compromise formula along these lines. But these ideas proved to be of no avail since in the meantime the Turkish side absolutely rejected the British proposal and emphasised once more that only acceptance of a fully fledged system of geographical federation would meet their demands.

Next, at the suggestion of Mr Callaghan, a meeting took place between Mr Clerides, Mr Denktash and the British Foreign Secretary, and it was here that Mr Denktash put forward his proposals regarding the constitutional future of Cyprus. These proposals came to be known as the Attila I plan, and indeed details of it had already appeared in various newspapers. The Denktash proposals asked for 'a fundamental revision of the constitutional structure of the republic of Cyprus' and demanded that this revision should result in the establishment of a federal system of government based on the following elements: First, the republic should be an independent binational state 'composed of two federated states with full control and autonomy within their respective geographical boundaries', and, secondly, 'the area of the Turkish Cypriot federated state', should cover '34 per centum of the territory of the republic'. The Denktash plan also provided that, pending an agreement on the final constitutional structure of the republic, 'the two autonomous administrations should immediately take over the full administrative authority within their respective areas'. This proposal was of course unacceptable to the Greek Cypriot side and was immediately rejected by Mr Clerides. Mr Callaghan then made the following points in an apparent effort to narrow the gulf between the two sides:

(1) The basic problem was that of security. The achievement of security for both communities should be the paramount objective of all concerned.

(2) The idea of 'groupings of villages and/or areas' should be investigated.

(3) It was imperative that demilitarisation of the island should be an essential part of any settlement.

(4) Dr Kissinger was in close contact with him throughout and was in agreement with him. Other avenues should therefore be explored for breaking the deadlock.

At a private meeting with Mr Clerides that followed, Mr Callaghan commented on the absence until then of any concrete Greek Cypriot proposals. He did not disagree with the view put forward during the first session of the plenary conference that the guarantors had no competence to impose a constitution on the people of Cyprus. At the same time it would appear 'bad' if the Greek Cypriot delegation refused to submit any plans whatsoever. It was obvious to the Greek Cypriot side that there was some Anglo-American initiative to save the conference and it was clearly wrong not to give it the opportunity to manifest itself fully. It was therefore decided that Greek Cypriot constitutional proposals should be prepared but that these should be submitted directly to the Turkish Cypriot leadership, and not to the guarantors. Note was also taken of the fact that the British Foreign Secretary believed that the ideas of groupings of villages and administrative areas should be pursued further.

Later on, during the evening of Monday, 12 August, a new plan, the Gunes plan,[5] was informally communicated to the Greek and Greek Cypriot delegations. This was also leaked to the press at about the same time by the Turkish Foreign Secretary who indicated that it had to be accepted by the next plenary conference which he had himself called for 10.00 p.m. of that same night – because, as he put it, he had to be in Ankara

[5] It has since been told to me (in private conversation with Mr Arthur Hartman, the American Under Secretary of State, who attended the Geneva conference as an observer) that this Plan was only submitted at the conference after intense behind-the-scenes American pressure. On this version, developments seem to have been as follows: Turkey went to Geneva with the Denktash plan (the Attila plan). This of course was basically the old plan that had also been submitted to the 1964 London conference and had been proposed to Dr Plaza in 1965. When this plan was unequivocally rejected by the Greek Cypriot side, Turkey made preparations for immediate military intervention. Then Dr Kissinger exerted pressure on the Turkish government which finally accepted that alternative plans, of a cantonal nature, should be submitted. These plans were hastily prepared and leaked on Monday late afternoon. They were expressly declared to be non-negotiable and it was demanded that they should be accepted within a derisory time limit. And, during the second plenary session, Mr Denktash cleverly brought the discussion back to bizonal plans. All the above make it almost certain that the Turkish government had decided to submit the cantonal plans only for satisfying the Americans and not for the purpose of holding genuine negotiations on them.

the following day. The Gunes plan provided for the establishment of a Turkish Cypriot autonomous zone consisting of a main Turkish Cypriot district in the north of the island and five other smaller districts or cantons in other areas. The extent of this Turkish Cypriot autonomous zone would also be nearly 34 per cent of the republic's territory. The Gunes plan expressly provided for each administration to have 'entire control of its own area within its geographical boundaries'. The Gunes plan was open to substantially the same objections as the Denktash one, and the Greek and Greek Cypriot delegations were unanimous in agreeing that it could not possibly be considered, let alone accepted. Mr Clerides was at that point visited by members of the British delegation who informed him that there was intense diplomatic activity behind the scenes to save the conference and asked him not to make any statements rejecting the Turkish plan. Mr Callaghan's message to the Acting President was that 'it would be helpful' if the Greek Cypriot delegation agreed to the plenary conference being convened and suggested that Greek Cypriot proposals should immediately be drafted and that they should certainly contain, inter alia, the following elements: the need for a fundamental revision of the constitution; the need for cooperation between the two communities; the bicommunal character of the Cypriot state; some acceptance of the principle of communal autonomy; the existence of a central government; the recognition of Turkish groups of villages and areas of regional administration; the holding of discussions in Nicosia in order to set up a new constitutional structure; and the acceptance of a time limit within which to report on the progress of these local talks.

Following the suggestion of the British Foreign Secretary, Mr Clerides asked for a postponement of the conference until the next day, announcing at the same time that Greek Cypriot proposals on the constitutional reconstruction of Cyprus would then be given to Mr Denktash. These, as prepared during the night, provided that the constitutional order of Cyprus should retain its 'bicommunal character based on the coexistence of the Greek and Turkish communities within the framework of a sovereign, independent and integral republic'. Para. 3 went on to say that the coexistence of the two communities should be achieved 'in the context of institutional arrangements regarding an agreed allocation of powers and functions between the central government having competence over state affairs and the respective autonomous communal administrations exercising their powers on all other matters within areas to be established'; and in para. 5 it was stated that the Greek and Turkish communal administrations should exercise their powers and functions 'in areas consisting respectively of the purely Greek and Turkish villages and municipalities'. For the purposes of communal administration such villages and municipalities were to be grouped together by the respective communal authorities. For the same purpose mixed villages were to come under the communal authorities of the community to which the majority of their inhabitants belonged. In this way it became possible to mention and make provision for the concepts of communal autonomy and 'areas', without substantially deviating from the principles of an integral state. It was nowhere specified in the Greek Cypriot proposals precisely what matters would come within the ambit of communal administration but the line drawn between state matters and communal ones was intended to demonstrate that communal administration would be carefully delineated so as not to lead to the fragmentation of the state and the disintegration of central authority.

The Greek Cypriot side knew there was virtually no possibility of their proposals being seriously considered by the Turks. These of course made many concessions to the Turkish side; they recognised Turkish 'groups' of villages and Turkish administrative 'areas', and prominently mentioned 'bicommunality'. Yet, to judge from the Turkish proposals, nothing but a full geographical federation with almost complete communal separation would be acceptable; and definite reports were now coming through that Turkey was preparing to launch further military operations and had already ordered mobilisation of her forces. Captured Turkish documents made this only too obvious. Orders had already been given to advance and occupy much more territory 'when the conference fails'. In such circumstances, Mr Clerides emphasised, there should be no illusions about Turkish intentions. The Greek Foreign Secretary agreed with Mr Clerides' evaluation of the situation. He could see no way out of the impasse brought about by Turkish intransigence and blackmail. If Turkey attacked, and it was very likely that she would do this in view of the public pronouncements of the Turkish Foreign Secretary, and America continued in her passivity, then Greece would withdraw from NATO and adopt a different attitude towards the United States. As regards tactics, it was decided by the Greek and Greek Cypriot sides not to precipitate a crisis but let the Turkish side appear to be the one breaking up the conference. It was also resolved that as soon as the Turkish ultimatum was given, the Acting President should announce that the Cyprus government was bringing the matter before the UN. Despite increasing pessimism, Mr Clerides, on the morning of Tuesday, 13 August, attended a meeting with Mr Callaghan and Mr Mavros and submitted to the British Foreign Secretary the proposals of the Greek Cypriot delegation. Mr Callaghan then conveyed the following to him:

(a) He was in constant communication with Dr Kissinger. The American Secretary of State could not undertake to exert any 'further' pressure on Turkey in order to prevent a further expansion of the area under the control of the forces of occupation. America, Dr Kissinger said, was not even prepared to threaten a halt in American military aid to Turkey.

(b) Great Britain was prepared, with US support, or in the context of a concerted UN operation, to use her forces in Cyprus in order to check the feared Turkish advance but neither Dr Kissinger nor Dr Waldheim, Mr Callaghan reported, could promise such support.

(c) Mr Callaghan observed that the Greek Cypriot proposals were not 'enough' and could not possibly save the conference. If the conference were to fail, there would in all probability be further Turkish military operations and much bloodshed; and by now, he told Mr Clerides, he had no illusions about Turkish policy and plans. He himself (and Dr Kissinger agreed with him) thought that it was imperative to recognise the necessity for an area to be put under the control of the Turks – the Turks themselves preferred a solid, cohesive area rather than a number of cantons far removed from each other. The extent of this area was to be negotiable and the figures mentioned were between 20 per cent and 30 per cent. Mr Callaghan said that if the Greek Cypriot delegation were to agree to this proposal, both he and Dr Kissinger would undertake to exert great pressure on the Turks so that the area to be ceded would not exceed about 20–22 per cent of Cypriot territory. Mr Denktash seems also to have told him that the Turkish Cypriot side would be satisfied with an area considerably smaller than 34 per cent but it was not made clear whether the Turkish delegation under Mr Gunes were privy to this suggestion. This moreover had been an informal statement, Mr Denktash and Mr Gunes continuing to demand both in public and in private consultations with the Greek side an area of 34 per cent and making this demand non negotiable. Mr Callaghan repeated most emphatically that it was necessary to go beyond the Greek Cypriot proposals; approval should be given to the structuring of the state along the lines of a geographical federation. Nothing short of this would save the conference. Given such an initial step, the US and Great Britain would be prepared to guarantee both the extent of the area to be eventually ceded and the inviolability of the rest of Cypriot territory.

Mr Clerides' first reaction, as he informed the Greek Cypriot delegation later, was to reject all such proposals. But under the circumstances he thought that a different course should be followed. He knew that time was running out. He regarded further Turkish military action as inevitable and had no doubt that, whatever the possible support that might be obtained from elsewhere, great bloodshed and consequent misery would ensue. If the Turks were to implement the Attila I plan, something which seemed increasingly likely, then he estimated that the number of refugees would rise to 180,000, a staggering figure for Cyprus. Given these considerations, and after consultation with the Greek Foreign Secretary, the Cypriot Acting President decided to embark on the following steps. He and Mr Mavros would ask for an adjournment of between 36 and 48 hours during which they would first go to Athens for consultations with the Greek government; Mr Clerides would then go to Cyprus where he would seek the views of leaders of the Greek Cypriot community, a general meeting of whom would meanwhile be convened. Simultaneously, a member of the Greek Cypriot delegation would go to London to confer with Archbishop Makarios. In the light of all the views that would be collected a decision would then be taken as to whether a geographical solution should be accepted. But since it was very unlikely that Turkey could be held back, or that she would be satisfied with mere acceptance of a geographical basis for future constitutional arrangements (as opposed to unconditional acceptance of a strictly defined geographical system one of the two regions of which would come under the immediate control of the Turkish military forces), Mr Clerides also said that before going to Greece and Cyprus he intended to contact the Russian observer and ask for Soviet military assistance in the event of further Turkish aggression. If a limited Russian military presence could be established on the island then it was very unlikely that the Turkish forces would unthinkingly embark on fresh military operations. Further, the Greek government would be called upon to assist Cyprus militarily for the purpose of repelling aggression. It was not necessary, the Greek Cypriot delegation thought, for Greece to engage in a full scale war against Turkey. But if Greece could be induced to send e.g. some military aircraft to Cyprus, as was her right and indeed duty under the treaty of guarantee, the whole picture might change dramatically, for, faced with the prospect of war between its two NATO allies, the American government was likely to reconsider its position and make at last some meaningful effort to avert Turkish expansion in the island.

In accordance with this, Mr Clerides, before attending the plenary session of the conference, met the Russian observer Mr Victor Menin, and brought up the question of possible Soviet military assistance if Cyprus was attacked further. The Russian observer asked whether the Greek Cypriot delegation had considered all the possible repercussions of its request being accepted. The Acting President replied in the affirmative. The Russian observer further asked whether this request had been 'cleared' with the Americans, thus indicating that unilateral Russian military action in Cyprus was unlikely and that there may have been an 'understanding' with the United States ruling out unilateral military intervention on either side. The Russian observer said that he would bring up the Greek Cypriot request with the Soviet leadership. Nothing more was heard from that quarter.

5. *Second session of the plenary conference (Tuesday, 13 August)*

6.45 – 10.00 p.m.

After some discussion of preliminary matters, Mr Gunes immediately turned his attention to the 'substantive constitutional problem'. He demanded an immediate answer to the Turkish proposals. Would they be accepted or not? Mr Clerides suggested that it would be appropriate if the conference were to adjourn for 36–48 hours. He would then have time to go back and consult the people of Cyprus; he promised to return within 36 hours and bring with him definite answers. Meanwhile, committees would be set up to deal with the various humanitarian problems that had not yet been resolved. Both Mr Callaghan and Mr Mavros accepted Mr Clerides' proposal, but Mr Gunes absolutely refused to do so. The Turkish proposals, he said, were well known to everybody. There was need for an immediate answer. He could see no reason for an adjournment.

Mr Callaghan reminded the Turkish Foreign Secretary that if the conference, so far, had not yielded the results that people expected, this was entirely due to Turkish unreasonableness; time and time again Mr Gunes had engaged in dilatory tactics; time and time again he had asked for unnecessary adjournments. Mr Gunes, Mr Callaghan continued, had waited four whole days before he submitted his proposals. There had not been enough time to study them. Surely a short adjournment was justified, particularly when Acting President Clerides gave a firm commitment to be back within 48 hours with definite answers to the questions raised. Mr Mavros expressed total agreement with the views of the British Foreign Secretary. The Cypriot problem, he pointed out characteristically, was being discussed and fought over for at least 20 years. Would 48 more hours be too much?

In answer to a plea from Mr Denktash who stressed the need for security for both communities, Mr Callaghan made the following important statement. 'Why were the guarantors at Geneva?', he asked. The answer was simple. It was 'to restore constitutional order'. If the guarantors did not infringe the prohibition against the imposition of a constitution on the people of Cyprus, 'there was no harm in discussion'. Turkey must remember under what article of the treaty of guarantee its action had allegedly been taken. This was Article 4 and the sole aim of such intervention was the reestablishment of the state of affairs brought about by the 1960 constitution. Turkey could do no more. It was the same when one forgot 'the legal aridities of the situation' and went to 'the common sense element of the matter'. Britain could not agree with what the Turkish position effectively amounted to, namely that the guarantors could impose new constitutional solutions on the parties. It was true that today the island was the prisoner of the army; but Turkey should not forget, the Foreign Secretary warned, that 'tomorrow the army might be the prisoner of the island'. The English themselves had some experience of this. Both communities were on the verge of ruin. Failure here would solve nothing. He himself saw the need for some Turkish geographical zone, but he wanted further time to study the various proposals. So would Mr Clerides. It was monstrous, Mr Callaghan concluded, to dictate to him in such a matter. He was wholeheartedly in support of the adjournment requested. The diplomatic channels had not yet been exhausted.

Acting President Clerides agreed. But he wanted to say something more. He deprecated the conflict between the two communities. The settlement at Zurich was in large measure to blame for Cyprus' present troubles. It had, in a way, been imposed from above. It was therefore absolutely necessary for any new settlement not to be imposed in a similar way but to flow from the people, and it would be nothing short of disastrous for a new solution to be dictated to Cyprus. The people of Cyprus, he went on, had not been as proud of their sovereignty as they should. The sovereignty of an independent and integral state was not something that should be despised. Many mistakes, the Acting President continued, had been committed in the past. Not enough flexibility had been shown. The main Greek Cypriot mistake had been in not realising the need for greater understanding for the minority. If these mistakes were not going to be repeated, it was absolutely imperative that arrangements for the future should be freely acceded to. 'Otherwise there could be fighting for generations to come'. He was not, the Acting President concluded, at the present stage either accepting or rejecting anything. He was only asking for some time to return to Cyprus and hold consultations. Mr Mavros reported that the Greek delegation could not possibly accept any ultimatums or time limits. He had heard on Ankara radio that unless the Turkish demands were accepted the Turkish armies would renew their offensive. Was this true? Mr Gunes refused to accept that he was delivering an ultimatum; but he seemed to agree that Turkey had set a time limit within which a solution had to be found – and this was on the point of expiry.

10.20 p.m. – 12.50 a.m.

Mr Gunes analysed the various Turkish proposals. He believed that 'after the experience the island had lived through' a new constitutional structure was required. This new constitutional structure should make it possible for the two communities in the island to have zones or geographical regions where two independent administrations, a Greek administration and a Turkish administration, would function. Names were not important but 'to facilitate matters' he would call the system he was proposing 'a federal system'. Why was he proposing this federal solution? 'The whole of the experience accumulated to this date has shown the ineffectiveness of all the systems that have been devised in spite of good will'. No other system was viable. When he spoke of federalism, various questions arose. First of all, which would be the regions and what would be their extent? Secondly, what would be the various governmental competencies and the powers and prerogatives of the regional/federal administrations? Many difficult problems of detail would arise with the importation of federalism and these problems could be left to specialists and the like. But essential principles had to be agreed upon immediately. Mr Gunes proceeded to sketch out the Denktash (bizonal) plan and his own (the cantonal one). The two plans, he said, differed in some respects but were based on the same premises. There was no Cypriot nation but two nations within the island, and events had made a geographical separation inevitable. Indeed, this geographical separation would make both enosis and partition unlikely in as much as there would be a balance of fear and restraint. Mr Gunes then demanded immediate recognition (a) of a federal geographic system and (b) of 34 per cent of Cypriot territory being the approximate area of the Turkish zone. The final demarcation would depend on studies to be made in the future, but the problem of the actual and specific demarcation was not to be confused with 'a general rough fixing of areas and their size'. There was no ultimatum contained in his pronouncements, he insisted, but the final position was that contained in his latest proposals. The exact sizes of the cantons were negotiable. But the principle of geographical separation and the approximate extent of the Turkish regions were not.

At 11.05 p.m. a member of the British delegation approached Mr Clerides and said that at that very moment the American ambassador in Ankara was with the Turkish Prime Minister and that, given some concessions on the part of the Greek Cypriot delegation, the adjournment requested by the Greek Cypriots might still be possible. He hoped that the Greek Cypriot delegation would not reject the Gunes proposals out of hand but that its leader would 'go on talking' so that time would be gained. Mr Clerides naturally did as was suggested. He turned his attention to the Gunes plan. Most parts of it had been put forward as non negotiable. It was demanded of him that he should immediately accept the concept of geographical separation, the existence of completely autonomous Turkish authorities and that the extent of the Turkish Cypriot zone should be approximately 34 per cent of Cyprus territory. What was this but a flagrant attempt to impose a solution on the republic of Cyprus? But Mr Gunes was not only asking him to accept a geographical federation; he was asking him to do so without adequate information. What would the powers and functions of the autonomous administrations be? When would the Turkish forces be withdrawn? What would the population composition of the regions be? So, even Mr Gunes' assertion that his plan was known did not correspond to fact. Before the recent invasion of Cyprus, Mr Ecevit, the Turkish Prime Minister, had said that he did not have in mind a geographical solution involving an exchange of populations but that what he aimed for was increased autonomy and security for the Turkish community. So, the Acting President remarked, there had been a drastic change in Turkish plans. That is precisely why he wanted time to go back and consider the new developments.

At this point Dr Kissinger sent a message which was read to the conference by Mr Gunes. The Kissinger proclamation stressed the following points:

(a) The US had been playing an active role in the negotiations on Cyprus. Dr Kissinger had spoken four times by telephone to Mr Ecevit during the last 24 hours; he had also been in touch with Mr Callaghan, with Prime Minister Karamanlis and with the Cypriot leaders.

(b) The US believed that the position of the Turkish community required considerable improvement and protection.

(c) There was need for a greater degree of autonomy for them.

(d) The parties were 'negotiating on one or more Turkish autonomous areas'. (This, of course, was not a description of fact but rather what Dr Kissinger hoped the parties would start negotiations on).

(e) The avenues of diplomacy had not been exhausted and the United States would therefore consider a resort to military action unjustified.

Mr Gunes took this proclamation as support for his suggested plan. His proposals, he continued, had been communicated to many countries, the Community of Nine, the countries of NATO, and others. They were by now well known. No adjournment was justified. Further delay would make matters worse. The Cyprus problem would become 'a chronic disease'. He was prepared to stay in Geneva and continue negotiations *provided* Mr Clerides declared that he viewed his proposals 'with some sympathy', and he himself was convinced that this 'sympathy' was not theoretical but practical and genuine. As soon as such a declaration was made, further progress would be swift.

Mr Clerides, who spoke next, could not accept this. He first expressed surprise that Mr Gunes had discussed his plan with so many countries; but how could this be relevant? The attitude of the Turkish Foreign Secretary, the Acting President remarked, was that everybody had a right to know his plans but the Greek Cypriots. 'We are neither a colony of NATO nor of America'. The time when constitutions could be imposed was long past.

The fact that Mr Gunes had consulted others did not deprive him of his right to consult his people.

Mr Callaghan, again, strongly supported the request for an adjournment. The avenues of diplomacy, he said, had not yet been exhausted. Mr Gunes knew well that he was not unsympathetic to Mr Denktash's proposals. He urged, therefore, 'strongly, very strongly,' that an adjournment should be agreed to by the Turks. At this point there was an interesting development in the Turkish approach. Mr Denktash reverted once more to his own plan which contemplated one region. The pendulum was now swinging back to such a concept, he suggested, because one cohesive region would provide more security. Mr Clerides agreed that the fundamental problem was that of security. How could the security of both communities best be achieved? Security would not be improved by the establishment of a Turkish Cypriot zone. Would that be a fortified area or would it merely be an administrative line? Mr Denktash had implied that it would be the latter. In that case, how would you get increased protection? Was it worth moving people around (because considerable movement, whatever the Turkish statements on the point were, there would have to be) simply to create an artificial line? Why not investigate further, the Acting President asked, the question of administrative groupings and administrative areas? He was now making it clear that the Greek Cypriot side would willingly discuss both the recognition of administrative regions and regional patterns of decentralization of power. In any case at the present time he only wanted a short adjournment to go back to Cyprus for consultations. He would be back within 36–48 hours with definite answers.

When, again, Mr Gunes refused any such adjournment and, among other things, said that he suspected the motives of both the Greek Government and of the 'Greek Cypriot administration', Mr Callaghan, in a stern tone, castigated Turkish obduracy and warned Mr Gunes that it was futile to believe that he could get a solution by military means. 'You will only get a solution round the negotiating table', he said. Bloodshed would be the result of Turkish refusals to negotiate. What would happen if the Turks, as seemed increasingly likely, broke up the conference? There would be many unanswered questions; there would almost certainly be a resort to force. Mr Clerides' attitude, Mr Callaghan continued, was a positive one. What the Cypriot Acting President had said should be put on record. Mr Clerides had accepted:

(a) that the 1960 constitution was unworkable and demanded fundamental revision;

(b) that considerable autonomy should be recognised for both communities; and

(c) that the Cypriot state should be a bicommunal one.

This was a major step, Mr Callaghan concluded. It should be put on record that this was the position of the Greek Cypriot side and that all other parties, with the exception of Mr Gunes, were prepared to grant the adjournment requested. The Turkish Foreign Secretary should be aware that it was he who was breaking up the conference.

Again, Mr Gunes would not be moved. The Greek Cypriot delegation had to accept his terms now. If not, he would consider that diplomatic means had failed. And then what?

Mr Clerides, at this point, emphasised once more, and in strong terms, his refusal to bow to pressure. 'I refuse to be cornered. I will not succumb to pressure'. Mr Gunes was trying, as he had done all along, to intimidate and pressurise him. Well, this was his answer. He would refuse to negotiate at gun point. He would not give in.

At 1.40 a.m. a short adjournment was called, and a last effort was made by Mr Callaghan to save the conference. By this time information had come to the Greek side from the British delegation that the Turkish army was already preparing to move and would certainly do so unless agreement was reached. With the approval of Dr Kissinger, the British Foreign Secretary asked Mr Clerides to sign a statement that he would go back to Cyprus for the purpose of 'favourably considering' the concept of geographical separation. Mr Clerides was not prepared to go that far. The maximum he would do, he informed Mr Callaghan, was to agree to go back to Cyprus in order to consider 'carefully and with an open mind' the various proposals. This was then communicated to the conference, but Mr Gunes did not think that this was a positive reply. There had to be some acceptance of his plan. Nothing else was good enough. Mr Clerides had to accept his plan that very night.

The last moments of the conference were tense. Mr Callaghan could not agree that the Greek Cypriot reply was negative. 'Mr Clerides has said that he is prepared to consider carefully and with an open mind the Turkish proposals and give a reply in 48 hours. Mr Clerides is using the English language, which I know, and "open mind" means that you have no fixed prejudices against an idea. It means that you are ready to consider it on its merits'. That, in diplomacy, was a positive response.

Mr Mavros: 'I have made my position clear. We do not have a right as guarantors to impose a constitution on Cyprus. The two communities must themselves agree on this.' He would come back to the conference as requested by Mr Callaghan.

Mr Callaghan: 'Mr Gunes, I would like an answer. Are you ready to come back on Thursday morning?'

Mr Gunes: 'I consider that I have had a negative answer to my proposals. Accordingly, I am unable to agree to a continuation of the conference'.

Mr Callaghan: 'I do not agree. I do not think that you have had a negative answer to your proposals. If somebody says "I will consider carefully and with an open mind something", that is no negative answer.' Mr Gunes remained silent.

Mr Clerides: 'I have nothing more to say except what I have said from the beginning. I have said that I was prepared to examine with an open mind every possible solution. I was only given the Gunes proposals very late last night. He also made certain parts of his proposals non negotiable. Am I now to take it that Mr Gunes is saying that this conference has failed because I have asked for 48 hours to consider his proposals? I am directing my question to Mr Gunes. Is he declaring that the conference has failed because one of the parties sitting here has asked for 48 hours to consider with an open mind his proposals? If so, I want his answer recorded'.

Mr Gunes: 'No. It is because Mr Clerides has been continuously asking for further "48 hours" and it is also because the UK cannot provide any guarantee or improve the confidence of the Turkish government'. There could be no adjournment, there could be no delay, there could be no further negotiation. Acceptance of his plan was the only solution.

Mr Clerides: 'I have only asked for one adjournment while Mr Gunes has repeatedly asked for many so that he could consult his Council of Ministers, etc. I have attended all the sessions of the conference. Mr Gunes only sent his proposals to us yesterday. I asked for the adjournment some time ago but we have been kept waiting till now for an answer. Delaying tactics have been used by Mr Gunes and not by myself.'

Before the conference finally broke up, Mr Clerides asked a final question of the British Foreign Secretary. What would Great Britain's position be if the Turks began, if they had not already done so, military operations? Would they take any action to protect the integrity of Cyprus or would they sit back and tolerate the dismemberment of a sovereign state whose independence they had guaranteed? Mr Callaghan answered that he deprecated strongly any resumption of hostilities. In his view the diplomatic avenues had not yet been exhausted. As to the question of military operations, Britain had offered to put her troops at the disposal of the UN. More than that Great Britain could not do.

At 2.45 a.m. Mr Callaghan asked again: 'Will my colleagues return to the conference on Thursday morning?'

Mr Clerides: 'I am willing to return to this conference on Thursday morning.'

Mr Mavros: 'I am prepared to return.'

Mr Callaghan: 'I am prepared to return, too.'

Mr Denktash: 'I would like to say that if Turkey comes, I will come.'

Mr Gunes stayed silent.

Mr Callaghan: 'This is the reality of facts. The three of us are prepared to come. The fourth will come if Turkey comes. It does not seem likely that the Turkish side will be coming.'

The conference broke up at approximately 3.00 a.m. The Turkish forces began military operations, including the bombing of towns, at 4.30 a.m.[6]

6. *Evaluation*

In retrospect the Geneva conference was always doomed to failure. It had been preceded by war, no serious diplomatic preparation aimed at narrowing the differences between the parties had taken place before it was called, the American administration was at this time experiencing the last convulsions of the Watergate scandal and was either unable or unwilling to act decisively, and the British Foreign Secretary, despite his belated appreciation of the fact that what the Turks wanted was not to negotiate but rather to break up the conference and occupy all of northern Cyprus, was not strong enough to influence events. Most important of all, at the time of the conference the Turks were enjoying overwhelming military superiority on the ground and were not prepared to come to any agreement unless this reflected the political and strategic advantage which they had obtained in consequence of their invasion. In short, the Geneva conference failed not because of its unclear legal and constitutional framework but mainly because of Turkey's preconceived decisions and tactics on the one hand and the ineffectiveness of western powers in exerting pressure on the Turkish government on the other. This does not mean that it does not deserve careful study. In this connection two levels

[6]On its way back to Cyprus from Geneva the Greek Cypriot delegation met with the Premier of Greece, Mr Karamanlis. At that time the Turkish forces were on the move, Turkish aircraft were mercilessly bombing towns and villages, and 200,000 Greek Cypriots were being expelled from their homes and driven into the remaining Greek areas. Naturally Greek military assistance to Cyprus was requested. Indeed, under the Treaty of Guarantee, Greece, together with Great Britain, was under a legal obligation to take all necessary measures for the protection of the independence and security of Cyprus. As is well known, no military assistance was sent. What apparently happened was that Prime Minister Karamanlis, as soon as military operations began, was in favour of dispatching to Cyprus some military support, e.g. a small number of military aircraft, which would, if nothing else, encourage the Greek Cypriots in their desperate struggle against insuperable odds and possibly bring the American government into the picture. The Greek armed forces however were discovered to be in such an appalling condition in consequence of the disastrous dictatorial mismanagement of the preceding seven years that even this limited exertion was beyond their power; and it was felt that even a limited engagement might encourage, or even give the pretext to, the Turkish government to launch an all out offensive against Greece. Indeed, it was apparently the heads of the military services who 'overruled' (by pointing out its impossibility and its very likely prejudicial consequences) the Karamanlis decision to send some token military assistance to Cyprus.

have to be distinguished – the jurisdictional and constitutional level, and the political one.

(a) *Jurisdictional and constitutional aspects*

What, first of all, was the competence and the precise duties of the Geneva conference? There was of course general agreement that it was a conference of the guarantors, attended, in addition to the three Foreign Secretaries of the guarantor powers, by representatives of the two communities; but various versions regarding its competence and duties were canvassed.

The Turkish Foreign Secretary suggested at the very beginning of the conference that it was for the guarantors to give a constitution to Cyprus. He soon modified this position in deference to strong British objections. He then maintained that he was there not in order to impose a solution but only in order to 'assist' the two communities in their efforts to solve the constitutional problem. But, anyway, the conference was not limited to the restoration of the 1960 constitution as alleged by the Greek Cypriot side. A new constitution or at least a fundamental elaboration of 'existing constitutional principles' had to be produced, and it was for the Geneva conference to provide what was needed. Positive 'assistance' in this respect should be offered to the two communities. Indeed, the lead should be taken by the guarantors and Greek and Turkish Cypriots should be asked to accept what the guarantors came up with. At the end of course all pretence was abandoned. Turkish constitutional plans were produced and it was demanded of the Greek Cypriot leadership that it should accept them without delay.

A slightly different thesis explicitly premised upon what the Turkish Cypriot leader regarded as the political realities of the situation was advanced by Mr Denktash. He did not really see the problem in terms of legal obligations and rights accruing from a treaty. Cypriots were Greeks and Turks and therefore had to rely in moments of difficulty on Greece and Turkey. 'I am a Turk in Cyprus and I know', he said during the second session of the conference, 'that without Turkish help I cannot stand on my legs; I cannot defend myself. Mr Clerides knows, as he has also said, that, without the active diplomatic help of Greece, Greek Cypriots are in the relevant strategic area a very small minority.' What existed was 'a double parenthood' and from this the two communities could benefit. The initiative had to come from Greece and Turkey (assisted, perhaps, by Great Britain), and the two communities should follow.

At the outset of the conference Mr Clerides made his position very clear. Cyprus was an independent republic. No constitution could be given to it without its peoples' wishes and the guarantors had no competence to consider any constitutional matter other than immediate return to the order that had been disturbed, namely the 1960 constitution. In consequence of insistent British persuasion a somewhat milder thesis regarding the conference's competence was advanced by Mr Clerides during the second session. The republic of Cyprus was an independent sovereign republic, he said, and no one could impose a constitutional solution upon it, but if what was to take place was 'a discussion in an effort to help finding a solution, then, obviously, if that discussion (was) to be done in good faith, nobody (could) object to its taking place'. And by the end of the conference the Greek Cypriot delegation not surprisingly came round to the view that, whatever the correct legal position, Turkish and British insistence on agreed principles regarding the constitutional future of Cyprus could no longer be resisted. But any such statement or declaration should preferably be issued by Messrs Clerides and Denktash rather than by the guarantors themselves.

Mr Callaghan, as appears from the exchanges set out above, had strong views regarding the jurisdiction and competence of the conference. He had 'a clear answer' to these problems, he said at one point. 'Cyprus is a sovereign republic and a member of the United Nations and the Commonwealth. We are here (both) as guarantors and pursuant to Resolution 353 of the Security Council. Both Resolution 353 and the declaration of Geneva call for negotiations for the restoration of constitutional government in Cyprus.' This was also the guarantors' duty under the treaty. They could not impose a new settlement; but they could exchange views, put forward suggestions and help the representatives of the two communities. Further, 'a basis' perhaps could be reached as to the future constitutional reconstruction of Cyprus in the context of the Geneva conference, Mr Callaghan suggested, provided that 'the constitutional position of Cyprus as an independent republic' was not infringed.

Closely related to the competence and duties of the Geneva conference were the two issues of the continued validity of the 1960 constitution and of the precise impact upon it of the Geneva declaration.

The first question was that of the 'existing' constitutional structure of the republic. Cyprus clearly had a constitution and this could be none other than the 1960 constitution, the Greek Cypriot, Greek and British delegations maintained. The 1960 constitution had not been abrogated, Mr Clerides pointed out; so it existed. It was true that it had not been possible to apply this constitution fully and that the courts had qualified it by the doctrine of necessity. But this did not mean that it did not exist or that it had lost its validity. Conscientious efforts to implement it fully had been made but as a result of abnormal political circumstances these did not succeed. Indeed, as Mr Clerides pointed out, how could Turkey invoke the treaty of guarantee, an integral part of the 1960 constitution, in attempted justification of its military intervention, and, at the same time, as had been the case with Mr Gunes, declare the non-existence of this constitution? The only possible way Turkey could proceed in attempting to justify the invasion was, first, by upholding the validity of the existing constitutional arrangements and, secondly, by proceeding to a restoration of the allegedly disturbed 1960 constitution by, among other things, consenting to its immediate reactivation and the phased withdrawal from the island of Turkish troops. Likewise, and on precisely the same arguments, Turkish forces in Cyprus should not interfere with the administration of the area over which they gained temporary control; the maximum they could claim was a limited and strictly temporary presence in order to ensure that the 1960 constitutional order was being reestablished and that the rights of the Turkish community under this constitution were being observed.

The Turkish dilemma on this issue was precisely the one set out by Mr Clerides. Turkish policy was based on two apparently contradictory points, first, that there was no constitution and that therefore a new one had to be set up, and, secondly, that the invasion of Cyprus was legal. But if one thing was clear, it was that the invasion could only be legal under the 1960 constitutional arrangements which were now alleged not to exist. Mr Gunes now proposed a new constitutional theory for reconciling these conflicting positions. The 1960 constitution, he said, was dead. This was because this constitution had ceased to be applied. What had to be reestablished was constitutional government and constitutional legitimacy, not the 1960 constitution. Cyprus, he admitted, was still an independent country but its constitutional structure was a peculiar one, consisting only of what he regarded as the most fundamental of principles, such as the independence and sovereignty of the republic, on the one hand, and the autonomous existence and functioning of the two communities, on the other. How did these principles exist? The answer of Mr Gunes seemed to be either that those principles were the only surviving elements of the Zurich constitutional arrangements or, alternatively, that the 1960 constitution had met with complete extinction, but not before transmitting to Cypriot society the 'fundamental' principles on which it was based and which now formed the foundation stone of Turkish policy. For it was the 1960 constitution that had recognised the 'partnership status' of the Turkish community and therefore a way had to be found whereby that 'recognition' would survive the general constitutional demise now suggested. In effect, according to the Turkish side, the events of 1963, the resulting separation of the two communities and the consequent establishment of the 'Turkish Cypriot administration' had brought about the disintegration of central government authority and the irrevocable division of the state into its two component parts, namely the two communities. What was now called for was the recognition and establishment of a completely new system of government based on a rigid geographical federation.

There was equal divergence of view with regard to the Geneva declaration. Turkey regarded it as a fundamental constitutional and political document which extended recognition both to the autonomous status of the Turkish Cypriot administration and to the new military and political 'realities'. The republic of Cyprus had been dissolved in consequence of the events of the preceding years, this had finally been recognised by the guarantors at their first meeting at Geneva, and what was now called for was the reconstitution of the state along radically different lines. For the Greek Cypriot side the Geneva declaration was not the landmark which the Turks thought it to be, but rather a patchy compromise aimed at bringing about a ceasefire and organising further discussions. Further, it was a serious mixture of contradictions, affirmations, ambiguities and concessions. It emanated from the three guarantors. Hence, nothing in it should run counter to the treaty of guarantee, the three Foreign Ministers having no competence either to dictate a settlement or to insist on any particular solution. They could only, consistently with their duties regarding the maintenance of the independence, territorial integrity and security of Cyprus, take some immediate measures for the normalisation of the situation, and order and ensure an immediate return to the constitutional order which they had pledged themselves to protect. Instead of the above, the declaration appeared to contemplate only a phased reduction of Turkish troops, seemed to extend some recognition to a legally nonexistent Turkish Cypriot administration, contained no real reference to the state of Cyprus as such but merely called upon the representatives of the two communities to 'participate in the talks relating to the constitution', and exacted many concessions from the Greek and Greek Cypriot sides alike, such as the demand for the immediate evacuation of the Turkish enclaves, without at the same time taking effective measures to ensure the adequate implementation of the ceasefire and the prevention of further Turkish aggression. Also, it was not exactly clear what subsequent discussions the three ministers had in mind when they called for further talks at Geneva. At one point it seems that the restoration of peace and the reestablishment of the 1960 constitution would be the only topics for discussion at these other meetings. But a little later the declaration is worded in a rather ambiguous way as if other matters too would be discussed. These points of course, the Greek Cypriot side was quick to point out, were counterbalanced by others. For a start, there was only a de facto recognition of the Turkish Cypriot administration and the juridical existence of the republic of Cyprus was throughout taken for granted. Then (this being the Greek Cypriots' strongest card) para. 5 contemplated a return to constitutional legitimacy (which clearly indicated the 1960 constitution), and there were repeated references, as the framework for any discussions, to the 1960 agreements. Yet, despite the above, as the Greek Cypriot side well knew, the declaration of Geneva was prejudicial to its cause, not only by demanding the immediate evacuation of the Turkish enclaves without imposing, on the face of it, any obligation on the Turkish side to allow the Greek Cypriot refugees to go back to their homes, but also by representing in its totality an insufficiently resisted Turkish attempt to bring about the dissolution of the republic. For this reason the Greek Cypriot side decided before the Geneva conference that every effort would be made to downgrade it politically and bring the discussion back to what for them was the sounder footing of the 1960 constitution and the very limited 'powers' of the guarantors under the treaty of guarantee. At one point Mr Clerides even toyed with the idea of completely repudiating the Geneva declaration, but, not surprisingly, this risky and unpredictable course that was unlikely to carry favour with Great Britain or even Greece was not followed. But the Greek Cypriot leader pointedly mentioned at the first plenary session that the declaration had been signed as a result of negotiations not participated in by the Greek Cypriots or by representatives of the republic. Nor indeed, as he observed, was the declaration the sole document or agreement embodying the parties' entitlements or obligations. Thus, one could not ignore either the treaty of guarantee which imposed clear duties on the three guarantors, including Turkey, or the relevant Security Council resolutions.

(b) *Evaluation of constitutional proposals*

Many misunderstandings still exist about the Geneva conference. Should the Gunes proposals have been accepted? Should further proposals on the part of the Greek Cypriot delegation have been given?

It should first be made clear that the central issue at Geneva was whether the geographical federation of Cyprus should be accepted. Two alternative Turkish plans were given for this purpose, the Denktash proposals and the Gunes ones. These differed in many respects, the most important of which was their geographical basis, the Denktash proposals being bi-regional and the Gunes ones cantonal. But undoubtedly their common features outnumbered their differences. Thus, both aimed at the geographical federation of Cyprus; the area that was to come under the control of the Turkish Cypriot administration was, in both cases, to be in the region of 34 per cent of the total territory of the republic; the two federated states were to have full control and autonomy within their respective geographical boundaries; it was made abundantly obvious that the competence of the central government in both sets of proposals would be severely restricted, if it were to exist at all; and an inevitable outcome of both proposals would have been a vast and compulsory population movement, the Greek Cypriot inhabitants of the areas to come under the Turkish administration facing certain expulsion so that the overwhelming majority of their new residents could become Turkish.

Further, there were pronounced 'procedural' similarities between the two plans, the following:

(i) The basic parts of both sets of proposals were not open to negotiation. Thus, the extent of the area to come under the Turkish administration as well as the geographical basis of the plans were expressly declared to be non-negotiable. What was said to be a negotiable issue was the exact demarcation of boundaries which would be left to expert committees and subsequent detailed discussions. But both the extent of the Turkish zones and 'a rough fixing of such areas', in the words of Mr Gunes, had to be acceded to.

(ii) Both plans were to be implemented immediately and without further discussion. Thus, as the Turkish Foreign Secretary put it, 'the Turkish areas to be' were to be evacuated at once by all Greek and Greek Cypriot forces, and 'their administration, order and security' immediately be taken over by the Turkish Cypriot administration. And what this meant was that Turkish Cypriot 'security forces' *and* Turkish military forces would be sent to these areas in order to assume their administrative supervision and military control.

(iii) Pending agreement on the final constitutional structure of the republic, the two autonomous administrations, in both sets of proposals, were immediately to take over full administrative authority within their respective areas and take jointly the necessary measures with a view to normalising and stabilising life in the island. What this clearly implied was, first, that all governmental officials and representatives of the state should immediately depart from the 'Turkish areas', and, secondly, that a kind of transitional government composed equally of Greeks and Turks would assume authority over the island as a whole.

(iv) The envisaged evacuation of the Turkish areas by Greek Cypriot forces and the fixing of the necessary lines would be done under the supervision of the Turkish armed forces. If this evacuation were not completed on time (within 24 hours), the Turkish armed forces would reserve the right to occupy the region (regions) in question. Also, the Turkish armed forces would reserve the right to control by their air force all evacuation operations; and 'any hostile act', Mr Gunes emphasised, would provoke immediate and massive Turkish retaliation.

(v) Another striking similarity of the plans was of course their mode of presentation. As was again made clear by Mr Gunes during the second session of the conference, both were coupled with time-limits within which they had to be accepted, and what the shortness of the time-limit meant was that they had to be accepted immediately. There could not even be full discussion or adequate opportunity to examine them. There first had to be unqualified acceptance of their basic elements and only then, and after their implementation, could there be further discussion.

(vi) Finally, both plans had no reference either to a withdrawal of the Turkish troops from the island or to a return of the refugees to their homes, elements that were regarded as fundamental by the Greek Cypriot side.

It can thus be seen that the similarities of the Denktash and Gunes plans far outweighed their differences. It may indeed be said that the Gunes plan was the more objectionable of the two, essentially for two reasons. To begin with, it was not really a cantonal plan because, as was made clear by the Turkish Foreign Secretary, all the Turkish Cypriot areas were to come under the undivided authority of a single administration. In this way, the Turkish Cypriot administration would have under its control, first, one main autonomous zone in the northern part of the island which would be a substantial one (over 20 per cent of the island's territory) and which would also be its administrative and governmental centre, and, secondly, a number of other areas dispersed throughout the island and situated in its most fertile parts. The reality of the biregional solution would thus be combined with the disadvantages of cantonal ones. A more correct designation of the Gunes plan might therefore be that it was 'a bizonal solution plus cantons'. Then, and perhaps most important of all, the fact that even the smaller 'cantons' would come under the immediate 'protection' of Turkish forces meant that the whole of Cyprus would, effectively, come under Turkish occupation. Military and security forces would have been sent from the occupied northern part of the island to the smaller cantons which were strategically placed so as to control potentially the whole of Cyprus, and both the nature of this operation as well as the manner and circumstances in which it was to be performed would have made its successful implementation exceedingly hazardous, if not impossible. Friction and confrontation would have been unavoidable, and they would certainly have resulted in Turkish retaliation and, probably, total occupation of the island.

At the same time it is likely that if the Gunes plan had been presented in a different manner, it would have stood a far better chance of serious consideration by the Greek Cypriot side. Thus, *if* there were references in it to the return of the refugees, the withdrawal of the Turkish armed forces (even if this was only to be a phased one), and the speedy implementation of the Security Council resolutions; *if* the plan had not been presented as a federal or a geographical one, but as one based on the recognition of considerable local/regional autonomy for the Turkish Cypriots within 'areas'; *if* the latter did not exceed 20 – 22 per cent in extent and their delineation was to be done in a manner that would not have necessitated the creation of a serious refugee problem; *if* express provision had been made for full negotiation and deliberation concerning all its constituent elements (with proper safeguards so that the talks would not drag on for too long this time); and *if* the plan had not been presented in so unreasonable a way and did not envisage an immediate effectuation of its basic elements in circumstances where the Turkish army of occupation would be the master of the situation, but had instead been put forward as a starting point for a subsequent fuller consideration of the main issues, *then* it may be that serious study of the Gunes proposals would have been justified. But, as it clearly appears from the exchanges of the second session of the conference, what was demanded of the Greek Cypriot delegation was not consideration or willing acceptance but capitulation.

Study of the Greek Cypriot proposals at Geneva yields the following conclusions. These can be seen as an effort at two kinds of compromise: first, compromise between the Greek Cypriot position that the conference had no competence whatsoever regarding any constitutional matter other than the restoration of the 1960 constitution and Turkish insistence that the outlines of a completely new constitution should be immediately agreed upon, any further talks to be used only for elaboration of the outlines to be thus adopted; and, secondly, compromise between the basic Greek Cypriot position still upholding the unity of the state and Turkish proposals envisaging rigid kinds of geographical federation.

On the procedural issue, the Clerides proposals did not abandon Greek Cypriot emphasis on the limited jurisdictional competence of the conference nor did they represent an acknowledgement that the constitutional future of Cyprus was, after all, the responsibility of the guarantors. On the contrary, they still adhered to the basic principle that the future of Cyprus was the sole concern of the two communities, that the 1960 constitution was valid, and that the guarantors only had the right to restore and reactivate it. But they now signified, by their very submission, acceptance of the view that the conference could discuss Cyprus' constitutional prospects and that the two communities, in the context of a conference of the guarantors and with their participation and cooperation, could agree on a new constitutional direction for the republic, a direction that itself went further than any Greek Cypriot proposal until then but which, at the same time, did not lose contact with the basic Greek Cypriot doctrinal tenet, namely that the 1960 constitution was valid and that amendments to be freely agreed upon by the two communities would be required before any new constitutional policy could be implemented.

As to the substantive content of the Greek Cypriot proposals, it can be seen that these still clearly maintained the unequivocal rejection of any

federal geographical arrangement, and emphasised the integrity and indivisibility of the republic's territory; but willingness was now declared
to extend further autonomy and regional self-government to the
Turkish community. It may be of interest to compare these proposals with
the Greek Cypriot views during the intercommunal dialogue, for, even
though the Geneva conference was not a continuation of the intercommunal talks (in as much as Mr Clerides and Mr Denktash were there not as
negotiators but as the respective leaders of the two communities at the
time), the Greek Cypriot delegation in formulating their proposals clearly
proceeded on the basis of the results of the intercommunal negotiations.
The following matters must be particularly noticed. The Clerides
proposals began by providing that the constitutional order of Cyprus was
to retain 'its bicommunal character' based on the coexistence of the Greek
and Turkish communities 'within the framework of a sovereign, independent and integral republic'. Even though these proposals were not, as
submitted, a finalised legal text, it can be seen that 'unitary' state is
replaced by 'integral' state and that the element of bicommunality is
accorded prominent mention. Whereas, throughout the intercommunal
talks, the maximum that the Greek Cypriot side had gone in this direction
was to negotiate on the basis of 'a unitary state with balanced bicommunal
participation', the state is now effectively acknowledged to be 'an integral
and bicommunal one'. The basis of the envisaged constitutional structure
was the recognition of institutional arrangements regarding an agreed
allocation of powers and functions between the central government
having authority over state affairs and the respective autonomous
communal administrations exercising their powers on other matters
within 'areas' to be established. This type of governmental structure
diverges in important respects from the views of the Greek Cypriot side
during the intercommunal discussions without however completely
abandoning the principal premises of the 1968–1974 approach. On
the one hand, the Clerides proposals indicate readiness to extend
recognition to two communal authorities, these to consist of the
branches of the House and appropriate communal administrations.
In addition, the creation of Turkish 'areas' consisting of the purely
Turkish villages and municipalities is cheerfully agreed to, and
subordination of mixed settlements to communal authorities rather than to
unified state organs is now declared acceptable, these being positions
which had been staunchly resisted by the Greek Cypriot side through most
of the intercommunal dialogue. On the other hand, the Clerides proposals
clearly reject any federal geographic element, 'any areas' they sanction
being principally administrative ones; and emphasis on territorial 'integrity' is calculated to stress the need for appropriate co-ordination
procedures for integrating communal administration within the state.

Further, the Greek-Cypriot proposals at Geneva look at the problem as one of delegating governmental and administrative powers and functions to the communities, as contrasted both with the setting up of new structures on the basis of allegedly existing total communal and governmental autonomy, as the problem was presented by the Turkish side, or the mere decentralisation of state authority, as the Greek Cypriot side had approached constitutional reconstruction during most of the intercommunal discussions, and hence can accurately be described as proposals aiming at a 'functional communal system' within an integral state (as opposed to either a unitary system or a federal one).

But it cannot be repeated strongly enough that the central issue at Geneva was not disagreement on constitutional reconstruction or governmental organisation. It is of course correct to say that the most important *constitutional* matter was whether the geographical federation of Cyprus would be accepted. But what the conference was *really* about was whether the Greek Cypriot side would *capitulate* to Turkish pressure aimed at the effective partitioning of Cyprus in the wake of the invasion and occupation of the northern part of the island.

(c) *Parties, politics, responsibility*

It would have been a miracle if the Geneva conference was attended by anything other than failure. To begin with, it was taking place against a recent background which included a coup by the Greek junta against the government of Archbishop Makarios, a large-scale invasion by Turkey and continuing expansion of the area under the occupation of her forces, the demise of the junta itself and the advent to power of K. Karamanlis in Greece and Gl. Clerides in Cyprus, the continuing threat of war between Greece and Turkey, and frantic but rather spasmodic and half-hearted efforts at mediation by the United States and Great Britain. The Geneva conference was in theory a conference of the guarantors, attended additionally by the representatives of the two communities. But in reality it was a direct confrontation between Turkey and the Greek Cypriot side. For there was little doubt that the Turkish Cypriots would faithfully follow whatever line was charted by the Turkish government, Greece had already decided that the initiative was to be left to the Greek Cypriot leadership, and Great Britain was at no time more than a rather ineffective broker between the opposing sides. Further investigation of the political attitudes of the Turkish government and the Greek Cypriot side is therefore necessary.

Internally, the position of the Greek Cypriots and the legal government of the republic could only be characterised as desperate. Disintegration of the machinery of government as a result of the coup, widespread collapse of law and order, terrible dislocation in consequence of the inexorable advance of the Turkish army with tens of thousands of refugees being driven into the Greek areas, and many other factors made up a terrifying picture of a state in dissolution. The result was that by the beginning of the Geneva conference the Greek Cypriot side had lost the advantage of locally preponderant power which it had enjoyed until then and consequently the scales of power had turned decisively in Turkey's favour. Further, possibilities of mobilising outside military support on the Greek Cypriot side were fast dying out and international opinion had not yet fully comprehended the magnitude of the Turkish operation or Turkish expansionism. Many international circles still viewed with sympathy Turkey's initial action which, it was thought, was primarily aimed at neutralising the Greek military coup against Makarios, and, perhaps most important of all, the United States government, far from taking active steps to stem military aggression, was either at best exhibiting a demoralising passivity and resignation in the face of Turkish adventurism or at worst actually looking with glee upon the anticipated dismemberment of Cyprus that would at last bring it within the orbit of NATO and eliminate its irksome presence from the future politics of the eastern Mediterranean. Turkey's repeated violations of the ceasefire had been frowned upon but it was still most unlikely that effective international action would be taken to restrain her. And there was little doubt that what the Turks wanted was the imposition of a system of geographical federation that would effectively partition the island. Mr Clerides for one did not think that they would be satisfied with less, not with so strong a military presence in the island; and such a solution he could not himself accept. In these circumstances the Greek Cypriot side had no illusions about what could be expected at Geneva. They knew that unless strong international pressure was brought to bear on the Turkish government the negotiations would speedily collapse. Yet the conference could still serve a useful purpose, it was felt, even though it did not seem likely to arrive in terms of result at any positive outcome. Time could be saved and some success on other fronts might be achieved. Public opinion was becoming more favourably disposed towards the Greek Cypriots, and this attitude of goodwill might well become both more pronounced and more practical were the Turks to pursue (as Mr Clerides expected) a policy of blackmail and intimidation. Further, if the final demarcation lines envisaged by the Geneva declaration were soon agreed upon, as was also expected, there would be increased scope for UN involvement, and UN organs, whose various resolutions were openly defied by the Turkish army, could with time take a more activist role politically as well as militarily. Something else that could not be ignored was the position of Britain, which could not but perceive a threat to its interests, both strategic and political, were

Turkish expansion to continue; and even though the British government, as Mr Callaghan was later to admit, was unlikely to take it upon itself to stop the Turks, its influence with the Americans, who ultimately operated the levers of power and alone could exert restraint on the Turkish government, was a vital factor which it was well to take advantage of. It can therefore be seen that the objectives of the Greek Cypriot side were basically three: first, to gain time, since the more the time that elapsed the more difficult it would be for Turkey to attack again; secondly, to mobilise international opinion and try to sway Anglo-American policy towards firm acceptance of the view that since constitutional legitimacy had been restored hostilities had to end and meaningful negotiations be resumed; and, thirdly, to try (if at all possible) to conduct any negotiations that became necessary not on the basis of geographical separation but on the lines of an integral and bicommunal state.

Not surprisingly, Turkey's perception of the situation as a result of all that had happened was diametrically different. It was that she had the 'right' and power to dictate a settlement and that she was not going to be stopped from doing so by legalistic considerations. When Mr Callaghan pointed out that Turkey was in breach of the treaty of guarantee, Mr Gunes retorted that 'everybody has the right to interpret the articles of the treaty as one wishes'. There was no court from which 'one can request an interpretation in order to determine what would be the most appropriate behaviour or conduct under the treaty', he continued. 'Everyone is responsible for his actions'. There is indeed little doubt that throughout this period Turkey was not motivated to any perceptible degree by concern for legality or the demands of the international order or even the security of the Turkish Cypriot community. Strategic and political considerations were all important. Through a remarkable series of events a golden opportunity to achieve the long-cherished ambition of establishing an irrevocable military presence on Cyprus and partitioning the island had been presented, and this was the time for decisive action. The Turkish government knew the following: It had scored a military victory by invading and occupying a part of Cyprus; through subsequent military expansion and open and repeated violations of the Geneva declaration and the Security Council resolutions, which, perhaps to its surprise, had not yet met with strong international condemnation, it had consolidated its hold over the occupied territory and had placed itself in a good position to continue the offensive; Greece had been exposed as weak and disorganised, and it was most unlikely that she would assist Cyprus militarily in the event of a renewal of hostilities; neither Great Britain, because of military and political limitations, nor the US, because of unwillingness to offend an 'indispensable' ally, were likely to intervene militarily or even exert diplomatic pressure that could not easily be resisted; and the Greek

Cypriot community was still in a demoralised condition, problems of legitimacy, organisation and morale having clearly exacted a heavy toll on the endurance of both government and people. At the same time a number of factors worried Turkish strategists. To begin with, when the invasion had first taken place, the world had generally accepted that Turkey had some colourable justification for doing so. But in the meantime, so openly had Turkey continued offensive military operations in clear violation of both the Security Council resolutions and its own agreements, that many international circles, principally Great Britain, looked upon the Turkish government as the new aggressor, and this international pressure, Turkey well realised, was likely to increase with time; secondly, after the return of constitutional legitimacy in Cyprus by the fall from power of the coup leaders and the constitutional accession to the Presidency of Mr Clerides, some type of normality was returning to the island; and, thirdly, after the first round of fighting the Turkish forces found themselves concentrated in a rather narrow and militarily vulnerable triangle. For all these reasons, Turkey obviously decided to attend the Geneva conference only for the purpose of appearing to comply with the UN resolutions and the earlier Geneva declaration. There she would submit plans and proposals that not only envisaged unacceptable forms of geographical federation involving the creation of a severe refugee problem but which were also likely, if accepted, to result in the complete dissolution of the republic. It was highly improbable that these plans would be accepted, the Turkish government correctly predicted, and therefore further military operations were necessary for full implementation of the Attila plan and the effective partitioning of the island. But time was of the essence. By the beginning of the conference international opinion was turning against Turkey, the governments of Premier Karamanlis and Acting President Clerides were operating with greater confidence, and pressure on both America and Great Britain for some kind of active intervention in the crisis was steadily increasing. This is why Turkey gave its stark ultimatum during the second session of the conference and obstinately refused to grant the very short adjournment requested by Mr Clerides despite the fact that this was strongly supported by Great Britain and possibly, but certainly more lukewarmly, by the United States; and this is also why Turkey resorted to military action moments after, if not even before, the conference collapsed. Indeed, such was the intimidation employed by the Turkish side and so undisguised the blackmail policies they pursued at Geneva, that the whole conference, or at least Turkey's part in it, was exposed as nothing but smokescreen for their military preparations, as nothing but a cynical exercise in power politics and gunboat diplomacy the like of which has not been seen for a long time.

What about the policies and overall diplomatic performance of the western powers most intimately involved with the situation – Great Britain and the United States? America's involvement and role deserve special study since not surprisingly it was at virtually all times realised that if a further Turkish military advance was to be prevented, the American government, primarily because of its close ties with Turkey, had to face its responsibilities in a forthright manner, take if necessary decisive diplomatic action, and in any case exert sufficient pressure on all parties to show moderation and restraint.

There has been general agreement that American policy over Cyprus was at best one of hasty improvisation, its diplomatic efforts being throughout incredibly naive, insensitive and ineffective, and at worst (particularly in the later stages and during the second round of the Geneva talks) a coldly calculating one, aiming exclusively at a minimisation of disturbances within NATO and showing total disregard for the true dimensions, both political and human, of the crisis. Further, American responsibility for the Cyprus tragedy does not have to be based on any broad conspiratorial theory or view of events, nor even on the US's own commanding political and military position in the area, exercised through NATO commands and the Sixth Fleet. The main reason why Washington bears a heavy share of the blame for the Cyprus tragedy is to be found in its own diplomatic performance throughout the crisis.

To begin with, there are substantial grounds for believing that the US had an opportunity to prevent the fatal coup against President Makarios, but let it pass because of a long held dislike and distrust of the Archbishop and an unwillingness to offend the then military rulers of Greece, whom the US, it must not be forgotten, had helped and assisted throughout their repressive rule of Greece. Trying to establish what happened at this period is complicated by the fact that apparently American authorities were in the habit of communicating with the junta via the CIA station-chief, while the regular embassy channels in Athens were rarely used. In any case, much more forthright and forceful measures should and could have been employed at this early critical stage, for the half hearted, complacent tactics of the American government failed to deter the junta.[7] After the coup Washington might have persuaded Turkey to hold back on military intervention if Dr Kissinger had given prompt and vigorous support to Britain's refusal to recognise the Cyprus regime and also to London's demand that Athens should immediately recall the Greek officers who had directed the operation. If Washington had at this early time embarked upon determined initiatives directed towards a swift return to constitutional legitimacy, the invasion might well have been averted. But the US dragged its feet and calculatingly refrained from committing itself, the

[7] See Stern, supra n.1, 110–33; Polyviou, supra n.3, 83–8.

State Department spokesman calling for moderation and at the UN Ambassador Scali declaring that 'it would be a serious error to rush to judgment on an issue of this gravity'. It may well be that these early American pro-junta leanings were interpreted by Ankara as tacit US acceptance of the new state of affairs in Cyprus. In any case Ankara immediately prepared for a military operation against Cyprus. Instead of taking decisive action to avert the impending catastrophe, contemporaneously launching serious diplomatic initiatives for an early return to constitutional legitimacy, Under Secretary Sisco was dispatched to shuttle ineffectively between Athens and Ankara in a frantic effort to bring about a compromise. He does not seem to have seriously warned either the Greek dictators that they should immediately withdraw from Cyprus and allow the return of Archbishop Makarios to the island or the Turks that they should not without further consultations seek a military solution, even though one could easily see both that a Turkish operation would not really be aimed at a restoration of constitutional government and that its inevitable result would be a serious danger of war between Greece and Turkey. After the Turks invaded Cyprus and massively violated the early ceasefires, the pressing need was to dissuade Ankara from embarking on further reckless military adventures aimed at achieving by force the division of the island and the forced separation of the two communities. Here again Washington's reaction was too mild and too late. What was required at this stage was the kind of tough and clear message that President Johnson sent to Premier Inonu and which prevented a Turkish invasion in 1964. What instead appeared was first equivocation and then weakness. Forceful action was particularly called for at the later stages of the Geneva conference. Throughout the second round of the talks, as has already been seen, Turkey's arbitrary and unreasonable attitude was observed by all. But the US refused to join in this universal condemnation, refused at any stage even to threaten a halt in American military aid, and resolutely refused even to consider either a UN or a British sponsored initiative. Finally, in an incredible move of bad timing, the State Department, at the most crucial juncture of the talks, instead of exerting strong pressure on Turkey to remain at the negotiating table, issued a statement which stressed the equity of the Turkish position. What clearly appeared both from the timing of the Kissinger proclamation and from the stress put on the Turkish grievances was either that Washington was supporting Ankara's position at Geneva or that nothing more would be done by way of American efforts to ensure observance of the ceasefire. The results are well known. On 14 August the Turkish army, by then heavily reinforced and wielding the advantage of complete air superiority, slashed across Cyprus. 40 per cent of the island came under Turkish military occupation. This vicious military advance had both a devastating effect on the local population and serious international repercussions. Almost two hundred thousand Greek Cypriots became refugees, the island was effectively partitioned, a durable settlement of the Cyprus problem became more distant than ever, Greece withdrew militarily from NATO and threatened to abandon the western alliance for good, and not since American involvement in South East Asia was there such a spontaneous explosion of feeling against American foreign policy. Even after the second phase of Turkish military operations, when Turkish aggression was universally condemned, the United States government still did not acknowledge openly that the territorial integrity and sovereignty of Cyprus had been violated through the invasion and occupation of a substantial part of its territory, and indeed in statements that followed American spokesmen seemed to give tacit recognition to Turkey's fait accompli and to associate themselves, with undiplomatic haste, with a rigid biregional settlement.

There can be no question that there was American bias towards Turkey. Was this the product of miscalculation or design? It is thought that both were instrumental in the shaping of American policy. At first it seemed as if the State Department did not really comprehend the issues at stake and the dangers on the horizon. Later, when partly as a result of this incomprehension the Turks landed a substantial force in Cyprus and gained the initiative, American policy tilted decisively and consciously in favour of Turkey as it was thought that only in this way could losses within NATO be minimised and American strategic interests safeguarded. This policy, as is well known, failed in the end, not only in terms of human suffering in Cyprus itself, but also in terms of United States strategic and political interests, in the sense that the price the American government has paid for coming down so obviously on the side of Turkey in the Cyprus conflict has already been high and will almost certainly become higher.

Great Britain too must bear part of the responsibility for what happened.[8] Great Britain, as one of the three guarantor powers, is bound by the treaty of guarantee to recognise and guarantee the independence, territorial integrity and security of the republic. If the guarantee means anything, it must surely mean that the UK is bound, should the island be attacked, to come to the defence of the republic. The UK did not do this even though it had powerful forces stationed on the island. Indeed at Geneva there seemed to be both full recognition and explicit acknowledgement of Britain's legal and moral duty in the circumstances, but it was more than once suggested to the Greek Cypriot delegation that Britain, as a result of her weakened military position and other political constraints, could not unilaterally take action to prevent Turkey's anticipated military

[8] Polyviou, supra n.3, 88–9; Kellner and Hitchens, *Callaghan:The Road to Number Ten* (1976), 136–42.

expansion. Mr Callaghan, it will be remembered, told Mr Clerides that he would be fully prepared to place British troops in Cyprus under UN command were a concerted UN operation to be mounted; moreover, with American assistance and co-operation, which, as Dr Kissinger had already made clear to him, would not be forthcoming, he would once again have been prepared to commit himself to some kind of dynamic action against Turkey. What of course cannot be denied is that throughout the Geneva conference Mr Callaghan valiantly attempted to dissuade the Turks from abandoning the negotiating table; toiled hard to narrow the gap between Greeks and Turks; and eventually strongly criticised Turkish intransigence and bad faith. Despite all this, without American support British diplomatic efforts could not but be frustrated. None the less, had Britain exhibited some of her older decisiveness and either interfered or at least threatened to interfere immediately, events might have developed differently. To say, as some have said,[9] that British policy in the Cyprus affair differed little, if at all, from that policy of appeasement practised so assiduously by certain pre-war British governments is to put it rather too strongly. But what has to be clearly recognised is that Britain had an obligation to come to the assistance of Cyprus once its independence was threatened.[10] This obligation, perhaps for understandable military and political reasons, was never fulfilled.

The chief lesson of recent events in Cyprus is that when a country thinks its army can pull off a quick smash and grab, it is liable to leave the diplomats and their fine adjustments standing on the sidelines. For the advantage that modern technology gives to an army with great local superiority of power means that essential military business can be finished before the lumbering machinery of international discussion or dissuasion even starts to go into action. Nuclear weapons may have made big wars unlikely, but, as is obvious from the Cyprus crisis, there is still plenty of scope in today's world for the quick, small war. It may be that the ultimate lesson to be derived from this is that people who do not want to be grabbed or enslaved must take their precautions.

---

[9] In letters to *The Times* (London) of this period.

[10] See the *Report of the Parliamentary Select Committee on Cyprus* (April 1976) which unequivocally declared that 'Britain had a legal right, a moral obligation, and the military capacity to intervene in Cyprus during July and August 1974', and went on to criticise strongly the British government's failure to do so for reasons that were not given. The Committee's report was not accepted by the government (*Parl. Deb (H.C.)* 19 May 1976, cols. 1399–1403).

7

Political and Constitutional Reconstruction

1. *Federal 'negotiations'*

After the breakdown of the Geneva conference and the occupation of the northern part of the republic by Turkish military forces, the problem of Cyprus was once more taken before the United Nations. On 5 November 1974 the General Assembly unanimously adoped Resolution 3212. This demanded respect for Cyprus' sovereignty, independence and territorial integrity, urged the speedy withdrawal from the island of all foreign armed forces, considered that 'all the refugees should return to their homes in conditions of safety' and called upon the parties concerned to take urgent measures towards their rehabilitation. The Turkish side immediately declared that it was not bound by any of the provisions of the resolution which could be regarded as prejudicial to its security or the political settlement it desired and made clear that what it wanted was a biregional federal state with an almost total separation of the two communities. As to the return of the 200,000 refugees, this, Mr Denktash said, was 'an internal political matter', and in view of the political settlement that the Turkish government and the Turkish Cypriot leadership would insist upon, it was most unlikely that any substantial number of them would be allowed to return to their villages and homes. Indeed, on 13 February 1975, Mr Denktash proclaimed the creation of an independent federated state in the occupied territories and promulgated a 'constituent charter' for its government and administration, stating at the same time that this was not a unilateral declaration of independence and that his independent state was merely the Turkish Cypriot wing of the future federation of Cyprus. Once more, the matter was taken by the Cyprus government before the Security Council which condemned this unilateral move by the Turkish Cypriots and called on the two Cypriot sides to resume their negotiations under the auspices, and this time with the personal participation, of the UN Secretary-General.

The time had obviously come for a new Greek Cypriot policy. The Geneva proposals were clearly unacceptable to Turkey and the Turkish Cypriot leadership and were not regarded by the international community as 'realistic'. Moreover, an area of 40 per cent was under continuing military occupation, Turkish aggression had not abated, and there was no move on the part of any outside power to exert meaningful pressure on Turkey to withdraw. Already in December 1974 full consultations had taken place in Athens between the Greek government, Archbisop Makarios and Mr Clerides, then Acting President and Greek Cypriot negotiator. The general situation was assessed, prospects examined, policy reconsidered and new decisions taken. It was realised that new and far-reaching concessions had to be made if negotiations with Turkey and the Turkish Cypriots were to have any chance of success. Accomplished facts dictated a new line. Federation had become inevitable. Meanwhile, discussions, mainly on humanitarian issues, between Greek Cypriots and Turkish Cypriots were taking place as demanded by Resolution 3212 of the General Assembly and with time these discussions were gradually expanded by the inclusion in the agenda of substantive constitutional topics. Finally, at a series of meetings of the negotiators, again Mr Clerides and Mr Denktash, in February 1975, new 'federal' proposals 'on the constitutional aspect of the Cyprus problem' were exchanged.

The basic proposals the Greek Cypriot side first submitted then and elaborated further at later rounds of the intercommunal talks in Vienna (particularly in February 1976) and elsewhere can be summarised as follows:[1] Cyprus must continue as an independent and sovereign state but its constitution could be that of a bi-communal multi-regional federal state. A number of areas, including a substantial one in the north of the island and corresponding approximately to 20 per cent of the island's territory, should be placed under a Turkish Cypriot administration, and Turkish Cypriots would be allowed, if they wished, to move from all parts of the island to the Turkish Cypriot areas. At the same time, the Greek Cypriot side insisted, it was necessary first that there should be a strong central government consisting of members of both communities, secondly that all foreign military forces should be withdrawn, and thirdly that all refugees should be allowed to return to their homes in conditions of safety. Despite insistence on the implementation of UN resolutions there is no denying how far reaching were the concessions that the Greek Cypriots made on their previous position. Thus, for the first time, a geographical federation was accepted; the bicommunality of the state was explicitly recognised and indeed raised to the status of one of the identifying features of the governmental system the two sides would negotiate on; it was declared that areas to be administered by the Turkish Cypriots would in effect be ceded to the Turkish community; a population movement of Turkish Cypriots to these areas was permitted; and in this way the principle of communal separation was, to a considerable extent, accepted.

[1] These have been published in the form of a pamphlet under the title *Proposals of the Greek Cypriot side on the various aspects of the Cyprus problem* (Nicosia: Public Information Office, April 1976).

The Turkish views[2] however, both as formulated in February 1975 and as subsequently articulated in Vienna in February 1976, were far removed from what the Greek Cypriots could possibly accept since Mr Denktash's proposals envisaged not so much a genuine federation as a loose confederation or even outright partition. What was in fact proposed was that any future political settlement should be based on the following three principles: there should be a rigidly defined bizonal federation, with only very minor rectifications and readjustments being made to the existing boundaries between the two regions; any central government to be established should have very limited powers, most functions and responsibilities 'remaining' with the two communities; and the participation of the two communities in the central (federal) organs had to be on an equal footing despite their numerical disparity. No political solution which was not based on the complete physical separation of the two communities could be accepted, the Turkish side further declared, and as a result very few of the refugees were to be allowed to return to their homes. As to additional security for the two communities, the Turkish Cypriot leadership expressed the desire to keep armed contingents from Turkey and Greece in the respective sectors as guarantors of Cyprus' 'independence' and to allow them to intervene whenever a threat to this independence was perceived. In other words, 'partition' was demanded 'in all but in name'.[3] In view of such fundamental differences of opinion it was not easy to see how prospects for a settlement could be other than non-existent.

But in early 1977 a significant breakthrough seemed to take place with a meeting between Archbishop Makarios, President of the republic, and Mr Denktash, the Turkish Cypriot leader, and signs of a renewed American interest in the problem of Cyprus. Thus, on 12 February 1977, talks were held in Nicosia between President Makarios and Mr Denktash, on the initiative and in the presence of the UN Secretary-General, Dr Waldheim. At this meeting four guidelines on the basis of which subsequent intercommunal negotiations would proceed were agreed upon and recorded, and these were the following:

'(1) We are seeking an independent, non-aligned, bi-communal federal republic;

(2) The territory under the administration of each community should be discussed in the light of economic viability or productivity and land-ownership;

(3) Questions of principles like freedom of movement, freedom of

[2] These have appeared in mimeographed form under the title *Proposals of the Turkish Cypriot side on various aspects of the Cyprus problem* (Nicosia: April 1976).

[3] *The Times* (London), 8 September 1975.

settlement, the right of property and other specific matters are open for discussion taking into consideration the fundamental basis of a bi-communal federal system and certain practical difficulties which may arise for the Turkish Cypriot community;

(4) The powers and functions of the central federal government will be such as to safeguard the unity of the country, having regard to the bi-communal character of the state.'

It was quite generally accepted at the time that the Makarios-Denktash agreement was yet another grievous (and ill-judged) concession on the part of the Greek Cypriot side, all the more remarkable because no correspond-ing concession or even a reciprocal gesture of goodwill on the part of the Turkish government was at the same time either exacted or secured. Its three features that provoked the most adverse comment among sections of the Greek Cypriots were, first, the general watering down of previously expressed strong insistence on a fully sovereign and integral state, evidenced by such things as the noticeable failure to refer to the terms 'sovereign' and 'integral' in the description of the type of state which the two sides were seeking and the rather anaemic way in which the issue of central powers was dealt with; secondly, its unprecedented omission of the criterion of population regarding the eventual demarcation of regions, and its replacement by the vague standard of economic viability and the disputed arithmetic of land-ownership; and thirdly, its curious subordi-nation of the until then fundamental principles of freedom of movement and settlement and rights of property to the vagaries of further discussion which moreover was to take place in the light of unspecified 'practical difficulties' which the Turkish community might face but which in their context could only be understood as authorising substantial deviations from free movement, settlement and ownership in the name of 'the fundamental basis of a bicommunal federal system' that is now more openly than ever acknowledged to be the basic criterion of constitutional and political reconstruction. An effort to repair some of the damage was belatedly made by Archbishop Makarios in June and July of the same year when the Cypriot leader made a point of emphasising that the guidelines he agreed upon with Mr Denktash were not intended to displace the relevant UN resolutions with regard to Cyprus which called upon Turkey to respect Cyprus' territorial integrity, to withdraw her occupation forces from the island and to allow the refugees to return to their homes in conditions of safety. Rather, they were intended as negotiating 'guide-lines', to facilitate the task of the interlocutors and to speed up the quest for a settlement. But whatever the subsequent explanations, there can be little doubt that the Makarios-Denktash agreement was a serious error on the part of the Cypriot President. What seems to have happened, as he

himself candidly acknowledged in subsequent private conversations, was
that he wished, in a dramatic and unexpected gesture of conciliation, to
'win over' the new American President, Mr Carter, so that at last
meaningful pressure could be brought to bear on the Turkish government
and real progress made. In this he seriously miscalculated both the
nature of American politics and the obduracy of Turkish policy-
makers.

In any case, after the announcement of the Makarios-Denktash
agreement, concerted and sustained efforts were made for the resumption
of the intercommunal talks on the basis of the four guidelines. Since all
previous attempts had failed, it was agreed that this time the two sides
would undertake from the very beginning certain specific commitments,
so that the talks might really be rendered meaningful and substantive.
Further, following the long-awaited initiative on the part of President
Carter in February 1977, the Turkish government gave an undertaking to
Mr C. Clifford, the American President's special envoy, that it would
negotiate seriously and that it would do its best, despite the impending
Turkish elections, to ensure that the Turkish Cypriot side would produce
at Vienna concrete and realistic proposals on the constitutional arrange-
ments. It was particularly intimated to the interested parties that if Mr
Clifford could win agreement from the Greek Cypriot side as regards the
production of concrete territorial proposals on a map, then the Turkish
Cypriots would respond substantively and meaningfully. Assurances were
also given to Mr de Cuellar, the UN special representative, that the
Turkish Cypriot interlocutor would 'discuss the Greek Cypriot proposals
on the territorial issue in full, substantively and meaningfully'. In short, the
effective commitments undertaken by the two sides were that the Greek
Cypriot side would, during the talks, take the initiative on the territorial
aspect by submitting relevant proposals accompanied by a map, within the
framework of the four guidelines, and that the Turkish Cypriot side would
take the initiative on the constitutional aspect by submitting comprehensive proposals, again within the framework of the four guidelines.
Further, both sides solemnly undertook to discuss in a 'meaningful and
substantive way' each other's proposals.

On the first day of the Vienna talks[4] in April 1977 the Greek Cypriot side
submitted a map indicating the region (approximately 20–22 per cent of
the total territory of the republic) which they proposed to place under
Turkish Cypriot administration. In doing so the Greek Cypriots showed
willingness to accept, under certain important conditions, what they had
staunchly refused to reconcile themselves to until then, namely a biregional federal system under which two (and not more) regions would be

[4] I have enjoyed access to much unpublished documentation concerning the Vienna talks
of March/April 1977.

demarcated, to be placed under the administrative control of the Greek and Turkish Cypriot sides respectively. But the following points were also put forward by the Greek Cypriot side as the basis on which this map was prepared and submitted. First, the federal republic that would be established was to be a federation, and not a confederation, and should continue being the sole subject of international law, to the exclusion of its constituent parts; secondly, in the interests of economic viability and productivity, whatever the island's eventual administrative demarcation, there should be no rigid division of the available area into two separate economic or political zones, but on the contrary every effort should be made to safeguard the unity and cohesion of the country; and thirdly, as stated in the Makarios-Denktash guidelines themselves, in any future set up, whether it was of the biregional or multiregional type, there should be effective protection for rights to property, freedom of movement, and freedom of settlement, which naturally included both the right of the refugees to return to their homes and the right of the Turkish Cypriots to reside in the Turkish Cypriot region, if they so chose.

The reactions of the Turkish Cypriot interlocutor to the Greek Cypriot territorial proposals were limited simply to negative comments. On the basis of an argument regarding 'security requirements and economic viability', he excluded the restoration to the government of most occupied regions, described others as indispensable for the economic survival of his community, and finally called upon the Greek Cypriots to take into consideration other and different criteria when presenting a new map. As a result, during this round of talks, no picture of any kind emerged of Turkish territorial views. In fact, what the Turkish Cypriot representative expressly stated was that, as regards territory, they had not come to Vienna either to give anything back or to indicate what they intended to keep. No progress was therefore made on this despite effective Greek Cypriot acceptance of a biregional settlement.

As regards the constitutional aspect, the Turkish Cypriot side, on the second day of the Vienna talks, submitted their own proposals, and it did not take the Greek Cypriot delegation long to find out that no Turkish Cypriot 'constitutional' concession, however small, had been made in response to the provisional Greek Cypriot acceptance of a biregional federal system. The main features of the Turkish proposals were that Cyprus should become an independent bizonal federal republic composed of two federated states, one in the north for the Turkish community and one in the south for the Greeks; that sovereignty should be shared equally between the two national communities as 'co-founders of the republic'; that each federated state should have its own constitution and should be given the right to take all measures thought necessary for its security and administration; that residual legislative power should vest in the federated states and that the legislative organ of the federal republic should only be able to legislate on certain limited and well-defined matters; that on important matters, such as foreign affairs, the ratification of international agreements and external defence, separate absolute majorities of the Turkish and Greek members of the federal legislature should be required; and that the two Cypriot communities, despite their numerical difference, should be acknowledged as completely equal and should be accorded equal representation in the weak central government that was to be set up. The Greek Cypriot side expressed the view that these proposals were not substantive. Indeed, as the Greek Cypriot interlocutor stated, the Turkish constitutional proposals were 'contrary to and incompatible' with the guidelines of President Makarios and Mr Denktash in that they provided 'neither for the setting up of a genuinely federal state nor for the unity of the country'. Indeed these proposals were, in the eyes of the Greek Cypriots, a regression even on those of 1976, in that they went further in providing for two separate states. Nevertheless, the Greek Cypriot side did not limit itself to their rejection, even though in its view they did not comply with the four guidelines, but instead proceeded to submit both extensive comments on them and its own concrete constitutional counter-proposals.

What the Greek Cypriot side was now proposing was that Cyprus should be an independent, sovereign, non-aligned bicommunal federal republic consisting of the Greek Cypriot region and the Turkish Cypriot region (with state sovereignty being declared to be one and indivisible); that fundamental rights should apply 'without qualification', and further that the general rules of public international law should be an integral part of federal law, should take precedence over repugnant domestic law and should be allowed directly to create rights and duties for the inhabitants of the territory of the federal republic; that there should be a strong federation, with the legislative power of the federal republic being contained in a federal list, that of the regions in a regional list, and with all residual powers remaining in the federal republic; that federal legislative powers should be exercised by two legislative bodies, the 'Federal Council', representing the regions, and the 'House of Representatives', representing the people as a whole (with the members of the Federal Council being elected in each region by universal suffrage and the members of the House of Representatives by universal suffrage by the people in general); and that any amendments to the federal constitution should require a special majority of the members representing the regions in the Federal Council. It was also proposed that the federal republic should be recognised to be a single economic entity, with financial and fiscal arrangements being structured accordingly, and that the participation of the two communities both in the various federal organs and in the public service should as a rule be proportionate to the ratio of the population, subject to equitable safeguards on certain specific matters. These proposals were completely unacceptable to the Turkish Cypriot side and were completely rejected by them. Mr Onan, the Turkish Cypriot interlocutor, did not regard them as 'realistic', 'constructive' or 'logical', and emphasised that the essential thing was that the Greek Cypriot side should understand that 'they [could] not again impose their hegemony'. The constitutional proposals of the Greek Cypriot side, he concluded, did not provide for anything other than 'a system of administration of a unitary state', and could not therefore be accepted even as providing a basis for negotiation.

There was general outcry against the Turkish attitude and proposals of April 1977. Thus, Turkey and the Turkish Cypriots had submitted no proposals on the territorial aspect of the problem, their views on the constitutional issues were widely acknowledged to be totally unrealistic, and no effort had been made by them to respond to what on any account was a major Greek Cypriot concession, namely conditional acceptance of a biregional federation. Immediately after the failure of the Vienna 'talks' pressure was put on the Turkish government by Dr Waldheim, and early in January 1978 Mr Ecevit, once again Turkish Prime Minister after a spell in opposition, undertook that the Turkish side would submit 'concrete proposals' to the UN Secretary-General by the end of February. On 14 January Dr Waldheim visited Cyprus for talks with representatives of both the Cyprus government and the Turkish Cypriot community, and on his departure from the island on 16 January he expressed the optimistic view, on the basis of assurances from Mr Ecevit, that comprehensive Turkish proposals would be prepared on both the territorial and the constitutional aspects, that there was hope at last that 'the stalemate' could be overcome and that in that event it would become possible to resume the negotiating process 'in a meaningful and constructive way'.

In fact the Turkish proposals[5] were only handed to Dr Waldheim on 13 April 1978 and were a major disappointment. It was immediately apparent that they did not provide 'a convincing blueprint for a genuinely functioning federation',[6] and strong suspicions were expressed in international circles that 'the real object of the operation (was) not to initiate negotiations on the basis of specific proposals but simply to impress the United States Congress',[7] at that time considering President Carter's request that the arms embargo imposed on shipments of American arms to Turkey in the wake of the 1974 invasion should be lifted. The basic tenet

[5] There were two documents, *Main Aspects of the Turkish Cypriot Proposals* and *Explanatory Note of the Turkish Cypriot Proposals for the Solution of the Cyprus Problem*. The references that follow, unless otherwise indicated, are to these two documents.

[6] *The Times* (London), 15 April 1978, at 15 (leading article).

[7] Ibid.

of the Turkish side was that no solution could be accepted unless recognition was accorded to the right of each community both to full political autonomy and to economic and social development on its own territory. The only way to start, given 'the situation of mutual mistrust where each community has reservations about the goodwill of the other side', was with non-existent central powers and no meaningful common functions, and on the basis of the twin principles of strict territorial separation and the absolute equality of the two communities. It was, in other words, essential to keep as much power as possible in the hands of the separate federated (communal) states, while at the same time adopting strict parity as the basis of representation in the few federal organs that would be brought into existence (any concession to proportional principles of representation being ruled out since this might give the numerically superior Greek Cypriot community the balance of power). But if in the future confidence between the parties were to return, the powers of the central government might be increased by stages, but of course only after a new agreement between the two communities. This, according to the Turkish side, was the principle of 'growth of federation by evolution'. The substantive proposals that were then put forward can be grouped under three headings, the nature of the state, that of central powers and functions, and that of the institutions that would administer any agreed federal responsibilities. On the first issue the Turkish side proposed the following: Cyprus should become a bicommunal and bizonal federation based on the strict equality of the federated states, and state sovereignty should continue to be shared equally between the two national communities, as co-founders of the republic, through their respective states. Fundamental rights should be observed in principle, but since great difficulties would certainly be encountered with regard to freedom of movement and freedom of residence, these were to be subject to special provision. Thus, freedom of movement was to be 'respected', but it was only 'an ultimate objective' to be 'achieved step by step';[8] in particular it had to be understood that '(t)he progressive stages for the implementation of this freedom' were to be determined by the two federated states through mutually agreed provisions and measures that might be deemed necessary to protect, among other things, the security of the communities 'and the public order based on the maintenance and protection of the federated states and the bi-communality and bi-zonality of the federal republic'. Freedom of settlement was to be approached even more restrictively. For a start, this right was to be recognised not generally but 'primarily for humanitarian and professional purposes', was to remain subject to permanent limitations in order to preserve the homogeneity of the two

[8] This was said by Mr Ecevit, the Turkish Prime Minister, in a B.B.C. radio interview on Thursday, 13 April 1978 (*The Times* (London), 15 April 1978, at 15).

zones,[9] and in any case could only be partially implemented 'in clearly defined areas' by the adoption or enactment of appropriate legislative and administrative measures by the two states. Finally, although foreign affairs were to be regarded as a federal matter, the two states were to reserve the right to enter into any agreement with any country, particularly their respective 'motherlands'; and to this end the two federated states should be given the right to maintain their own diplomatic and consular contacts.

On the closely related issues of federal functions, federal legislation and federal legislative organs, the Turkish proposals declare readiness to allot foreign affairs (subject to the qualification mentioned above), external defence, banking, external communications, federal health services and a few other matters to the proposed federation, but immediately nullify this by providing not only that all residual legislative power will belong to the two federated states but also that *all* legislation should be introduced through the legislative assemblies of the states, the Federal Assembly (consisting of twenty members, ten from each community) being given only arbitrative and not true law-making functions. The Turkish legislative proposals are so remarkable that they deserve further attention. Their objective is to ensure that federal laws can only be passed upon receiving a simple majority vote in each of the legislative assemblies of the federated states. It is thus provided that federal bills may be introduced in either of the communal legislative assemblies and should first be debated in the one in which they are introduced; federal bills adopted with or without amendment by one of the legislative assemblies must be referred to the other; if a bill is rejected by one of the legislative assemblies, it must be deemed to be withdrawn; conversely, if a bill, adopted by one legislative assembly, is also adopted by the other without amendment, it must be transmitted to the presidents of the federated states for joint promulgation; but if a federal bill adopted by one of the legislative assemblies is only adopted with amendments by the other or if a bill introduced jointly by the presidents of the federated states is adopted by both legislative assemblies with different amendments, it must then be submitted to the Federal Assembly where bills can be adopted by a simple majority; in case of an equality of votes, the President of the Federal Assembly will have a casting vote; but if a federal bill is so adopted, the president of each federated state must then submit it to a separate referendum, and if this bill is then accepted in both states, it must be jointly promulgated by the two presidents. What is therefore abundantly clear is that, according to the Turkish proposals, the federal legislative power is to be exercised not by the proposed Federal Assembly but by the two (communal) assemblies. In

[9] Ibid.

similar fashion, as regards the other organs of the so-called federation, the Turkish proposals envisage a purely ceremonial federal president, the presidency to rotate between the two communities and all executive power to vest jointly in the two presidents, and a Federal Constitutional Court composed of six judges, three from each community.

The Turkish proposals were hardly more conciliatory on the 'political' questions of territory and external guarantees. As regards the former, it was confidently anticipated by many, including UN officials, that the Turkish side was at last about to make a major concession that would facilitate the resumption of the intercommunal negotiations. They were disappointed. The Turkish side did no more than indicate *readiness* to discuss the question of territory, and then only in the light of 'the underlying principle' of security (which in this instance meant that Greek and Turkish Cypriots had to continue living in strict communal separation and within distinct and rigidly defined geographical boundaries) and on the basis of certain 'economic facts', such as the predominantly agricultural nature of the Turkish community, which meant that only minor readjustments to the Attila line could be contemplated. Further, as political observers were quick to notice, the territorial modifications proposed by the Turkish side were 'so small as to be scarcely significant'.[10] Although a figure of 5 per cent was mentioned unofficially by the Turkish leadership as the percentage of the island's territory which they were proposing to withdraw from and return to the Greek Cypriots, even this could only be arrived at by the inclusion of the buffer zone, namely the area lying between the two sides and under the control of the UN military force, which by definition was not under Turkish occupation and therefore hardly for the Turkish side to concede; but even if there was a genuine Turkish withdrawal from 5 per cent of the island's territory, well over 30 per cent would still be under occupation, still wildly excessive for a population of about 20 per cent. Finally, on the question of guarantees, the Turkish side insisted that any settlement should be guaranteed, among others, by Turkey, as under the 1960 treaty of guarantee.

Not surprisingly, these proposals failed to provide a basis for substantive negotiations. On April 19 President Kyprianou, who had succeeded Archbishop Makarios on 3 August 1977, announced that they were 'totally unacceptable' and 'nothing but a propaganda exercise designed to extricate Turkey from its isolation and to facilitate the lifting of the arms embargo imposed on Turkey by the United States Congress', and declared that acceptance of them 'would be tantamount to a decision (on the part of the Greek Cypriots) to commit suicide', which they were not prepared to do. Finally, on 22 April, the Greek Cypriot representative at the

[10] *The Times* (London), 15 April 1978, at 15 (leading article).

intercommunal talks, Mr T. Papadopoulos, sent a lengthy document[11] to the UN Secretary-General formally announcing his side's rejection of the Turkish proposals.

Some of the many Greek Cypriot objections to the Turkish proposals were that these did not provide for the establishment of a true federal state, but for the creation of two separate states; that the direct relationship of the federal government to the citizen, 'an essential element of federation', was non-existent; that the individual would not be able to enjoy, irrespective of the community to which he belonged, his basic human rights throughout the territory of the republic, the implementation of the vital rights of freedom of movement and freedom of settlement in particular being made subject to mutual agreement (which, because of the deadlock provisions, either side would for ever be at liberty to withhold) and to such conditions and restrictions as would no doubt be calculated to render their enjoyment impossible; that all real powers had been conferred on the two communal administrations, even authority over federal matters being exercisable by the separate communal assemblies and not by a federal legislature; that the strict equality that was envisaged as the basis of participation in the federal organs was 'the surest recipe for bringing about continuous and insur-mountable deadlocks at all levels, leading to perpetual intercommunal friction, culminating, inevitably, in partition'; and that on the all important issue of territory no proposal was now being made beyond what had been proposed before, namely an insignificant 'readjustment of the line'. There could therefore be no doubt that what the Turks were demanding was not the setting up of a genuine federation but the partitioning of the island. It followed that their proposals could not be viewed as providing any basis for negotiation and the resumption of the intercommunal talks.

Two further events which followed the collapse of the initiative of Dr Waldheim were, first, the decision of the United States Senate in July 1978 to accede to President Carter's request that the embargo on arms sales to Turkey should be lifted (but subject to a requirement that the American government should exert efforts towards bringing about a solution of the Cyprus problem and submit regular reports on the progress of such efforts), and secondly, the fresh endorsement of the Greek Cypriot case by the United Nations Assembly early in November 1978 by a vote of 110 to 4. The importance of the first of these events lay not only in that it apparently made the Turkish government somewhat more amenable to American mediation, Mr Ecevit acknowledging in an interviw in November that the United States was in recent months adopting 'a helpful attitude towards Turkey', but also in that it encouraged and indeed put an obligation on the

[11] *Observations on the (Turkish) Documents* (1978).

American administration to show some positive interest in the matter, if for no other reason so as to be able to put something in its reports to Congress. As regards the UN resolution of November 1978 which reaffirmed respect for Cyprus' sovereignty and territorial integrity and repeated the demand that the Turkish occupation forces should be withdrawn from the island, its main significance, despite the political impossibility of securing its implementation, was that it was 'an impressive reminder of Turkey's virtual isolation'[12] on the Cyprus issue.

Prompted by these developments the American administration in late November 1978, with assistance it seems from the British and Canadian governments, prepared and submitted to the interested parties a set of proposals as a framework for resumed negotiations under the auspices of the United Nations. The American suggestions, purporting to be a distillation and blending of the views and positions held by the two sides and aiming to provide both of them with an opportunity to escape from their entrenched positions, envisaged a bizonal federation, consisting of two ethnic regions, the specific territory constituting each region to be negotiated both in the light of security and economic viability (traditionally Turkish Cypriot criteria) and on the basis of population and land ownership (criteria that have been suggested by the Greek Cypriots). A key proposal on the question of territory urged the Turkish side to agree to 'significant geographical readjustments' in favour of the Greek Cypriot side. In principle, citizens would be free to move and settle in either region, and displaced persons would be allowed to return to their properties, but all these rights would apparently only be exercisable subject to certain qualifications and limitations and 'to the extent feasible and consistent with the bicommunal character of the republic'. As regards the central government, the American framework proposed that there should be a president and a vice-president, each from a different community, who would jointly appoint the ministers, neither community obtaining less than 30 per cent of the ministerial portfolios; a legislature which would consist of two chambers, the two communities to be represented equally in one and in proportion to population in the other; and a supreme court of three judges – one Greek Cypriot, one Turkish Cypriot and one non-Cypriot – appointed jointly by the president and the vice-president. It was also proposed, first, that the federal government should handle a reasonable number of matters, including foreign affairs, external defence, currency and central banking, interregional and foreign commerce, customs and immigration, secondly, that 'powers and functions not explicitly granted to the federal government' should be reserved to the two constituent regions, and, thirdly, that there should be a complex system of checks and

---

[12] *The Times* (London), 23 November 1978, at 19 (leading article).

balances to prevent domination of the representatives of the Turkish Cypriot community by those of the Greek Cypriot one.[13] All in all, the American proposals envisaged a federal government and parliament which would exercise some real powers and discharge meaningful functions, but which at the same time would not be able to override the strong opposition on specific issues of the Turkish Cypriot side. Two other sections of the American framework that were significant were, first, that, 'in order to promote an atmosphere of goodwill and to resolve pressing humanitarian problems', the Varosha area should be resettled (obviously by displaced Greek Cypriots) under UN auspices, this to be initiated 'in phase with the resumption of full intercommunal negotiations on a comprehensive agreement', and, secondly, that as part of a final settlement all foreign troops should be withdrawn from the island, 'except those specifically agreed to'. Initial reactions to the American proposals seemed to be favourable. But then, after meetings with representatives of the American government, there was long silence on the part of both the Turkish and Cyprus governments. Not long afterwards Turkey reiterated her official view that third parties should stay out of the Cyprus problem and leave it to those directly concerned, and shortly thereafter it was announced in the Turkish press that the attitude of Turkish governmental circles was 'negative'. The Greek Cypriot side too, it seems, made it known to American officials and Dr Waldheim that even though some parts of the plan were constructive and on the right lines others of its suggestions were objectionable and unacceptable. Unfortunately the two sides did not find it possible to accept the plan in principle, that is as a general framework for negotiation and without prejudice to their interests, at the same time expressing if need be strong disagreement with specific parts and without committing themselves to any of its concrete elements in advance. But the American proposals nevertheless, which on one version had Dr Waldheim's tacit approval, have not been rejected outright and might conceivably be resuscitated in the future, at least if in the meantime the American government engages in more effective behind-the-scenes diplomacy, coaxing Turkey into offering something which the Greek Cypriots can reasonably be asked to accept.

Early in 1979 Dr Waldheim himself once more took the initiative and began fresh consultations, and finally on 19 May at a meeting under his chairmanship between President Kyprianou and the Turkish leader Mr Denktash a new ten point document was agreed upon. This reaffirmed the guidelines negotiated between the late President Archbishop Makarios and

---

[13] It was thus provided that in the event that a majority in the upper chamber failed to concur in a bill passed by the lower chamber, a subsequent affirmative two-thirds vote in the lower chamber would be sufficient to enact, provided that at least three-eighths of the representatives from each community concurred therein.

Mr Denktash in February 1977, but now added the UN resolutions relevant to the Cyprus question as forming part of the basis for resumed talks. In another important development both parties pledged 'to abstain from any action which might jeopardise the outcome of the talks' and to give special importance 'to initial practical measures to promote goodwill, mutual confidence and the return to normal conditions'. Also significantly, the two sides agreed first that in any new settlement there should be respect for human rights and fundamental freedoms and secondly that there should be eventual demilitarisation. Finally the document stressed that 'the independence, sovereignty, territorial integrity and non-alignment of the republic should be adequately guaranteed' both against union in whole or in part with any other country and against any form of partition or secession. As regards the procedural aspect, the ten point plan provided that the intercommunal talks would now be carried on in 'a continuing and sustained manner' which, as President Kyprianou later explained, is a departure from the previous procedure of having successive rounds of talks. But early optimism that this was a major breakthrough and that meaningful negotiations would now be put on a solid basis was soon dissipated by new disagreements. On the resumption of the talks in June 1979 the Turkish side demanded, as a precondition to the holding of further negotiations, that the Greek Cypriot side should accept the addition to the Makarios-Denktash guidelines of the terms 'bizonality' and 'security for the Turkish Cypriots'. The Greek Cypriot side rejected this, particularly since the Turkish side had in the past ascribed meanings to both terms destroying the notion of 'federation' that underlay the guidelines, but reiterated first that it was committed to the establishment of a true federal system composed if necessary of two constituent parts, and secondly that the Turkish side could raise at the negotiating table any matter, including 'bizonality' and 'security', in precisely the same way that the Greek Cypriots could raise any other issue, such as that of the security of Cyprus as a whole 'the importance of which has been eloquently illustrated by the Turkish invasion'.

2. *A political and constitutional settlement*

Even though it has now become abundantly clear that an acceptable settlement cannot be brought about except through decisive action by the international community,[14] one can hardly afford the luxury of waiting for external mediation, and in any case all that one can realistically expect from foreign powers and the international community is the meaningful

---

[14] The all-important international dimension of the Cyprus problem is dealt with in Polyviou 'Cyprus: What is to be done?' 1976 *International Affairs* 582, at 592–5.

and bona fide exertion of efforts towards bringing the two sides, Turkey and the Greek Cypriots, closer together, in this way breaking the currently existing deadlock. But numerous difficult issues and thorny problems to be solved by the parties primarily involved in the dispute will remain, and our discussion of these can profitably be divided into two sections, that of the fundamental principles on the basis of which any settlement must proceed, and that of internal constitutional arrangements.[15]

(a) *The principles on which a solution must be based*

Any settlement of the Cyprus problem must be based on certain well-defined and understood criteria. Foremost among them are those which emerge explicitly or implicitly from the recent UN resolutions on Cyprus; also vital are criteria deriving from the actual circumstances of Cyprus and the realities and security requirements of the area. Any settlement must therefore be based upon the following considerations:

(i) The Cyprus problem, as has been accepted by all parties, can only be solved on the basis of an independent, sovereign and non-aligned state. Enosis, partition or any kind of separatist independence must be excluded both in the interests of the security and peace of the area and for the sake of the well-being of the people of Cyprus, Greeks and Turks alike. In this connection, it must be made clear – as has been uniformly accepted by the international agencies and organisations that have pronounced on the issue – that the republic of Cyprus has not been dissolved as a result of the Turkish invasion and occupation,[16] which in turn means that the political and constitutional reconstruction of Cyprus cannot start either from the premise of the existence of 'two autonomous administrations' on an equal footing or from the preexistence of federated states, because these do not exist. At the same time it goes without saying that what will eventually emerge from the negotiations between Greek and Turkish Cypriots will be a new constitutional structure for the republic, a federal system of government, which, when it is put into effect, will supersede all previous constitutional and political arrangements.

(ii) Secondly, no settlement should be negotiated elsewhere than in the context of the United Nations and in basic accordance with its broad

[15] See Polyviou, *Cyprus, In Search of a Constitution* (1976), 381 et seq. In November 1977 I attended a seminar in Rome organised by the Centre for Mediterranean Studies on the *Institutional Framework of a Federally Structured Cyprus*. The *Report* was prepared by Dr Dennison I. Rusinow, and I found his observations very helpful.

[16] See the way in which the European Commission of Human Rights has dealt with this matter (6780/74 and 6950/75). Reference may also be made to the various resolutions of the Security Council (starting from that of 4 March 1964) and of the General Assembly of the United Nations (starting from that of 18 December 1965).

principles; and a necessary start in this direction should be the implementation of the relevant UN resolutions. Particularly important are the provisions that the refugees should be allowed to return to their homes in safety and that urgent measures should be taken for the withdrawal of all foreign troops. As regards this first issue, every possible effort must be made to ensure that as many displaced persons as possible return to their homes. If the implementation of the federal principle to the circumstances of Cyprus means that not all are able to return to their properties, generous compensation should be made available to those who are unable or do not choose to return. As regards the second issue, it is thought that an integral part of a final settlement should be not only the withdrawal of non-Cypriot armed forces from the territory of Cyprus but also the permanent demilitarisation of the republic. This must take place in a phased manner and in a way that is best calculated to ensure the security of the republic and the safety of all its citizens. Demilitarisation of course is not inconsistent with the maintenance of police forces or even lightly armed security forces entrusted with the function of maintaining law and order either within the territory of Cyprus as a whole or within each region.

(iii) More broadly, any eventual settlement must be consistent with the provisions and principles of the UN charter, of which of course particular resolutions are specific expressions. In particular, the following UN principles seem very relevant: the purposes, principles and obligations relating to the maintenance of international peace and security, the peaceful settlement of disputes, respect for human rights, recognition of the sovereign equality of states, abstention from the threat or use of force against the integrity or security of any state, and respect for treaty obligations and the charter itself. No settlement should be accepted if it clearly violates any of these principles, and any proposed solution must be judged with them in mind. A confederation, for instance, or a rigid bizonal federation based on the compulsory separation of populations, and attended by the virtual absence of those central powers whose existence alone can guarantee the preservation of an independent state, would fall foul of almost all of them. Thus, such a system would be likely to endanger international peace and security, would seriously disturb and in fact render impossible respect for human rights, cannot be based otherwise than on force and faits accomplis, and would clearly fly in the face of treaties and international agreements. At the same time, in view of current realities, any governmental system that is adopted must recognise considerable autonomy for the two communities, and accordingly substantial powers and responsibilities should be given to the areas which will eventually be demarcated so that the legitimate interests and concerns of members of both communities can be adequately recognised and protected. It is such considerations that have necessitated adoption of a federal system as the basis for the intercommunal discussions. But the ultimate objective must be an independent, sovereign, non-aligned, integral and bi-communal republic the institutional arrangements of which should be conducive to a gradual evolution towards a more united Cyprus whose citizens, with time, will feel themselves to be Cypriots first and Greeks or Turks second. This entails arrangements and procedures which, without sacrificing security, will encourage the growth of a 'Cypriot consciousness' or 'Cypriot identity' that will superimpose itself on but not in the foreseeable future completely replace the additional cultural or ethnic self-identification of Cypriots as 'Greek Cypriots' and 'Turkish Cypriots'.

(iv) Any settlement must also be based, to a great extent, on the security requirements of the two communities and the republic of Cyprus. The main complication here is that 'security', particularly in its relationship to the other criterion of federal reconstruction, namely the workability of the federal system, means different and indeed contradictory things to the two communities. The Greek Cypriots regard the functional efficacy of the federal system and the essential territorial and governmental unity of the island as the central guarantees of their security. Turkish Cypriots tend to see in that same functional capacity and governmental unity the main threat to theirs. This fundamental disagreement appears clearly in the insistence of the Turkish Cypriot leadership that they cannot tolerate a 'strong' federal government until prolonged and happy experience with cohabitation under a weaker one has decisively changed the climate on the island and disarmed their suspicions, and in the Greek Cypriot conviction that a 'weak' federal government will encourage centrifugal forces and lead either to partition or to partial or even total annexation by Turkey. But what is undeniable, despite all these differences, is that for all concerned, particularly for the Greek and Turkish Cypriots, 'security' is the central problem in the Cyprus dispute, and therefore one of the primary issues is what must be done in order to create both the reality and the psychological assurance of security. Given the deep divergence of view of the two sides, one cannot do much more than try to set out certain tentative guidelines as to how this issue should be approached. For a start, one should not take a narrow or short-term view of the requirements or the concept of 'security'. Thus, if disguised partition accompanied by the perpetuation of the refugee problem is legitimised and becomes Cyprus' governmental and political structure, the displaced persons will almost certainly remain a source of bitterness and instability and will thus be a major danger to the durability of any settlement. Further, any rigid line of division between the two communities, particularly the one at present envisaged by Turkey, is likely to be the cause not only of endless administrative difficulties but also of much friction. In addition, if, as a result of the organisation and structure of the new federal government and constitution, the dependence of the two federated states on Greece and Turkey respectively is likely to be such that in fact a new frontier between them has come into existence, yet another and potent source of danger to the security of the area will have arisen. At the same time the tasks of constitutional reconstruction and administrative demarcation must be discharged with special sensitivity and appreciation for the special and understandable fears which any minority, and particularly the Turkish Cypriot one, must feel in a state where it is overwhelmingly outnumbered by the predominant ethnic group. To summarise, the security of the republic of Cyprus and of its people demands both a sensible and workable internal structure that will not be the cause of domestic unrest and further foreign involvement, and adequate and reliable external guarantees, if possible given directly by the Security Council.[17]

(v) Further, any solution must promote the well-being of the people and the island as a whole. It must be capable of providing for the adequate protection of the legitimate rights and interests of all Cypriots, Greeks and Turks alike, and must be conducive to the prosperity and progress of both communities. The form of government currently put forward by Turkey would not fulfil these requirements. Indeed, the restructuring of the Cypriot state on the basis of the Turkish proposals appears utterly impossible in practice and a sure recipe for future disaster. Such a rigid geographical separation as the Turks are now suggesting would result in the artificial creation on the one hand of areas rich in certain resources and on the other of areas completely barren, and would inevitably bring about the economic breakdown of the whole island and of both communities; and economic stagnation and depression are certain to impede the development of a peacefully united people. There is little doubt that from an economic point of view Cyprus is an economic entity characterised by the great interdependence of its regions and resources, and only by a sensible distribution of powers and a sane demarcation of regions can its full potential be realised.

(vi) Finally, any lasting settlement must be a genuinely 'agreed' one. This means that it should be truly capable of securing the support of all the parties identified by the General Assembly and Security Council resolutions on the Cyprus problem, namely the two Cyprus communities and the governments of Cyprus, Greece and Turkey.

These then are the criteria which must govern any solution of the Cyprus problem; and it is only in their light and the guidance they afford that one can usefully consider federal constitutional reconstruction.

[17] This was suggested by Dr Plaza, the UN mediator (*Report of the United Nations Mediator on Cyprus to the Secretary-General*, UN doc. S/6253).

(b) *The internal constitutional arrangements*

The pivotal factor here is the acceptance of a federal system of government. What are the implications of this? It is thought that some of these implications are entailed by traditional understandings of the concept of federal government; others emerge from the particular circumstances of Cyprus. The following observations on both may be offered.

Federal government[18] comes in a considerable variety of forms and a great number of institutional variations is possible. But some essential characteristics of federalism which constitute the 'skeleton model'[19] of federal government are the following:

(a) There are two levels of government, the central and the regional. The powers of these governments are defined by a constituent charter.

(b) Powers, functions and authority are assigned to the two levels of government on a coordinate and normally independent basis. Each government is independent of the other within its own sphere.

(c) Each government has control over certain sources of revenue or is assigned some such sources so that it may perform the tasks assigned to it by the constitution and, in so doing, be financially independent of the other.

(d) Both central and regional powers and other essential aspects of the federal system are set out in a written constitution which is supreme law, in the sense that neither the central institutions nor the component parts or regions can exercise unilateral power in repealing, amending or modifying the basic constitutional arrangements. There is also normally an independent tribunal to interpret the constitution, adjudicate upon disputes between central and regional authorities, and declare invalid any legislation which is repugnant to the relevant constitutional provisions.

Proceeding from the above considerations, various definitions of federation, federal government and federal structure have been proposed, but the one that has secured the most support is the one put forward by Professor Wheare. For him federal government is the system embodying 'predominantly a division of powers between general and regional

---

[18] See Wheare, *Federal Government* (1962); A. W. Macmahon, ed., *Federalism, Mature and Emergent* (1959); Watts, *New Federations: Experiments in the Commonwealth* (1966); Friedrich, *Trends of Federalism in Theory and Practice* (1968); Birch, *Federalism, Finance and Social Legislation* (1955); Vile, *The Structure of American Federalism* (1961); S. P. Aiyar and U. Mehta, ed., *Essays on Indian Federalism* (1965); Austin, *The Indian Constitution* (1972); S. A. de Smith, *The New Commonwealth and its Constitutions*, Ch. 7 (1964); Reagan, *The New Federalism* (1972); Lower, Scott, ed., *Evolving Canadian Federalism* (1958); MacMahon, *Administering Federalism in a Democracy* (1972).

[19] Birch, op. cit., at 1.

authorities, each of which, in its own sphere, is coordinate with the others and independent of them'.[20] This definition can be used as a convenient starting point even though it may need some qualification in the light of modern circumstances. Its essential premise is the principle of non-subordination, namely that in a federation neither level of government is subordinate to the other, or, as it has been put more simply,[21] the main thing which distinguishes a unitary from a federal constitution is the location of the supreme legislative authority. In the case of a unitary constitution this is vested in one government. In the case of a federal constitution it is shared between the central government and the regional, provincial or state governments, all of which exercise the powers and functions given to them by the constitution directly upon the people and within assigned geographical areas.

A vitally important point to notice is that it is this non-subordination of powers exercisable within coequal and coordinate levels that the Greek Cypriot side has accepted by agreeing in principle to the establishment of a federal system, not that in future there should be three separate governments[22] or that there should be rigid separation in the exercise of regional and central powers. The fact that the intercommunal negotiations are now based on a federal model means that a territorial basis for the future government of Cyprus has been accepted and that in some areas there will necessarily be non-subordination of powers, i.e. some matters will be allocated exclusively and by direct constitutional grant to the regional administrations, and the central government will be incompetent either to interfere with this regional discharge of functions or to amend unilaterally the organic distribution of powers and responsibilities. Within these broad outlines, however, there is no set pattern to follow, no easy example to emulate. What is essential is that arrangements must be set up that will be capable of ensuring or at least not positively obstructing the preservation of an independent state and the development of a genuine sense of Cypriot nationhood divorced from ethnic allegiances and the enmities of the past.

[20] It must not be forgotten that Professor Wheare has attempted to define 'federal government'. Some necessary distinctions are drawn by Birch 'Approaches to the Study of Federalism', XIV *Political Studies* 1 (1966).

[21] Awolowo, *Thoughts on the Nigerian Constitution* (1966). On the problems raised by attempts to define Federalism, see Vile, op. cit., 187–201; Birch, op. cit., 304–306; and Riker, *Federalism: Origin, Operation, Significance* (1964).

[22] It must not be forgotten that the federal concept in the case of Cyprus will not be based exclusively or even primarily on topographical or geographical factors. It has in effect become necessary as a result of ethnic considerations and external involvement, mainly from Greece and Turkey. A future federal system for Cyprus is bound to be not so much a geographical as a communal one.

But it is undeniable that it will not be easy to work out the details of a federal system for Cyprus. Much thought should go into what has here been called 'federal reconstruction' and special efforts should be made so that the eventual federal structure, without of course involving any diminution in essential security, does not prove cumbersome, unduly expensive or unworkable. Some principles and suggestions on which, it is thought, the federal constitution of Cyprus should be based can be set out as follows:

(i) *General character of the state.* The republic of Cyprus should become a sovereign, independent, bicommunal federal state consisting of two areas or regions, one of which may be inhabited predominantly by Turkish Cypriots. State sovereignty should vest in the republic of Cyprus, not in the regions or communities, and it should be expressly provided that the territory of the republic should be indivisible and integral. Further, the independence, sovereignty, and territorial integrity of the republic should be positively guaranteed, if possible directly by the Security Council of the United Nations, the incorporation of all or any part of the republic into any other state must be prohibited, the island should be demilitarised, and its right to pursue a non-aligned policy should be solemnly recognised. Two other vital matters fall for consideration under this heading, the issue of the geographical basis and form of the federal system, and the issue of human rights. As regards the former, three points may be made. First, it would appear that even though various Greek-Cypriot proposals continue to speak of multiregional arrangements, the Greek Cypriot side has accepted an effectively biregional federal regime both by conceding as early as 1975 that there should be a main region of Turkish Cypriot administration and by submitting in April 1977 a map indicating willingness to accede, under certain important conditions, to a biregional set-up; secondly, the total extent of the area under Turkish Cypriot administration should be negotiated on the basis of criteria such as population, land ownership, economic viability and productivity, security, and historical factors, and should correspond approximately to 20–22 per cent of the territory of the republic; and thirdly, whether the federation is ultimately biregional or multiregional, the legal status of Greek Cypriots living in areas under Turkish Cypriot administration and that of Turkish Cypriots living in areas under Greek Cypriot administration must be defined and protected. This brings us to the question of human rights. It is strongly believed that effective protection for fundamental rights and liberties, including freedom of movement, freedom of settlement and the right to own property anywhere in the republic, must form an integral part of any overall settlement and be entrenched in the federal constitution, subject only to such transitional qualifications or modifications as are made necessary by the specific requirements of the federal system eventually adopted.

(ii) *The central government* What are the considerations on the basis of which this should be organised? It is thought that there should be a balanced and sensibly organised central federal government, composed of Greek and Turkish Cypriots. Subject to the formulation and adoption of satisfactory safeguards, it should be given all powers needed to deal with the economic and other problems that Cyprus is certain to face in the coming years. Further, the central government should be assigned sufficient financial resources to enable it to carry out its tasks satisfactorily and help the regions by grants, revenue-sharing, and so on; and appropriate devices and mechanisms should be adopted for the purpose of co-ordinating the exercise of governmental powers, central and local, and for ensuring that essential constitutional flexibility is retained. Two matters merit close attention, first the allocation of powers and functions between the central and regional administrations, and secondly the composition and structures of the central government.

As regards the allocation of powers and functions,[23] two distinct issues are raised, first, the form in which legislative authority should be distributed, and, secondly, the question of which specific legislative powers and responsibilities to allocate to the two governmental tiers, the central and the regional.

(a) On the question of distribution, many forms are possible and have been attempted in various federations. Only the main ones will be considered here. To begin with, there might be three lists of legislative powers, that is lists of central, regional and concurrent powers, with perhaps some additional arrangement regarding residual powers, namely that residual powers should be vested in either the central or the regional authorities. Secondly, there could be two legislative lists, one list enumerating exclusive central powers and the other regional ones, with residual powers again being vested in one or the other, or, alternatively, there could be two lists, one list enumerating exclusive central powers and the other concurrent ones, leaving the regional governments with exclusive authority over the unspecified residual field. Yet another way of dividing legislative authority is to draw up a single list of exclusive central powers, all residual powers being assigned to the states or regions. It is thought that two basic models of distribution of legislative authority offer themselves as serious candidates for adoption in Cyprus. One would be to have two legislative lists, one for the central government and the other for the regions. The other would be to have three lists, namely lists of central, regional and concurrent powers.

[23] Watts, op. cit., ch. 8; particular assistance was derived from a Memorandum on this subject prepared by M. A. Triantafyllides, President of the Supreme Court of Cyprus.

Two matters, it can confidently be anticipated, will prove especially troublesome, whether there should be a sphere of concurrent legislative activity and where residual power should reside. As regards concurrent powers,[24] that is areas of state activity where both central and regional governments may legislate but where the regional laws, when in conflict with applicable general laws, must give way to the extent of their repugnancy, two possible lines of argument might be advanced. It may be argued that the federal system for Cyprus must be as simple as possible and that the enactment of a separate list of concurrent powers will introduce unnecessary complications in that it will both increase the likelihood of jurisdictional friction and leave the regional authorities in doubt about the extent of their powers. In addition, it might be said that a suitable formulation of central and regional powers could deal with all the problems likely to arise, in which case the separate concurrent list would be nothing but a redundancy at best and at worst a dangerous sphere of potential conflict. On the other hand, as many of the new federal systems have discovered, a separate concurrent list has undeniable advantages that usually outweigh its disadvantages. To begin with, 'such a list enhances flexibility'.[25] Thus, it gives the opportunity to the central government to postpone taking any action until a specific problem has arisen *and* the states/regions have failed to deal with it effectively, and it also affords the chance to the regions to experiment with their own solutions and arrangements until such time as the relevant problems either prove too difficult or big for their resources or alternatively until the difficulties being faced are shown to be not so much local as interregional ones, calling for more effective and extensive remedies. Further, a concurrent list may in the long run facilitate cooperation between central and regional governments both by encouraging or indeed necessitating concerted and complementary rather than independent action and by allowing in effect the central government to assume overall superintendence of basic policy direction whilst leaving specific regulation to the regional authorities. All in all it is not an easy matter to decide whether there should be a concurrent list or not, but the view that there should be one seems preferable. After all, most human contrivances, including constitutional arrangements, must take some risks. Where residual legislative authority should vest is even more controversial. The Greek Cypriot side, regarding federal reconstruction as an attempt to make a federation out of a unitary state, maintains that residual powers should be vested in the central government and that any powers given to the regional administrations must be regarded as grants from the centre to the circumference. The Turkish side, supported strongly in this by western governments, insists that only powers and

[24] Watts, supra, 174–7.
[25] Ibid., 174.

responsibilities explicitly granted to the federal government should belong to it and that all others should be reserved to the two communities. It may well be that the only way out of this impasse will be to spell out both federal and regional powers in some detail and in such a manner that there is no need for a residual field.

What about the actual allocation of powers and functions between the central and regional administrations? This is perhaps the most difficult problem with the setting up of any federation, particularly the Cypriot one, for 'it is not easy to separate the activities of government into two parts which can be carried on independently of each other, and the more activities the state engages in, the more difficult (this) becomes'.[26] It is thought that distribution of powers and responsibilities should be based on the following considerations: Whatever concerns the people of Cyprus as a whole rather than the inhabitants of particular regions or the members of a particular community should be placed under central control or, to put it differently, whenever it can be seen that matters are interregional ones or that the needs of people in given areas of governmental activity are similar and not dependent either on locality or community, then such matters or areas of legislative activity must be entrusted to the central government; powers as a rule should be assigned to the authorities best able to administer them; the fragmentation of integral and interrelated functions must if possible be avoided; and attribution of functions and responsibilities should not lose sight of certain advantages that might nowadays depend upon central control. With such considerations in mind, the legislative list of the central government should include the following subjects:

(1) Foreign and external affairs, including treaty implementation, the recognition of states, diplomatic relations and all matters relating to citizenship, aliens, naturalisation, immigration and emigration.

(2) Defence and security, although if there is demilitarisation, there will be no need for an army. Communal police forces will be unavoidable but at least efforts should be made to retain an integrated command structure.

(3) Finance, economy, money, which should include the formulation of general economic policy, the preparation and administration of the federal budget, the raising of money by taxation, customs and excise duties, and so on.

(4) Trade, commerce and industry, with particular emphasis upon all aspects of international and inter-regional trade and commerce. In addition, the freedom of trade and commerce should be positively guaranteed throughout the island.

[26] Birch, op. cit., at 2.

(5) Preservation of the environment and utilisation of natural resources, including agriculture in its interregional aspects.

(6) Social services and labour.

(7) Communications and transport.

As for the regional list, this should include all the matters that had been recognised as local or regional ones during the intercommunal talks; the internal organisation of the Turkish Cypriot administration; the maintenance of public order and security on a local/regional level; local/regional trade, industry and commerce; local and regional works; regional agriculture; all communal affairs, and so on. Provision should also be made for the future transfer of further powers and functions initially exercised by the regional administrations to the federal government, provided the two sides agree.

(b) The composition and structures of the central government have unfortunately become politically controversial issues. To begin with, there is no rule or even presumption that the various constituent units of a federation are completely equal in the sense that they should be entitled to the same representation in the central government. This untenable proposition has been put forward by the Turkish side and has been called by them the principle of 'condominium'. But the two communities, which are in effect the real members of the federation, cannot be considered equal and should not therefore be accorded equal representation. Participation in the central federal government should generally be on the basis of the population strength of the two communities, but there will no doubt be deviations from this, principally for reasons of security and confidence, in particular areas. Insofar as the structures of the federation are concerned, the organs and institutions of the proposed federal system *need not* differ materially from the ones eventually agreed upon in the context of the intercommunal discussions. Executive power, that is, should belong to and be exercised by the President of the republic, the Turkish Vice-President and a council of ministers jointly appointed by them and composed either in proportion to the population of the island or on some other acceptable basis. 30 per cent of ministerial portfolios, for instance, might be allocated to the Turkish community or, again, it might be provided that certain ministries should always be occupied by Turkish Cypriots, even though this last course is not one that commends itself for its potential contribution to future political interaction between members of the two communities. It should further be provided that the President and the Vice-President should be elected through democratic processes, that in the event of the temporary absence or incapacity of the President the Vice-President should assume his position and act in his stead, and that a power of veto over federal legislative acts should belong to and be exercisable jointly by the President and the Vice-President, any executive veto, it goes without saying, to be overriden by a suitably reinforced majority of the House of Representatives (the lower house). In addition, fair provision, on the principles suggested above, should naturally be made for the participation of members of both communities in the federal civil service. In this connection it may be necessary to enact that certain senior public positions should belong exclusively to the Turkish community, and in any case certain appointments should only be made as a result of joint action on the part of the President and the Vice-President. As regards judicial power, this should be the domain of a unified system of courts at the apex of which a federal supreme court should be entrusted with the superintendence of the federal system, the protection of human rights and civil liberties throughout the island, and the ultimate interpretation and application of federal law. This federal supreme court should consist of one Greek Cypriot, one Turkish Cypriot, and one non-Cypriot appointed jointly by the President and the Vice-President. Alternatively, if either equality of judicial representation for Greek and Turkish Cypriots or the importation of a neutral President from abroad were thought to be undesirable and it was instead decided that the federal supreme court should be composed in some other way, for instance of three Greek Cypriot and two Turkish Cypriot judges, additional safeguards should be adopted to help combat intercommunal mistrust and assure the Turkish Cypriots of absolute impartiality at the hands of the judiciary. It might thus be thought advisable either to entrust the President of the International Court of Justice with giving (binding) advisory opinions on matters pertaining to the Constitution (particularly in those cases where strong judicial disagreement had manifested itself) or to institute some further appeal either to some international tribunal or the Privy Council. There should also be local/communal magistrates for the purpose of trying local offences and adjudicating upon communal claims.

As regards the all-important issue of the legislative organs, a number of arrangements might be attempted. A course that would normally commend itself would be to follow the intercommunal model and try to avoid three or even two distinct legislatures. On this model legislative power over central or inter-regional affairs would belong to and be exercised by a House of Representatives composed of Greek and Turkish representatives in proportion to their communities' respective populations, and this assembly would separate into its Greek and Turkish parts when any matter that is designated as regional or communal came up. If this model is adopted it would also be very important that the two branches of the House should be structured in such a way that they would in the final analysis be integral parts of the state legislature rather than separate bodies that only came together for specific and rather exceptional purposes. This proposed system has much to commend it as it is well calculated in the long run to make for a body of representatives conscious of the wider interests of the country as a whole rather than of narrower communal or regional concerns. But it is most unlikely that the Turkish side would ever agree to what might appear to be an effectively unicameral legislature. An alternative plan would therefore be to vest legislative authority in a bicameral legislature, the lower house or chamber (the House of Representatives) to represent the people of Cyprus as a whole and therefore to be elected in proportion to population, and the upper house (the Senate) to represent the two communities or regions and therefore to be either selected or otherwise chosen in some other way and on the basis of different criteria. Various additional safeguards relating to the exercise of legislative power should also be enacted for the protection of the Turkish Cypriots. To begin with, even though decisions of the lower house (the primary legislative organ) should as a rule be taken by simple majority vote, in a number of special areas to be agreed upon between the two sides a reinforced majority of the House should be required, including a specified number of Turkish representatives; further, in even more sensitive spheres, something akin to the 1960 system of separate majorities might well be instituted; finally, in the case of certain other topics, again to be defined by agreement, the concurrence of the upper chamber should be obtained before a bill passed by the lower house can become law, even though here too a subsequent affirmative vote of a two-thirds majority of the lower chamber, including perhaps a specified number or percentage of Turkish Cypriot representatives, should have the result of overriding what in effect amounts to a legislative veto exercisable by the upper house.

(iii) *Financial resources*   Financial arrangements in federal systems traditionally present great problems.[27] This is not the place for a detailed discussion but there are basically two ways of arranging the financial structure of a future federal Cyprus. One can either assign revenue sources to the two sides so that they will both be able, each in its own sphere, to carry out the functions and responsibilities assigned to them under the constitution. Alternatively, realising the impracticability of rigidly separating the limited financial resources of the island into two groups, one for each community, one may assign most of the major revenue sources to the central government and rely on either revenue sharing or on a system of grants to the regions/communities for the discharge of regional tasks. It is suggested that this latter mode of finance should basically be followed in

---

[27] See B. P. Adarkar, *The Principles and Problems of Federal Finance* (1933); G. F. Shirras, *Federal Finance in Peace and War* (1944); A. H. Birch, 'Intergovernmental financial relations in new federations', in U.K. Hicks and others, *Federalism and Economic Growth in Undeveloped Countries* (1961); Birch, op. cit.; Watts, op. cit.

Cyprus. The dominant considerations here must be those of efficient administration, availability of resources and the general economic welfare. If an effort is made to distribute financial resources and assign tax and other revenues between the two tiers of government in order to secure to each adequate and completely independent sources of finance, not only will there be serious waste and continuous conflicts of overlapping agencies, but also it will be very difficult, if not impossible, to secure adequate financing for numerous regional projects, with the result that the two communities, but particularly the Turkish one, will be forced to rely on Greece and Turkey, something that is not calculated to promote their future political cooperation. In order to avoid this and combine financial flexibility with the necessary autonomy, most of the major sources of revenue must, in a federal Cyprus, be assigned to the central government. This is also the trend in most of the new federations, these developments having clearly been dictated by considerations of efficiency and facility in administration, the necessity for an integrated and coherent overall financial policy, and the need to ensure interregional freedom of movement. As now regards the financing of regional projects, transfers of revenue from the central government must principally be relied upon. Some of these should be conditional, which means that they should be made for specific purposes, and others should be unconditional. But in general federal organs, composed of course by members of both communities, should not surrender all control over the expenditure of money raised by taxation and therefore both central and regional authorities should be ready to account for the way they have disposed of the funds transferred to them.

(iv) *Correlation of functions*   It is vital that a special effort must be made to avoid the wasteful duplication and overlapping of federal and regional administrative services, with all the consequent inefficiency and possibilities for friction that that would entail, and to encourage cooperation and profitable interaction between the central and regional units. A way to contribute to these two objectives would be to abandon a rigid compartmentalisation of functions and a strict correlation of executive jurisdiction and administrative powers on the one hand with legislative autonomy on the other. Normally of course the distribution of executive authority in federal systems is made co-extensive with the allocation of legislative responsibilities, in other words federal laws are executed and administered by federal agencies and regional laws are administered and implemented by regional ones, but it is not thought that the limited resources of Cyprus can possibly justify or warrant either the establishment of three distinct civil services, one for the state as a whole and one for each community, or adoption of a principle that all three governments, the central and the two regional ones, must separately and in their own spheres make and implement their own legislation. Indeed, as has already been suggested, it does not follow from acceptance of a federal governmental system that three distinct governments should in future operate in the republic of Cyprus. The economic resources of the island will support no such governmental structure. What has been agreed upon is the principle of a geographical or territorial basis for the future government of the island, not that Cyprus should bleed to death on the altar of federalism. In this connection one might profitably consider patterns of 'delegated administration', namely that the implementation of some federal legislation can be assigned to the regions.[28] The advantages of 'delegated administration' are, among others, that duplication is avoided, that the possibly feared impact of federal legislation is made both more palatable and more acceptable through the mediation of locally responsible agencies,[29] that it enables the federal government to draw towards it and thus 'federalise' locally entrenched administrative services and, perhaps most important of all, that it helps allay regional fears about the wide extent of federal legislative powers. The effect of course of vesting in regional authorities administrative powers over central or concurrent subjects will be to make administration much more decentralised than legislation, and this is normally thought to necessitate in most federal systems some federal supervision of regional administrative activities and the establishment of mechanisms and procedures for integration and coordination. The same need will no doubt exist in Cyprus.

The unavoidable fact is that strict compartmentalisation of functions is undesirable and in ultimate analysis impossible. The dualistic conception on which the older federations were based has given way to a new cooperative approach.[30] The two levels of government cannot but influence each other's activities in important respects, and since after all their joint task is to discharge the various governmental and administrative functions in a given state or territory, even though this territorial 'unit' is divided into smaller ones where alone the various regional authorities can operate, it is imperative that appropriate arrangements should be set up that both express and articulate this inevitable governmental interrelationship and help institutionalise it further. Thus, among other things, it may be thought advisable, first, to allow the central government in some spheres and after satisfaction of certain preconditions to issue specific directions to the regional authorities, secondly, to require in other matters consultations between central and regional governments before action either by the one

[28] See Friedrich, op. cit., part 1, ch. 8; see also the Basic Law (Constitution) of the Federal German Republic, Articles 83–91; Edward McWhinney, *Constitutionalism in Germany and the Federal Constitutional Court* (1962).

[29] Friedrich, op. cit., at 73.

[30] Birch, op. cit.; Reagan, op. cit.; Watts, op. cit.

or the other is taken, and thirdly to set up a number of intergovernmental agencies for discussing and taking action on selected general and specialised subjects alike. It may be thought particularly helpful to establish an essentially advisory council for communal reconciliation and regional co-operation, the main function of which would be to take all possible steps, especially in the educational, cultural and sporting fields, for promoting the unity of the nation.

(v) *Some final reflections on federal government*   Before we conclude our comments on the introduction of federal government to Cyprus, there is need for some additional remarks. One of the major causes of the breakdown of the 1960 constitution was the then prevailing limited vision of constitutionalism and constitutional government and the almost complete disregard for what one might call the dynamic aspects of government. The same error must not be committed again. To begin with, federal government must not be approached only from the institutional angle. One must also think of and regard federalism as a 'process', as a 'bargain', and as a 'compromise'.[31] Indeed, the problems of federalism begin rather than end with the introduction of a system of federal government. A federal order, namely the principle of organisation 'whereby a compromise is achieved between concurrent demands for union and for territorial diversity within a society',[32] cannot survive unless there come into existence and are allowed to continue both a firm determination to maintain a single overall political system and a willingness to respect diversities and, to an extent not incompatible with the preservation of the federal order, distinct territorial development and separate growth. Further, a working federal order must be based on 'loyalty and comity', loyalty in the sense of a basic commitment to the working needs of the federal system and comity in the sense of a readiness to compromise and adopt a pragmatic and non-legalistic approach to the solution of difficulties.[33] If these essential aspects of federalism are ignored and an effort is instead made to solve at the outset and forever all the problems that may arise, and if moreover a doctrinaire rigidity rather than a flexible pragmatism is sought to be made the guiding criterion, gradual governmental decline or abrupt political disintegration will be the inevitable outcome of 'federal' efforts.

Further, a federal constitution is primarily a compact, a bargain. The Cyprus federal system of course, if it is ever launched, will have come about as a result of the disintegration of a theoretically integral order rather than of the coming together of its previously 'independent' component parts; but in this case too, whatever the theory, the federal

[31] Friedrich, op. cit., at 173–84.
[32] Watts, op. cit., at 13
[33] Friedrich, op. cit., at 175.

process will have emerged as an uneasy political compromise between on the one hand some type of unitary governmental structure and on the other complete political and communal separation, and should therefore also be seen to involve, as in the case of more traditional types of federation, a new form of cooperative association which should be allowed to develop naturally so that it may eventually involve 'living' arrangements for working out solutions together, joint decisions, joint ventures, supplementary policies. For federalism refers to this process of continuous adaptation and readjustment as much as to the structures and governmental forms that are normally understood by its terminology. If it is therefore attempted to turn a blind eye to this dynamic aspect, and it is sought to exclude or stifle the pragmatic attitudes and cooperative ideas on which federal behaviour ultimately rests and which are themselves generated by it, the proposed federal constitution, or for that matter any federal or other constitution, will not work. The older federal constitutions, it is true, were allegedly based on the principle that federal and state governments should operate in watertight compartments, each completely independent of the other. But this is clearly now acknowledged to be impossible. 'Under the heat and pressure generated by social and economic change in the twentieth century, the distinct strata of the older federalism have begun to melt and flow into one another'.[34] The new federal constitutions accept that interaction between the central and regional levels is inevitable and desirable, and therefore make ample provision for its institutionalisation and furtherance. Making use of this experience, interdependence and cooperation should also be made the features of the Cyprus federal constitution. Only in this way will some semblance of constitutional rationality be retained. The future prosperity and peaceful coexistence of the people of Cyprus, Greeks and Turks alike, demand no less.

3. *A common or divided society?*[35]

This book can have no conclusion. The long search for a viable and durable political and constitutional settlement for Cyprus has not yet met with success. Efforts to break the deadlock continue, but in view of basic differences of opinion prospects for an early solution are discouraging, not to say non-existent. It is therefore time to turn to fundamentals. A constitution for Cyprus must be both 'vision' and 'estimate'. As 'vision', it must be essentially a moral act, a conception of goals. As 'estimate', it must

[34] J. A. Corry, 'Constitutional trends and federalism', in Lower and Scott, eds, *Evolving Canadian Federalism* (1958), 92–125.
[35] See Cowen, *The Foundations of Freedom* (1961).

be based on a pragmatic assessment of realities. And the two must be related. For a 'vision' of the future cannot be transmitted directly nor can its 'truth' be automatically validated or realised. Both transmission and realisation can only be achieved if the operative social forces and political realities are understood and if this knowledge is made to serve the goals already identified. Equally, a constitution must be more than an attempt to settle immediate and outstanding problems of political and governmental organisation, and if it is not to be devoured from within by apathy or cynical legalism, it must be animated by a spirit or conception of the social order it is intended first to bring about and then to serve.

What should our 'vision' of a future Cyprus be? It should surely be based upon the twin objectives of genuine and long term security, both for Cyprus and the two communities, and the need to create a 'common society'. On this last point, before the Greek Cypriot side had acceped a federal constitution, I had written the following:[36]

> 'As I see it, the one and only hopeful alternative to the disastrous policy of separatism pursued in the past and its poor relations such as geographical federation is a policy whose long-term goal is a democracy in which all men, irrespective of ethnic origin or communal affiliation, can enjoy in peace and security the basic human freedoms and political rights in one integrated society. A strategy for integration – this is what we need in Cyprus. It is plain that there can be no real progress along the road to true peace and harmonious integration without a wholly fresh start – without the excision from the constitutional, legal and social arrangements, and, indeed, in the course of time, from men's hearts both of the gross distortion of ethnic prejudice and the pernicious influence of blind communalism'.

Even at that time, when all that the Greek Cypriot side had conceded was the introduction of regionalism, namely reinforced communal and local autonomy, it was realised that to speak unqualifiedly of 'integration' might be to court serious danger of misunderstanding as this terminology, it was feared, might conjure up notions of an unacceptable assimilation or illiberal absorption of the Turkish Cypriot community with a consequent loss of its distinctive characteristics and culture. 'Balanced partnership' was therefore considered a more appropriate expression for denoting the kind of social policy that it was realistic to pursue.

It is now feared that acceptance of a geographical federation will impede even further social and political integration. For what acceptance of a federal system of government based on communal considerations means is that the principle of separate communal development on a territorial basis has been sanctioned. Has then the future been completely lost? Are the people of Cyprus forever condemned to live in different

[36] Polyviou, *Cyprus, The Tragedy and the Challenge* (1975), at 164.

regions of the island, fortified barriers separating the two communities, the psychological impediments to future cohabitation and coexistence multiplying as the years go by, the forced suppression of everyday human contacts and relations and the inevitable frustration of any healthy movement of ideas or progressive initiatives breeding distrust, bitterness and intransigence? One should be reluctant to accept defeat. There is still time, it is thought, to build *a common society*. Separate development need not result in total schism nor in a permanently divided island. If certain conditions are not ignored, there may still be hope for future developments in the direction of a more united state and a more cohesive society.

But to achieve this two factors must be given particular attention. There is first the level of constitutional reconstruction. Much on this has already been said. Federal constitutional arrangements should try to maximise the interdependence and future interaction of the two communities without the loss of essential security, whether actual or psychological; they should be flexible and workable; they should contain all possible guarantees and safeguards of human and communal rights; and, by paying attention both to the underlying social and economic forces upon which any structure of organised government ultimately rests and to the surely imperative need for communal reconciliation within an independent and integral Cyprus, they should attempt to provide a viable and durable framework for future peaceful development and common progress.

But, to come to the second level, much more will have to be done if the twin goals of a future politically united island and a genuinely common society are to stand any hope of being realised. Rational constitution-making is of course essential but is neither all nor even a substantial part of the total effort that will be required. What in fact is needed is nothing less than a social revolution, particularly in habits of thought and basic attitudes, and it is here that the major difficulties will be faced. But whatever these may be, there is little doubt that in the long run it will be attitudes and beliefs, the education of public conscience and the development of a sense of public responsibility, acceptance of each other by the two communities as partners and cohabitants rather than as grudging and unwelcome neighbours, a genuine desire to safeguard Cyprus' sovereignty and take pride in its independence, magnanimous use of power, on the one hand, and restraint and moderation, on the other, all this and much else besides that will ultimately determine constitutional success and political rejuvenation. And there can be no formal instruction in how to abandon intolerance, passion, arbitrariness, bad faith, suspicion and intransigence, and replace them instead with an enlightened and humane attitude both on the part of society as a whole and on the part of its organised political forces, with good sense and the salutary spirit of compromise and mutual accommodation, and ultimately with all those elusive factors that together make for an elevated public and private life. These attitudes usually have to be acquired through a laborious process of effort and failure, mistake and correction, frequent frustration and further attempt. The people of Cyprus, both through their own shortsighted policies and through the operation of forces beyond their control, have met with all the above. Do they now possess the good sense and necessary maturity, born of tragedy and now demanded by nothing less imperative than Cyprus' very survival, to reverse the legacy of the past? The article of faith of the present writer is that they do.

Cyprus

Greek

Turkish

The pre-1974 distribution of Greek and Turkish villages over the island

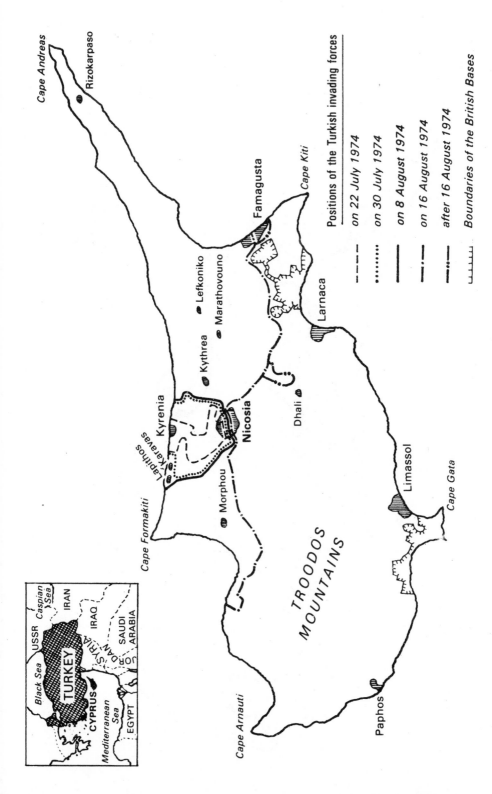

The area of Cyprus occupied by the Turkish forces

Positions of the Turkish invading forces

- – – on 22 July 1974
- · · · · on 30 July 1974
- —— on 8 August 1974
- –·–· on 16 August 1974
- —— after 16 August 1974
- ·······⊥ Boundaries of the British Bases

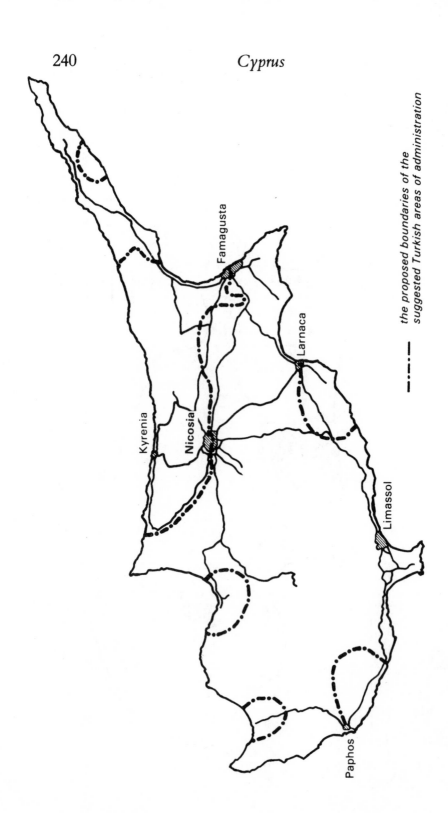

The effect of the proposal of the Turkish Foreign Secretary put forward at Geneva, August 1974 (the Gunes Plan)

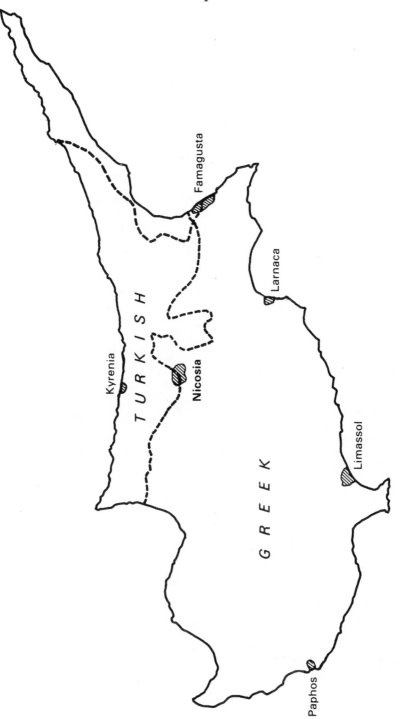

Greek Cypriot territorial proposals put forward at Vienna, March–April 1977

Index

Vienna talks (between Greek and Turkish Cypriot sides in March–April 1977), 207–10

vision of Cyprus, 234–7

Waldheim, Kurt, 104–5, 161, 210, 214, 216

Wheare, Professor, 222

Zurich agreement: negotiation, 12–15; position of Makarios on, 14, 36–7; position of Turkish side on, 39–40, 88–90; breakdown, 25–35